Unleashing Hope

Also by Sister Timothy Marie Kenndy, O.C.D.,
from Sophia Institute Press:

*In the Face of Darkness: The Heroic Life
and Holy Death of Mother Luisita*

Sister Timothy Marie Kennedy, O.C.D.

Unleashing Hope

The Biography of Venerable Maria Luisa Josefa of the Most Blessed Sacrament

Foundress
Carmelitas del Sagrado Corazón of Mexico
Carmelite Sisters of the Most Sacred Heart of Los Angeles

SOPHIA INSTITUTE PRESS
Manchester, New Hampshire

Sophia Institute Press
Box 5284, Manchester, NH 03108
1-800-888-9344
www.SophiaInstitute.com

Sophia Institute Press is a registered trademark of Sophia Institute.

paperback ISBN 978-1-64413-492-4

ebook ISBN 978-1-64413-493-1

Library of Congress Control Number: 2022932435

First printing

To all those who are searching
for a deeper meaning in their lives,
and a reason to hope and trust again

We are all in God's hands.
There is no better place we can be.
Live in hope.

—Venerable Maria Luisa Josefa
of the Most Blessed Sacrament, O.C.D.
"Mother Luisita"

Contents

Foreword

I first "met" Mother Luisita when I came to Los Angeles in the spring of 2010. A friend told me about her, describing her as a virtually unknown local saint. I became captivated by the story of Venerable Mother Maria Luisa Josefa of the Most Blessed Sacrament.

A wife and widow from a privileged background, she became a contemplative nun who ran hospitals and orphanages for the poor before being driven underground and eventually into exile during the bloody persecution of the Mexican Church in the 1920s. She was welcomed to Los Angeles, along with thousands of refugees from the violence in Mexico, by my predecessor, Archbishop John J. Cantwell.

Mother Luisita and her Sisters ministered throughout the Archdiocese of Los Angeles, working without pay, teaching children, and caring for the poor and the sick. Working closely with local pastors, the Sisters shared in the poverty of those they served and responded with calm and grace to the occasional flare-ups of anti-immigrant prejudice they faced, even at times from fellow Catholics.

The émigré gifts that Mother Luisita brought to this city and this country are still bearing fruits. She founded the Carmelite Sisters of the Most Sacred Heart of Los Angeles, a unique and authentic expression of the ancient Carmelite tradition that joins the Carmelite thirst for union with God with a demanding apostolate to the poor.

The Carmelites continue to shape the spiritual identity and moral character of the Church in Los Angeles, and their friendship and collaboration is one of the blessings of my ministry as archbishop. Over the years, my devotion to their foundress has continued to deepen.

In my inaugural homily, I invoked her witness as a kind of "evangelical key" to understanding the Catholic mission in Los Angeles:

> Venerable Mother Luisita would tell everyone: "For greater things you were born!" That's it, my friends! That's the good news we are called to proclaim to our city, to our country, throughout this continent and world! Each of us has been made for love and for great and beautiful things. There is no soul that God does not long to touch with this message of His love! And He wants to touch those souls through us.

Later, I took these words of Mother Luisita for the title of my second pastoral letter, on the topic of the Incarnation and God's plan of love, Our Lord's call for all of us to seek the "greater things" of being saints—holy men and women living as children of God in the image of Jesus Christ.

I have come to see Mother Luisita as a saint sent to the Church in the Americas especially for these times. The background to her witness is the persecution of the Church by the Mexican government in the years following the Mexican Revolution.

It has always troubled me that this period in the history of the Americas seems largely forgotten. It is hardly mentioned in many contemporary histories of Mexico and Latin America. Even Mexico's renowned public intellectuals and men of letters, Carlos

Fuentes and Octavio Paz, have never had much to say about this dark stain on Mexico's conscience.

When people write about the "murder ideologies" of the twentieth century, they speak of Nazism and atheistic communism in Europe, China, and Southeast Asia. They seem not to know that also during that century, thousands of Mexicans, some as young as teenagers, were imprisoned, tortured, and murdered in the name of an atheist-socialist ideology.

It is curious, too, that Catholic religious-freedom advocates in the United States often invoke as patrons the martyrs of England's anti-Catholic purges in the sixteenth century, great saints such as Thomas More, John Fisher, and Edmund Campion. They seem unaware of the martyrs who fell to an anti-Catholic regime in our own hemisphere just a hundred years ago.

I learned the names of these martyrs and their stories as a boy growing up in Monterrey. Among them are Blessed Miguel Pro, maybe the only martyr in the history of the Church whose execution was photographed; the child-martyr Saint José Sánchez del Río; Blessed Salvador Huerta Gutiérrez, the only auto mechanic in the Communion of Saints. There was also Saint Toribio Romo González, the martyred priest who has become the patron of immigrants and refugees from Mexico. And so many more, such as the beautiful catechist, the Servant of God María de la Luz Cirenia Camacho González. When the soldiers came to burn down her church in Coyoacán, she stood in front of the door, arms stretched wide, and proclaimed, "!Viva Cristo Rey!" They shot her dead. But the church was somehow spared.

The history of the Americas has never witnessed persecution on such an epic scale as that waged against the Catholic Church in Mexico in the 1920s and 1930s. The post-revolutionary regime had adopted a constitution that outlawed the public practice of the

Catholic Faith. And this was enforced ruthlessly, from the highest levels of the Mexican government. The decade that followed was a reign of terror.

Across Mexico, churches, seminaries, and convents were desecrated and destroyed. Public worship was outlawed, leaving tabernacles empty of the presence of Christ for the first time in nearly four hundred years. Hundreds of priests were tortured and killed during the persecution — many strung up on poles along the highways, others shot while celebrating Mass.

The revolutionary president Plutarco Elías Calles boasted of having killed priests and said he could wipe the memory of Christianity from the Mexican consciousness in a single generation. He was wrong. In the forge of his persecution, saints were made. This exceptional book tells the story of one of them.

Writing a biography of Mother Luisita is not an easy task. We know only the fragmented outlines of her life, and there is little by way of secondary sources. She spent many years during the persecution ministering in exile or in hiding. Hundreds of her letters survive, but these, while rich with spiritual insight, tell us precious little about her life or her state of mind.

Despite the obstacles, Sister Timothy Marie Kennedy, O.C.D., has emerged as among the foremost experts on the life and spirituality of Mother Luisita. She is a fine biographer, with a novelist's eye for the telling detail and the keen instincts of a historian. For this book, she has returned to the primary sources, including the reminiscences of Mother Luisita's sisters and other contemporaries, and she tells her story with a rich knowledge of Mexican history, especially the period of the reign of terror.

We know from historians such as Jesuit Father Wilfrid Parsons that Mother Luisita's agriculture-rich home state of Jalisco was the site of some of the bloodiest attacks and the most courageous resistance. In his *Mexican Martyrdom* (1936), Parsons tells how government forces in Jalisco's capital, Guadalajara, rounded up forty elderly men and women, marched them to the cemetery in the dead of night, and shot them. Their crime was going to Mass.

Parsons tells another story about a heroic Jalisco priest, Father Francisco Vera. There is a harrowing photograph that you can still find on the Internet, distributed back then by government propagandists. It shows Father Vera in his priestly vestments and biretta facing a firing squad. Four soldiers train their rifles on him as he looks them in the eye, hands folded in prayer.

Sister Timothy Marie evokes all this tension and danger, as Mother Luisita sought to minister in a world turned upside down. The book you hold in your hands tells the story of a holy life lived in unholy times.

Much of Mother Luisita's spiritual legacy was handed down in the form of letters written on the backs of envelopes and on scraps of paper and carried secretly across the border to her sisters still ministering in Mexico. She wrote in code to avoid giving away their hiding places. In her letters, the persecuted Church is called "grandmother"; my predecessor, Archbishop Cantwell, is "Papa Juanito" or "grandfather."

The saint you will meet in these pages is a shrewd, practical foundress, a mystic of everyday life, and, above all, a wise observer and keen guide of souls. With a wry sense of humor worthy of her spiritual mother, the great Saint Teresa of Ávila, she once told a young sister: "Try not to neglect your spiritual reading, prayer, and examination of conscience—and have some fun, also."

We find in Mother Luisita a deep appreciation for the wisdom of Saint Thérèse of Lisieux's "Little Way" as well. She lived in close intimacy with God, aware that she was always in His presence. She taught her sisters to have a rock-solid trust in God's loving providence and urged them to abandon themselves to seek His will in everything.

"May you use every day of your life to love Him, to serve Him, and to thank Him for the love He has for you," she said. "May His will be done. Place yourself in His hands, for you are His, and He will allow to happen whatever is most pleasing to Him."

Mother Luisita told her sisters that their holiness and salvation would be found in serving Jesus in the poor and the sick and in trying to perform even the smallest labors of daily life for the love of God. "All for You, my God," was her prayer. She urged her sisters to stay faithful to their daily duties and work for "little victories" over their selfishness and weaknesses. "Be a little better, more and more each day," she would say.

Always, Mother Luisita would call her sisters, and all of us, to set our minds on things above, the things of God. "For greater things you were born," she wrote. "Pray for me. I want to be what I should be." And what she should be—what God made each of us to be—is a great saint.

She wrote these words long before the Second Vatican Council would restore the "universal call to holiness" as the vital mark of Christian identity. Mother Luisita is one of the prophets of holiness whom God raised up in those decades before the Council. Her life and works deserve to be studied alongside those of St. Josemaría Escrivá, Venerable Madeleine Delbrêl, Servant of God Dorothy Day, Blessed Charles de Foucauld, and others from those years who called us to live as saints in everyday life, with our hearts open to the sufferings of the poor and the forgotten.

Sister Timothy Marie has given us an important book for this moment in the Church.

Reading history through the lives of the saints, we see that indeed the saints are the true agents of history. God raises up saints in every time and place to bear the light of Christ and scatter the darkness that would turn our hearts from God and His plan for our lives and the world.

The Mexican Revolution and its aftermath were a time of martyrs and saints and countless hidden heroes for the Faith. Ordinary Catholics became Cristeros, courageous defenders of Jesus Christ. Many felt compelled to take up arms to defend their rights in what became known as the Cristero War. Others chose nonviolent means to bear witness to Christ.

"I die, but God does not die," Blessed Anacleto González Flores said before his execution. His words were prophetic. The Cristeros' blood became the seed for the Church of future generations in Mexico.

And, as we see in this fine book, this period of persecution also shaped the growth of the Church in the United States. When I became an archbishop in San Antonio, I began to see the great gift of faith that had been brought to this country by the many refugees from the persecution.

I had already known of Saint Rafael Guízar Valencia, a bishop who ran a clandestine seminary in Mexico during the early years of the persecution. Later he was driven into exile, and he even spent some time preaching and teaching in San Antonio. It was always humbling to me to reflect that this heroic priest once preached in the same pulpit I used to preach in every Sunday at San Fernando Cathedral. I still wear a pectoral cross that is a replica of Saint Rafael's and contains a relic of the saint. I try to wear it often, especially when I am with my seminarians.

In Los Angeles, in addition to the vibrant Carmelite Sisters of the Most Sacred Heart Order that Mother Luisita established, we have the Poor Clare Missionary Sisters, founded by another holy refugee of the persecutions, Blessed María Inés Teresa Arias.

At a time when the Church in this country is more and more shaped by the experience of immigrants and refugees from Latin America, Mother Luisita's story reminds us that our spiritual bonds with Mexico run deep. In fact, it was Hispanic missionaries, including the great "Apostle of California," Saint Junípero Serra, who came up from Mexico and first evangelized this country. Our country continues to be renewed by the spiritual contributions of men and women from Mexico and Latin America.

In this context, Mother Luisita brings us a spirituality that is fully Catholic and authentically Hispanic. From out of the darkness of the worst persecution the Church has ever seen in the Americas, she teaches us how to live out heroic Christianity, surrendering ourselves to God's will and living only for Him. "Sorrow precedes joy, fear precedes conviction, weakness precedes strength, and all redounds to the welfare of those who love God," she tells us.

Mother Luisita, I continue to believe, is a saint for these times. She brings us a message of spiritual renewal that begins with interior conversion of the heart and is manifested in works of mercy and compassion. She shows us the way to be contemplatives in the midst of the world's sufferings, living in the presence of God, working to advance the dignity and transcendent destiny of the human person, especially those whom Jesus most identified with—the hungry and the homeless, the sick, the immigrant, and the imprisoned.

Mother Luisita comes to challenge us, as she challenged her sisters. And make no mistake, she could be tough in reminding us that God is calling each of us to live our lives beautifully and for Him alone.

> Are you becoming a saint? God our Lord has given you a soul for that very purpose, and woe to you if you do not correspond to the graces that He has granted you. You've

been especially chosen through the predilection of a great God. Don't be a coward, my daughter. Fight in a manly manner against your passions. Overcome yourself! Seek sanctity through the ordinary duties of daily life, and don't let any occasion that presents itself to you take control of you or have any dominion over you. If you follow this advice, I can assure you that in a very short time you'll gather so much spiritual wealth that even you will be surprised. Don't doubt it. And not with just a little bit of effort, either, but with perseverance. Adelante, my daughter! Onward!

I pray that this book will introduce many to this unknown saint of Los Angeles and the Americas. May her witness renew our commitment to speak out and work tirelessly to defend human dignity, especially the dignity of those who are persecuted for their religion. I pray, too, that Mother Luisita's witness may inspire a deep spiritual renewal in every Catholic, through a new commitment to the greater things, to becoming the saints we are born to be.

—Most Reverend José H. Gomez,
Archbishop of Los Angeles
February 11, 2022, Memorial of Our Lady of Lourdes,
85th Anniversary of the Death of Mother Luisita

Acknowledgments

My deepest thanks to all the patient people who put up with me as I learned how to write a biography: Mother Gloria Therese, our superior general, for her support and encouragement all the way to the finish line; Archbishop José Gomez for his profound foreword and for use of quoted materials; my generous and charitable sisters at our Holy Innocents and Casa convents, who gave me the time and space to write and assumed my convent duties, big and small, so generously; Marilyn Finnerty, O.C.D.S., for her innumerable phone conversations about commas and redundancies and such; Father Donald Kinney for his gentle finesse in leading me to better writing, especially the sections on Carmelite spirituality; Sister Joseph Louise and Sister Juana Teresa for the Spanish translations and Sister Antonia Teresa for their assistance in understanding nuances of Spanish expressions and smoothing out transitions; Sister Judith and Sister Carmelina for their valued suggestions and encouragement; Sister Mariella for her "spot-on" recommendations; Sister Regina Marie, Sister Vincent Marie, Sister Mary Clare, Sister Mary Jeanne, Sister Martin Marie, Sister Noella, Sister Madonna Joseph, Sister Rosario Therese, Tracey Ertl, and Carmen Sanchez for going over and commenting on the various drafts; and Selin Polat and Sister Anita Mary for their help with photos. And a thank-you to the Carmelitas del Sagrado Corazón of Mexico for their collaboration and to Father José de Jesus Orozco Mosqueda, O.C.D., author of the recently published definitive biography *Rostro de Bondad: Biografía de la madre María Luisa de la Peña*, which provided a wealth of added information on her life.

My special gratitude to Barbara Hanna and Jo De La Torre, who accompanied me throughout the writing of this book with editing scissors that never stopped cutting and the encouragement that lifts up and spurs on.

Nora Malone, now I know why authors acclaim their editors so highly and thank them so profusely. You are the best! Thank you for your faithful help. All our Carmelite Sisters join me with prayerful gratitude as we thank Charlie McKinney and the many people at Sophia Institute Press for their help and guidance in publishing this biography that was a long time in coming and, hopefully, will prove to be well worth the wait.

Note from the Author

It was a cold February morning years ago. I was praying quietly in the Church of San Miguel Arcángel in the small town of Atotonilco el Alto in the state of Jalisco, Mexico, when I felt a slight tug on my sleeve. Opening my eyes, I turned to my right and noticed a woman trying to get my attention. While speaking to me in Spanish, she maneuvered a young boy, about five or six years old, along the wooden kneeler until he was standing at my side. Then she looked directly at me. Her unforgettable expression remains with me to this day.

"Please help me," her eyes pleaded.

I looked around for another Carmelite Sister, one who knew Spanish, but the church was nearly empty. Delving into my high school Spanish vocabulary, I haltingly asked her to speak more slowly. Listening intently, I got the gist of what she was asking. She wanted me to pray for the healing of the young boy, her son, who was born deaf. I let her know that my Spanish was extremely poor. Somehow, I managed to convey the fact that other sisters would be arriving at any moment and that Spanish was their native language.

She would have none of it.

She looked at me and said slowly in Spanish, "You are one of Mother Luisita's Carmelites, yes?"

I nodded.

"That is enough for me," she answered. "I trust you."

It became clear to me that I was the one she wanted to pray for her son. So, I nodded and prayed silently and sincerely for him as I cradled his head in my hands. How could I refuse those pleading eyes?

"*Gracias, madrecita, gracias,* thank you, little mother, thank you," the mother said as a wide smile of contentment spread across her face. "*Gracias.*"

And the two stood up and left me.

Mother Luisita had died more than eighty years before. That is three generations' worth of years. This young mother had obviously never met her, yet Mother Luisita was as alive and real to her as if she were sitting next to us in the church.

Why?

And I thought about that as I continued praying. Why do these people still remember her?

Introduction

No two people are exactly alike, and thus, no two saints are the same. Just look at a random sample of some saints in the Catholic Church. Impetuous Saint Peter. Fiery Saint Teresa of Ávila. Comical Saint Philip Neri. Zealous Saint Paul. Humble Saint Teresa of Calcutta. Eccentric Saint Benedict Joseph Labre. Mystical Saint John of the Cross. Trust-filled Saint Thérèse of the Child Jesus. The list goes on and on. How encouraging it is to discover that people of every temperament can lead virtuous, moral lives. If the saints can do it, so can we.

Saints are persons who are raised up by the Catholic Church as models, examples, and mentors for the rest of us. Learning about them and their responses to life's joys and sorrows, hurdles and challenges, reveals life paths that are manageable, paths that we can follow in our own life journeys.

When the Catholic Church determines that a person should be considered for sainthood, a process is set in motion. The Church closely examines testimonies, writings, miracles, and other factors pointing to the person's holiness before the title *Saint* is given to that person.

Like us, saints lived during periods in history, under specific circumstances, and they responded uniquely to life events according to their temperaments and characters. As Saint Paul tells us:

> We are God's work of art, created in Christ to live the good life as from the beginning He had meant us to live it. (Eph. 2:10)[1]

To live the good life. The saints teach us how to live the good life, and that lesson is about choices. Saints chose virtue and integrity over moral compromises, and if they slipped and fell, they got up. Being a saint is about continually growing in a relationship with God and saying yes to His inspirations even when we would prefer to say no. Life becomes a journey of trust — trust in God no matter what happens during that journey.

This book is the story of one woman and the choices she made: a woman who left her privileged life in the distinguished upper class to live and work among the poor and needy; a woman who freely chose a simple life dedicated to loving and serving the poor as a married woman, as a widow, and finally as a consecrated religious who suffered greatly during the religious persecution in Mexico.

People affectionately called her Mother Luisita and looked to her for encouragement and advice, especially during the extraordinary challenges of the Mexican Revolution and the subsequent Cristiada.[2] Mother Luisita encountered one obstacle after another, yet her amazing resilience allowed her to remain peaceful amid the chaos she faced. She seemed to be anchored in strength beyond

---

[1] Jerusalem Bible, 1966 edition.

[2] The Cristiada (1926-1929), also known as the Cristero Uprising, or the Cristero War, was a widespread struggle in many central-western Mexican states against the secularist, anti-Catholic, and anticlerical policies of the Mexican government. It was the Mexican people's war for religious freedom.

her own capacity and was an anchor of hope for all who came to her, especially the poor and the downtrodden.

At the time of the writing of this book, waves of the COVID-19 pandemic are submerging our world. Many people are discouraged, and some say that they have lost all hope. A shroud of discouragement blanketed our world even before the pandemic. People seem to have lost their sense of identity, purpose, and trust. It shows in their body language, in the words they speak and the choices they make. Yet there *is* hope.

There is always hope. Always.

May this story of Mother Luisita's life be a catalyst for *unleashing hope* in the hearts of all its readers.

Background regarding the *Sisters'* *Remembrances* in This Book

Many of the stories in *Unleashing Hope* come from a gathering held in the summer of 1958, twenty-one years after Mother Luisita's death, at the motherhouse of the Carmelitas del Sagrado Corazón in Atotonilco el Alto, Jalisco, Mexico. Mother Beatriz of Jesus Ochoa Lopez, superior general,[3] had gathered twenty-eight sisters who had entered the community between 1904 and 1936 and had lived with or had personally known Mother Luisita. The purpose of the gathering was to collect information for the Spanish biography *A Zaga de Su Huella*, by Father Jaime de la Cruz, O.C.D., which was published in June 1961.

Mother Mary of the Eucharist Nuñez, vicar-general,[4] presided. Sister Elisa Graciela of the Sacred Heart Gonzalez oversaw recording everything. Most of these twenty-eight sisters had not responded in writing to a questionnaire that had been sent to them.

---

[3] A superior general, or general superior, is the leader or head of a religious institute in the Roman Catholic Church. The superior general usually holds supreme executive authority in the religious order.

[4] A vicar-general is the sister next in rank to the superior general and is usually empowered to act in her absence or disability.

Sisters who had been novices[5] together in the beginning years of the community clarified and verified their remembrances in small groups. Other important data was made available to each group to help them remember details. These very intense gatherings, which lasted one month, were both stimulating and emotional because the memories of the sisters touched the delicate fibers of their hearts.

The original transcripts in Spanish from the 1958 gathering (called *Sisters' Remembrances* in *Unleashing Hope*) are kept in the general archives in Guadalajara, Jalisco, Mexico. The English translation of these transcripts that was used in *Unleashing Hope* is found in the archives of the Carmelite Sisters of the Most Sacred Heart of Los Angeles at their motherhouse in Alhambra, California.

In addition to the personal remembrances of the founding sisters, *Unleashing Hope* was written using other primary documents: the more than six hundred personal letters of Mother Luisita, which, thanks be to God, have been preserved in the general archives in Guadalajara. Copies can be found in the general archives of the Carmelite Sisters of the Most Sacred Heart of Los Angeles in Alhambra.

Particularly helpful were the first articles and books written on the life of Mother Luisita: *Biografía de Mi Muy Amada Tía, Luisa Josefa del Santísimo Sacramentado*, written by her nephew, Carlos Hector de la Peña in 1945, eight years after her death; *The Flower of Guadalajara* (1956), by Helenita Colbert; *The Doctor's Widow* (1956), by William Queen; and *A Zaga de Su Huella* (1961), by Jaime de la Cruz, O.C.D. Special mention must be given to the definitive biography of Mother Luisita, *Rostro de Bondad: Biografía*

---

[5] A novice is in the second stage of initial formation in the religious life. The novitiate usually lasts from one to two years, according to the constitutions of each community.

de la madre María Luisa de la Peña Navarro (2021), by Fray José de Jesús Orozco Mosqueda, O.C.D. Other essential resources were the original letters between Mother Luisita and the Christian Brothers in Moraga, California, during 1928 and 1929, as well as her original letters to Father Pedro Heriz, O.C.D., and Father José Refugio Huerta, in 1929 and 1930, and the three archbishops of Guadalajara during her lifetime. Included also are stories and traditions that have come to us through the documented oral history of Mother Luisita's two communities.

History is multifaceted and can become complicated in the unraveling of its many perspectives. The history that unfolded during the lifetime of Mother Luisita is told in this biography specifically through the lens of the people of the Los Altos region of Jalisco, Mexico, and Mother Luisita and her Carmelite Sisters.

Unleashing Hope

Part 1

The Formative Years
(1866–1896)

Birth through Marriage

Two women arrived at our Sacred Heart Retreat Center that day, escorted by their friend, who introduced them to us. I remember that we were sitting in the morning shade of the north side of Mater Dei Hall. The air was crisp, and we enjoyed a leisurely brunch in this lovely garden setting. Soon we were talking about life. The women spoke about their families, and we shared about our lives as Carmelite Sisters: our hopes and dreams, our successes and challenges. The conversation was grace-filled.

We arranged to meet again and began to go our separate ways. That's when one of our new friends turned and told us, "You sisters give me hope."

—Author

Chapter 1

The Best Rose of the Garden

Luisita has changed. This daughter of mine
impresses me and I respect her for it;
when she is around, I speak differently.[6]

—Don Epigmenio de la Peña, Mother Luisita's father

Memories fill the little Mexican town of Atotonilco el Alto in Jalisco, Mexico. Like ghosts, they hover over the cobblestones as emotions emerge among the townspeople. Loss. Gratitude. Revenge. Deeper emotions that have no name. As the people come together to tell their stories, feelings flow quite unconsciously into the telling. It cannot be helped. Deeply embedded emotions rise unbidden to the surface as the account is told again. The people will not let it die.

Walking through the town's narrow streets is painful. The old stones are uneven now, and the holes cause imbalance, so travelers need to move carefully. Walls flank the streets, obscuring the homes and the property they guard. Aged bricks crumble from the

---

[6] Ariadne Katherine Caravacci, *Loving Kindness* (Alhambra, CA: Carmelite Sisters' Printing, 1983), 21.

ravages of time. On one of the peeling walls is a simple inscription embedded into a single terra-cotta tile:

Mother Luisita
(Maria Luisa de la Peña Navarro)
was born in this house on June 21, 1866.
"The Best Rose of the Garden."

Simple words. Straightforward. Beautiful. Like her. At her name, faces light up. Townsfolk still discuss the genteel, quiet manner and strong moral character that brought power and credibility to her words and actions.

Decades later, people still recall with affection and gratitude this spiritual mother who was there for anyone who needed her hand and her heart, which she readily gave, time and time again. She provided shelter, education, and health care and helped them when their precious land became killing fields and their families, friends, and neighbors found themselves victims of the atrocities of war. She showed them how close God is and how to find Him even in the darkest of times. She unleashed the hope that lay paralyzed within traumatized hearts.

Mother Luisita was a petite Mexican woman, sickly her entire life, who accomplished so much that it is hard to figure out how she did it all. Born into wealth, she gave her money, her time, and her life in service to those in dire straits, to people who were homeless, poor, or sick, and especially to children. Despite stumbling stones and roadblocks at almost every step of her life's journey, she continued quietly and steadfastly with her eyes on her goal—not on the difficulties in reaching it. She was authentic. She truly cared, and people responded to that.

Although Mother Luisita's contemplative nature thrived in times of silence and prayer, her life was not a quiet one. It reads much like a novel with the main theme intertwined among a variety of subplots. It was precisely these often-complicated interactions that brought out a hidden quality within Mother Luisita. What was this hidden quality that intrigued those around her and revealed her to be a source of hope during difficult days?

Mother Luisita, married at fifteen, widowed at twenty-nine, foundress of a new religious community of contemplative-apostolic Carmelites at fifty-five, and an exiled refugee during her later years, is a woman deeply respected and dearly loved. Her amazing personal relationship with God and her calling to begin a new community of Catholic sisters within the family of the Carmelite Order,[7] at the very time Catholics were being persecuted and killed for practicing their religion, form the heart of her life story. She was a quiet light that pierced the darkness. She was a beloved spiritual mother.

In this biography of Mother Luisita, the word *evil* is used according to the Catholic understanding of evil as defined by Saint Thomas Aquinas: evil is the absence, lack, or privation of a good that should be present in something. With astute clarity, Saint Thomas competently synthesizes this complex concept in these few words.

Much suffering appears in *Unleashing Hope*, both physical and moral: lack of health care, education, or necessities of life, and the torture, murder, and persecution of Catholics. The word *darkness* is used interchangeably with *evil* in this telling of the life of Mother Luisita.

The Catholic Church has begun the process to determine whether Mother Luisita should receive the title *Saint*. In 2000,

---

[7] The origin of the Carmelite Order can be traced to Mount Carmel in northwestern Israel, where several devout men, apparently former pilgrims and Crusaders, established themselves near the traditional fountain of Elijah about 1155.

Pope Saint John Paul II, following the process for beatification and canonization of saints, proclaimed her *Venerable*. This English biography of Mother Luisita was written at the request of Father Romano Gambalunga, O.C.D., the former postulator of the cause for her beatification and canonization.[8]

∞

The first light of dawn etched its way across the night sky above Atotonilco el Alto, Jalisco, Mexico, announcing the arrival of the summer solstice, the day with the most hours of sunlight—a fitting day for the birth of one who would grow up to battle the darkness. It was five in the morning on June 21, 1866, and the Angelus bells from the nearby Catholic church were ringing as Luisa de la Peña was born. Her parents, Epigmenio de la Peña and Luisa Navarro, were from Los Altos, also known as the Highlands of Jalisco.

On a clear day, viewed from a plane, Los Altos is an undulating landscape dotted with ranches tucked away in its folds. The region called Atotonilco el Alto is made up of twelve small towns, with Old World names, scattered throughout the valley and into the highlands. Even today, most of these small towns consist primarily of ranches in the northeastern part of Jalisco, about eighty miles east of Guadalajara. In the late 1800s, when Luisita de la Peña was born, the rugged journey into the nearby hills from one ranch to another could be made only atop slow-moving, sure-footed burros.

One of the towns bears the same name as the region. Atotonilco (ah-toe-toe-NEEL-co) means "the place of hot waters" in the native

---

[8] The *posulator of the cause*, according to Catholic Church law, is the legal person to represent a cause for sainthood with all its accompanying documents, interviews, and so forth to the Congregation for the Causes of Saints.

language of Náhuatl. An early native legend claims that the waters have healing properties.

Luisa de la Peña's father, Epigmenio, was also a native son of Atotonilco. In his late twenties, he married Arcadia Romo, a beautiful and gracious young woman from a family of wealthy landowners. But at only twenty-eight years old, Arcadia died bearing their daughter, Gabriela. Gabriela's death followed soon after her mother's. Epigmenio grieved profoundly. Infant mortality was no stranger in the late 1800s, when life was hard and survival never guaranteed.

As time went on, in God's providence, Don[9] Epigmenio met Luisa Navarro, who would become his second wife and Luisita's mother. Luisa Navarro lived in the town of Capilla de Guadalupe[10] about twenty-two miles north of Atotonilco, an arduous trek further up into the hills. Capilla de Guadalupe was the center of the region's commerce in the 1800s, and Don Epigmenio traveled there often on business matters related to his agricultural empire. He and his brother, José Maria, often rode into town astride their fine horses sporting Jalisco's traditional *charro* attire.[11] It was thus that he met Luisa.

Epigmenio followed the traditional custom of asking Luisa's father for her hand in marriage. When Epigmenio and Luisa exchanged their wedding vows in the parish church of Capilla de Guadalupe on June 15, 1859, their holdings merged, and their wealth increased. Epigmenio was twenty-nine and Luisa Navarro was fifteen at the time of their marriage.

---

[9] *Don* is a title that was originally used to show a man's nobility, and *Doña* was used to show a woman's nobility. Today the terms are comparable to the English *sir* and *madam*.

[10] Named after Our Lady of Guadalupe, patroness of the town.

[11] A *charro* is a skilled Mexican horseman typically dressed in an elaborately decorated outfit of close-fitting pants, jacket, and sombrero.

A month after their wedding, the couple traveled back down the hills to make their home together. It was a 150-mile trek for the newlyweds as they descended from the highlands into the Atotonilco valley on El Camino Real, the King's Highway. In those days, *King's Highway* was applied to any road that had been built by Spain during Mexican colonial times, in the sixteenth century.

Don Epigmenio and Doña Luisa soon welcomed two daughters, Maria Magdalena Clotilde del Refugio, who was born on their estate of La Labor in 1861, and Maria Clotilde de Jesus, born in Atotonilco in 1864. Both died in infancy. Two years later, in 1866, the couple's third child, Luisa,[12] was born on her mother's birthday. Following the custom at that time, both mother and daughter were named after the patron saint of the day, Saint Aloysius Gonzaga — Luisa being a feminine derivative of Aloysius. Everyone called the new baby Luisita, which means "little Luisa."[13]

Six days after her birth, Luisita's health declined, and her alarmed parents hurriedly arranged her Baptism. On June 27, 1866, the tiny infant was baptized by Father Juan Munguía, vicar of the parish of San Miguel Arcángel. According to her baptismal certificate, her godparents were Manuel Rojas, an uncle, and Doña Rafaela de la Peña, her aunt. Some of the earlier biographies of Luisita mention that her Baptism was done so soon that the de la Peña gardener stood in as proxy for her godfather, who could not come to the ceremony on such short notice.

---

[12] Previous books state that Mother Luisita's given name was Luisa. Her birth, baptismal, Confirmation, and marriage certificates, as well as her passport, show her name as Luisa de la Peña.

[13] In this biography, Mother Luisita's mother is referred to as Doña Luisa.

Who could have known that this frail, sickly infant would live out her baptismal consecration in dire times of revolution and religious persecution? Or that, as the years passed, the infant would grow up to fulfill her life's mission faithfully and steadfastly as a single woman, a wife, a widow, and, ultimately, foundress of a new Carmelite community in the Catholic Church? Or that she would come to be known as "the Best Rose of the Garden" or "the Heart and Soul of Atotonilco"? At the time of her Baptism, the prayers of her parents and relatives were simply that she would live.

∞

Atotonilco was a devoutly Catholic town at the time of Luisita's birth. San Miguel's stately spires dominated the landscape. Not only was the church the tallest and best building in the town, but it was in the center as if to proclaim that Catholicism was central to every aspect of daily life. The huge bell tower called the people to prayer every morning, noon, and evening. Resonant clanging from the campanile alerted the townsfolk whenever Mass was ready to begin. Weddings, special holy days, and holidays were celebrated with the jubilant ringing of the San Miguel Arcángel bells. At funerals, their heavy, deep-throated toll echoed the heartfelt loss of loved ones and called the people to prayer for their souls. The church doors remained open during the day, and the townspeople often walked inside to pray. The women wore delicately created mantillas, and the men removed their wide-brimmed sombreros that shielded them from Atotonilco's beating sun.

Don Epigmenio and Doña Luisa, fervent Catholics, wanted to pass their Catholic Faith along to their children. The couple wove Catholic customs and beliefs seamlessly into their daily family life, providing their children with a solid religious formation. This impacted Luisita powerfully. As a sunflower turns its face toward the sun, she turned her face toward the beauty of life, both within and outside of her home, and absorbed God's grace. She was dearly loved, and she knew it. The influence of her exemplary parents, their deep faith, devout adherence to the teachings of the Gospel and Holy Mother Church, and outstanding charity toward the poor and the needy, inspired Luisita and helped to form her character.

Descriptions of Luisita's parents reveal their character traits. Luisita's father, Don Epigmenio, was born into a family distinguished in Jalisco ever since colonial times, in the 1600s, and was known for his expansive and outgoing personality. A hard worker and a good businessperson, he took his responsibilities as a landowner seriously. Although he was popular among the townspeople and dearly loved by his family, his strong character would sometimes cause Doña Luisa, who also had a strong temperament, although a quieter one than her husband's, to tremble.

Doña Luisa, on the other hand, was quiet, steady, and reflective. She was strong and resolute, dominating and determined. Less restless than Don Epigmenio, she had innate prudence. Her light, gentle eyes and small, expressive mouth were framed within a perfectly oval face. Her movements were graceful. She radiated an inner beauty of soul. Doña Luisa was a woman who knew how to fit in, whatever the situation or the circumstance.

Don Epigmenio and Doña Luisa had fourteen children in all, but only nine lived—Luisita, Carlota, Maria del Refugio, Epigmenio, Maria, Maria Concepción, Maria Guadalupe, Aurelio Salvador, and José. The parents' personalities, though vastly different, complemented each other and helped them in the formation and education of their children.

∞

Luisita was nine years old when, in 1875, twin sisters, Maria Refugio and Carlota were born. Doña Luisa soon discovered that she needed someone to help nurse the newborn girls and asked Señora Rivera, who had a daughter about Luisita's age, to assist her by nursing one of the infants. Señora Rivera's daughter was named Francisca, but the family called her Pachita. Pachita and her mother remained in the de la Peña household for decades. Luisita and Pachita became close friends, and Luisita was Pachita's Confirmation sponsor.

When Pachita, at an advanced age, was interviewed by the author of a Spanish biography of Mother Luisita, *A Zaga de Su Huella* (Following in her footsteps), her colorful and precise recollections provided vivid portraits of Mother Luisita and her parents. Pachita said that every Saturday morning, Doña Luisa gave Luisita money, food, and clothing to pass along to the poor, as well as signed notes for the families living on the outlying ranches so they could buy necessities on her credit. She also paid many people's rents. According to Pachita, Luisita's mother was a very devout Catholic. She was devoted to Our Lady of Mount Carmel and prayed fifteen decades of the Rosary daily with her family.

Jalisco is peaceful now, but make no mistake about it, its people have suffered through many uprisings. Over a period of four centuries, from the Spanish conquest of Mexico by Cortés in the 1500s until the mid-twentieth century, battle after battle was fought on Jalisco's soil. The struggle for land, freedom, and justice that sparked these uprisings carried over into the life and times of the de la Peñas. The undercurrent from this long-standing, complicated relationship between conqueror and conquered affected Mother Luisita's life and the lives of those around her.

Luisita grew up in the lush, agricultural oasis in eastern Jalisco, far away from the political intrigues of the larger cities. Her father owned many large ranches in Los Altos, each one specializing in products of the fertile land: limes, guavas, apples, lemons, oranges, and grapefruits, as well as several varieties of trees. His fields, which sprawled across the vast agricultural region, also yielded beans, potatoes, corn, carrots, onions, chilis, and tomatoes.[14]

Luisita loved flowers—especially yellow ones, as yellow was, by far, her favorite color. Atotonilco's climate produces magnificent flowers that explode into vibrant colors. Bouquets made with Atotonilco's flowers are exquisite, with a beauty that almost takes your breath away. The townsfolk call one particularly fragrant blossom Santa Maria. It grows in vivid yellow and orange clusters, and children love to hide in its branches. Another favorite is jasmine. Every year on the solemnity of the birth of Saint John the Baptist, on June 24, the townspeople climb the mountains to gather the first jasmines of the season.

Like Atotonilco's fragrant jasmine, which releases its exquisite fragrance in the dark of night, as Luisita matured, her unwavering trust in God's goodness, providence, and mercy became a healing balm in the darkness of the lives of those who suffered, bringing them hope.

Land was important, then and now, and the Spanish conquest shifted ownership of land that belonged by right to the native people into the hands of the Spaniards. The local people were forced to work for the Spanish conquerors. This gave birth to the Mexican hacienda system, which lasted many centuries and has been compared by some to the feudal system in medieval Europe. In the feudal system, people who worked on the land, called serfs,

---

[14] Author's interview with Sister Patrocinio of Our Lady of Mount Carmel Gonzalez, Duarte, California, July 2016.

were servants of the lord of the manor, who owned the land and pocketed the profits of their backbreaking labor.

The landowners were known as *hacendados*. Wealth, political power, and access to education were concentrated among a handful of these elite families. *Hacendados* owned vast landholdings, most often acquired from taking over land they had conquered. Most of the other people in Mexico were landless peasant farmers called *campesinos* who worked on these vast estates. Many *hacendados* were corrupt and self-seeking. Don Epigmenio, however, was just and charitable, as were several other *hacendados* sprinkled here and there throughout Mexico.

As the influence of Catholicism spread throughout Mexico, religious fiestas (which honored saints or commemorated religious events), holy days, and weddings increased in number. People came on foot or by oxcart, burro, mule, horse, wagon, or carriage from distant haciendas and towns for these celebrations. The journeys were worth the time and effort as the people loved to get together to catch up on the news and to sing, dance, and trade stories. The people looked forward to the celebrations and their spirit of festivity and solidarity. Warm and hospitable, friendly and expressive, fiestas were important to family, faith, and cultural heritage.

When Don Epigmenio and Doña Luisa married, they placed their home under the patronage of Saint Joseph and every year hosted a grand fiesta on March 19, Saint Joseph's feast day. They celebrated with their family and field workers. De la Peña descendants still come together each year on the feast of Saint Joseph and bring donations for the ministries of Mother Luisita's community. The special day always begins with a family Mass and is followed by a dinner with music and entertainment.

The Mexican culture in which the de la Peña family lived was vibrant and strong. Work was hard during the week, but on Sundays the work stopped. In the 1800s, Sundays always began with

Mass at San Miguel's. After Mass, the people gathered in the plaza, which was filled with vendors' tables. Everyone enjoyed *pan dulce*, *dulces*, *atole*, *champurrado*, *tamales*, and a variety of fresh fruit and vegetables. Live music filled the plaza, and young and old enjoyed themselves throughout the long afternoon and evening.

∞

Mexico, then and now, remains a land of contrasts and conflicts. In this culture where great wealth and extreme poverty exist side by side, squalor and disease reign where opulence and comfort stop. Although Atotonilco el Alto was a charming place to live, the townsfolk understood there were people who lived in nearby hillside caves or wherever they could find shelter. Many families throughout Mexico lived in misery at the mercy of the elements and through the generosity of the rich.

This endless cycle of poverty that began with the Spanish conquest in 1519 continued for hundreds of years because of the widespread use of the *encomienda*, a grant from the Spanish Crown to the conquering Spaniards. It gave the conquerors the right to demand tribute and forced labor from the native inhabitants of the area, together with the handing over of all land rights. It was held in perpetuity by the Spanish grant holders and their descendants, who were called *encomenderos*.

Most of the Mexican people resented not only the *encomienda* but the whole hacienda system that it created. It is easy to understand how this caused the unrest and instability that existed for centuries. An inevitable war for independence came about in 1821, three hundred years after the Spaniards took power and forty-five years before Luisita's birth. But Mexico's independence from Spain did not bring stability to Jalisco. "Between 1825 and 1885, Jalisco witnessed twenty-seven peasant rebellions. Seventeen of these uprisings occurred within one decade, 1855–64, and the year 1857 witnessed ten separate revolts. The cause of these waves of unrest, popular protests, and open rebellions arose out of the political and social struggles among classes."[15]

At the time of Luisita's birth in 1866, the hacienda system was in full swing. Luisita, the *hacendado*'s daughter, was assured of the luxuries of the distinguished upper class. When she was old enough to begin school, her parents enrolled her in Señorita Lupe Escoto's elite school for girls of privileged families, but they soon discovered that Luisita was too sickly to attend with the other children. Because of her physical weakness, she could not be around large crowds, so her parents provided Luisita with a private tutor, an unmarried member of Don Epigmenio's family.

Her tutor's name was Agapita, but to Luisita, she was always just Pita. Luisita's relationship with Agapita impacted her life profoundly. Agapita was well-educated, self-disciplined, and amiable. More importantly, she was deeply spiritual. Agapita quickly became Luisita's confidante and a trusted friend, who guided her into a life of deep prayer. Whenever they were together, Luisita quietly observed Agapita's heart-to-heart conversations with God. Pita, who received Holy Communion every day during a period in history when daily Communion was extraordinary, carefully prepared Luisita for her First Holy Communion. She taught Luisita to say, "The great day of my First Communion is coming! The great day is coming!"[16]

---

[15] Donna S. Morales and John P. Schmall, *The History of Jalisco* (Houston: Houston Institute for Culture, 2004), 5.

[16] Although the exact date of Luisita's First Communion is unknown, she was confirmed sometime between June 6 and June 29, 1874, by Don Pedro Loza y Pardavé, archbishop of Guadalajara, during his pastoral visit to Atotonilco.

Pita influenced many children in Atotonilco and directed them wisely toward the practice of virtue. Pita and Luisita would often sit together in the backyard of the de la Peña home, amusing themselves for hours by sorting out the family's holy pictures and novenas. At other times, they would study the natural world around them and then discuss its mysteries. At night, they would watch the stars come out. Often the two would kneel together, with hands folded and eyes closed, and pray quietly. Simply and naturally, under Agapita's guidance, Luisita learned how to live in the presence of God, which allowed her to discover God in all that would happen in her life.

In 1876, when Luisita was only ten years old, General Porfirio Díaz took power as Mexico's president. Mexico was an isolated, unstable country at that time. During the *Porfiriato*, the name given to the thirty-four years during which Porfirio Díaz was in power, improvements were made, the wealth of the country increased, and cities were modernized and beautified. However, most of the people continued to live in extreme poverty. They suffered hunger and injustice, and if they voiced their rights or spoke of political freedom, they were persecuted. Education was available only to the middle and upper classes. In order to control the people, Díaz suppressed freedom of speech, the press, and the right of assembly. The so-called privileged classes of society monopolized any prosperity, while the rest of the people, the majority, deprived of medical attention and social service, cried at the top of their voices to demand their rights.

Luisita heard their cries, and as the years passed, she became aware that she was called to alleviate their sad existence.

Chapter 2

Vocation

My God, give me a holy heart
with a pure intention to please You.[17]

—Mother Luisita

In the Atotonilco valley, an endlessly blue sky meets the horizon, creating a backdrop for the luscious fruit trees—laden with apples, oranges, lemons, limes, and grapefruit—with their varying tones of green. Enticing citrus fragrances fill the air. The whole environment breathes forth peace and a sense of well-being. For those who work the land, God seems so close that prayer rises spontaneously from the heart.

The de la Peñas lived in such a setting, and the daily rhythm of life was shaped by the agricultural seasons: preparing the fields, planting, cultivating, and harvesting. Conversations were unhurried, and life was simpler—though, with Don Epigmenio's penchant for organizing fiestas, it was never dull.

As Luisita grew older, she tended to isolate herself because most of the time she preferred to be alone. Doña Luisa and Don

---

[17] Caravacci, *Loving Kindness*, 28.

21

Epigmenio began to wonder why. Was it her poor health that drew her into seclusion? She seemed to be utterly content just playing quietly or reading in a corner. When she grew older, as often as her health permitted, she slipped away to ride her spirited horse across Atotonilco's expansive landscape. In time, she became a skilled rider.

As Luisita advanced through her childhood years, her mother watched and waited as she continued to observe Luisita's isolation, and a more worrisome trait—her haughtiness. Doña Luisa slowly and methodically began the demanding task of Luisita's character formation, which the determined mother had decided would take the form of various tests of obedience. One of these tests is mentioned in Ariadne Caravacci's biography of Mother Luisita, *Loving Kindness*.

Aside from her haughtiness, Luisita was like all other youngsters her age. A share of whims accompanied her vanity. Mama Luisa was aware of all those characteristics and confronted them on an afternoon of bullfights. Luisita was dressed for a celebration and was visibly restless because of a fear that all children have of not being noticed. It was finally time to leave.

"It happens that you cannot go" her mother said.

"I want to go to the bullfights!" cried Luisita.

Doña Luisa retorted with, "So, you are going to leave me alone?" With those words she had touched a sensitive chord in her daughter's heart. Luisita loved her mother very much and could not bear to leave her alone.

"But what about the bullfights?" Luisita asked.

Luisita preferred not to hear the answer and changed the subject. She concluded with, "I want to listen to music."

"That's fine, the two of us can listen to it from here," her mother answered. It was true that the fiery Spanish pasa doble, which gave a unique flavor to a wild fiesta, was audible from the de la Peña house. Just some steps away and around the corner a temporary plaza was under construction.

It was too much for Luisita to bear. She had the usual look of a child who is about to cry.

Her mother commanded, "Stop crying; save your tears for the time of my death!"

Luisita answered, "I am ashamed to stop crying since I already started. It is all your fault because you didn't let me go to the bullfights!"[18]

Don Epigmenio also noticed the haughtiness that Luisita was displaying and provided his daughter with valuable character lessons. One family story relates how Don Epigmenio bought a beautiful and very expensive cloak for Luisita to wear at special fiestas. Later, he was appalled to see her putting the cloak on a donkey's back and running off to play. He punished her by buying a roll of very cheap material and telling her to make herself another cloak out of that cloth.

Another story that has come down to us through her family tells of one day when father and daughter went horseback riding together. Don Epigmenio and Luisita mounted their horses and headed for their ranches. Don Epigmenio greeted each worker with a pleasant *Buenos días* (Good morning). When the fieldworkers greeted Luisita, she turned her head away and pretended not to hear them. This happened several times. One day, Don Epigmenio turned and looked at her and said, "Luisita, why can't you simply greet these people?"

[18] Caravacci, *Loving Kindness*, 20.

Later in life, Mother Luisita shared that that was the day she began to change her ways. After the incident with her father, she strove to tame her self-centeredness and to learn compassion. Although her health and stamina were fragile, her moral character and willpower were strong, and little by little, she changed.

Several factors came together to support Luisita's desire to become a more caring person: her God-given gifts and talents, Agapita's friendship and guidance, the natural beauty of Atotonilco's countryside, her experience of growing up in a closely knit Catholic family, and her cooperation with God's grace in her life.

As she contemplated the beauty of creation in the Atotonilco countryside surrounding her hacienda, Luisita grew in her understanding of God as Creator and Father. Agapita helped her by leading her to a deeper awareness that God not only created everything in the world but also sustains everything by His power. She helped Luisita to discover the mystery of God in every creature and taught her to meditate and to have Heart-to-heart conversations with God.

Her family's deep faith impacted Luisita greatly, giving her a moral compass. Later in life, when referring to her spiritual growth, Mother Luisita used simple analogies from nature that she learned as a child to explain the quiet workings of the Holy Spirit within the soul. "Look," she would say. "These little leaves are close to the fountain, but if you look closely, you will see that they do not have much life; it is the same with us; we should take care not only to be close to the Fountain, but we also need to drink of the grace of God."[19] Finally, over and above all these, Luisita's openness to the promptings of the Holy Spirit helped her to accept and respond

---

[19] Personal remembrance of Sister Rosa Maria de la Inmaculada Hernandez Vasquez.

to God's grace. Her spiritual life was further strengthened when she received the Sacrament of Confirmation, which took place sometime between June 6 and June 29, 1874, and was administered by Archbishop Pedro Loza y Pardavé during his pastoral visit to Atotonilco. The exact date of her Confirmation or of her First Communion remains unknown.

When Luisita entered her teen years, her relationship with God was loving and comfortable. She thought of God spontaneously throughout the day and cherished her silent conversations with Him.

Vain and self-centered Luisita de la Peña, whose childhood behavior had been characterized as not easy to govern and as haughty, overly sensitive, and conveniently withdrawn, had changed. Grace builds on nature, or better still, grace completes or fulfills nature. Luisita began to make better choices and to form new habits of unselfishness and charity toward others. Her brother and sisters called her "Mama Luisita," because of the great respect they had for her.

A new Luisita had emerged during her early teens: a young woman who mounted her horse and galloped through the *haciendas del valle* (haciendas of the valley), who loved to dance cultural dances such as the *jarabe tapatío*, who sang well, and who, at her father's request, would walk to the bandstand and sing for the crowd as the mariachis played.

Teenage Luisita led an active social life, participated in the fiestas organized by her father, and was once chosen as the Queen of the Grand Fiesta. That day she wore an intricate black hair comb with a costly Sevillian mantilla and carried a fan with a bouquet of carnations. Yet her family tells us that even as Queen of the Grand Fiesta, Luisita still felt that the other girls who formed her court were more beautiful than she. Although she had come a long way in overcoming her self-centered tendencies, she had not yet accepted herself the way she was, as a unique person with both strengths and weaknesses. Luisita struggled against pride and vanity her whole life.

Years later, one of the Carmelite Sisters, after listening to Mother Luisita talk about her mother's strong discipline, remarked that Doña Luisa had acted unreasonably and too harshly. Mother Luisita answered, "Actually, my mother was very devoted to me, but she knew that my stubbornness had to be corrected. I had to learn to accept the denial of my own will. My mother let me know by experience what these cost. Besides, I'm sure that God was active in all of this. I was destined to become a religious sister. And the sculptor cannot carve a crucifix without blows."[20]

Luisita's health still worried her parents and her doctor. They ordered her to take daily walks and cautioned her to be sure to get enough rest and relaxation. Dutifully, during her free hours, she went for walks in the country, or through the orchards, usually with Agapita. Some days, these outings took place in an open carriage along the roads that joined the haciendas with the cultivated fields near the town.

Whenever a performance or concert was held in the plaza across from the de la Peña home, Don Epigmenio used to place about a dozen chairs around the petroleum lantern that hung from the ceiling of his front porch. Before long, all the chairs would be filled with family and friends. He opened the gated doors to the town's central plaza so his family could listen to music festivals. The plaza

[20] William M. Queen, *The Doctor's Widow* (Fresno: Academy Library Guild, 1956), 24.

was lit by lanterns of various sizes, with the larger ones placed in central areas and the smaller ones scattered among the trees, shops, and assorted ledges in and around the plaza. The scene replicated the exquisite beauty of the night sky with the lamps arranged like the stars in various constellations.

One evening, as the de la Peña family sat together enjoying the serenade, Luisita remained quiet and, with her eyes closed, whispered, "My God, give me a holy heart with a pure intention to please You."

These words, overheard by one of her sisters, open a window into her relationship with God. Luisita had always loved music and she relished the serenades, but now she preferred to pray quietly. Something new was stirring within her, something that she did not yet understand. The fiestas with their loud music no longer attracted her. The opposite was now true. They distracted her. She wanted to pray, and during these growing hours of communion with God, she felt herself led to follow another path — a path still unknown to her. Her thoughts gravitated toward her future.

Jaime de la Cruz, O.C.D., wrote a description of Luisita during this time of her life in *A Zaga de Su Huella*:

> There is nothing so relative as beauty and the language that expresses it. I have a picture of Mother Luisita on my desk. She was thirteen years old when it was taken. There is an indefinable expression on her face; it is the countenance of one who aspires to great things. Her gaze is not one of graciousness, but one of serene reflection, with a touch of sadness and severity. Her clear eyes look out from under the well-delineated, straight eyebrows. The naturalness of her lips is almost extraordinary. They are tightly closed and ready to utter a frank and positive statement at any

moment. Her whole demeanor reflects self-confidence and self-assurance. Her somewhat haughty expression was really a way to mask her shyness.[21]

Another description of Luisita is also found in Helenita Colbert's *The Flower of Guadalajara*: "She possessed a natural unadorned beauty. She was not very tall; in fact, she might be considered rather petite. Her frailty only accentuated her charm. Her skin was very fair, with an almost transparent quality. She dressed her dark hair in a graceful but simple style. From her childhood, she was inclined to be serious and thoughtful, yet she had developed an enjoyable sense of humor."[22] Luisita's hazel eyes were that rare combination of brown, green, and gold possessed by only 5 percent of the world's population.

Doctor Pascual Rojas, a frequent visitor to the de la Peña hacienda, was a good friend of Don Epigmenio. The Rojas family belonged to the distinguished upper class of Atotonilco el Alto, and the two families were related by marriage. One of Don Epigmenio's brothers, José Maria, had married Adelaide Rojas Santoscoy, who was Pascual's older sister. In her remembrances, Sister Luisa Maria Josefa Estrada remembered something that Mother Luisita had once told her. "I heard from her that one day when her mother was combing her hair, Doctor [Rojas] arrived at her home, and that she thought, 'I wonder who is going to marry him.'"[23]

Time would tell.

---

[21] Jaime de la Cruz, O.C.D., *A Zaga de Su Huella* (Mexico: Los Talleres Graficos de La Editorial Helio-México, S.A., 1961), 36.

[22] Helenita Colbert, *The Flower of Guadalajara* (Alhambra, CA: Carmelite Sisters' Printing, 1956), 4.

[23] Personal remembrance of Sister Luisa María Josefa del Niño Jesus Estrada Gonzalez.

Chapter 3

Protectors of Atotonilco

They not only respected and loved each other; they had not only become one through their marriage, but they now shared the same great ideal through their love for the poor. The doctor placed his medical knowledge and advice at their disposal, and Luisita provided them with food, clothing, and other indispensable items. Above all, she offered them kindness and affection.[24]

A group of curious tourists standing around a simple, hand-carved wooden trunk are visiting the Mother Luisita heritage room in Atotonilco. The trunk holds some items from Luisita and Pascual's fourteen-year marriage. The Carmelite Sister who conducts the tour closes the lid gently and points to the painted initials on the top. Originally, she explains, the letters were P. R., the initials of Pascual Rojas. It had been his trunk. Looking closely at the initials, the tourists could see how Luisita had painted over parts of each letter to change the initials to L. P., for Luisita and Pascual.

Back in the 1880s, privileged hacienda life came with its respon-sibilities. Doña Luisa had prepared Luisita well for her marriage.

---

[24] Caravacci, *Loving Kindness*, 45.

For years, Luisita had observed the management of servants and watched how daily schedules were made and distributed; she learned the many responsibilities that were a part of running a large household. At the same time, as Luisita continued along the steady path toward marriage, a path that had been traced out for her since birth, she experienced the Holy Spirit gently drawing her toward God. A quiet, persistent, interior calling to give herself completely to God alone resonated within her soul.

Some of the books and articles on Mother Luisita's life give the impression that she married Doctor Pascual Rojas Santoscoy only out of obedience to her parents and not out of love. But that was not the case. Luisita loved Pascual, and he loved her.[25] Sister Paulina of Jesus Flores Alvarez recalled that much later in her life, Mother Luisita had been asked by one of the sisters if she had loved "Pascualito," and her response was that she had loved him very much.[26] Their marriage had been arranged, it is true, according to the custom of the day. William Queen writes in *The Doctor's Widow* that "while Luisita was still in the cradle and Pascual still a boy at school, Mama Rojas implored the de la Peñas to reserve the hand of their daughter for her son."[27]

In an interview with the author of *A Zaga de Su Heulla* around 1960, many years after Mother Luisita's death, her youngest sister, Lupita, recalled, "One day I asked her, 'Why did you get married?'

[25] Author's February 1998 interview with de la Peña family members, whose oral tradition affirms the love of Pascual and Luisita. At the Synod on the Family in 1980, Cardinal Palazzini, prefect of the Congregation for the Causes of Saints, in two synodal interventions noted the marriage of Pascual and Luisita as a model of Catholic marriage.

[26] Personal remembrance of Sister Paulina of Jesus Alvarez.

[27] Queen, *The Doctor's Widow*, 29.

Mother Luisita answered, '... Because Mamá Rosarito [Doctor Rojas's mother] wanted me to marry Pascualito and she told my father; consequently, it came to be.' "[28] In the 1880s, this was the established custom throughout Mexico and, like the other families, the de la Peñas followed the tradition of arranged marriages. Luisita was fifteen and Pascual was thirty at the time of their marriage.

How strange it must have been for Luisita to experience at the same time the desire for two entirely different vocations—marriage and the consecrated life[29] of a religious Sister. Luisita did not have a spiritual director. Nor did she have any available books to help her find a point of reference regarding the life of total consecration to God. She had not taken any special catechism courses. No religious sisters served in Atotonilco at that time. She and Pascual accepted and followed the traditional, conservative Jalisco marriage protocols: the promenades, the serenades, and the formal asking of the father for the hand of his daughter in marriage.

The marriage of Luisita and Pascual was celebrated by everyone in the little town of Atotonilco. On February 7, 1882, their civil marriage took place at Don Epigmenio's hacienda, *La Labor*. Two days later, long before dawn, in the early hours of Thursday,

---

[28] Personal remembrance of Guadalupe de la Peña Ugarte, Mother Luisita's sister.

[29] "To consecrate something means to set it aside or devote it to a holy purpose. When a man or woman decides to accept Christ's invitation to leave everything and follow Him in a more radical way, they make vows to live like Jesus in poverty, chastity, and obedience. They promise Christ that they will live the rest of their lives dedicated exclusively to Him. These vows help them to live simply, to be more open with God, and to depend totally on Him." "What Is Consecrated Life?," Catholic Diocese of Raleigh, https://dioceseofraleigh.org/religious-orders/what-consecrated-life.

February 9, 1882, people from the various ranches throughout the surrounding hills plodded along the winding trails of Los Altos on their way to San Miguel Arcángel to attend the church wedding. San Miguel Arcángel Church was crowded to overflowing long before the wedding bells rang out joyfully from the campanile. Luisita had grown into a compassionate and empathetic young woman who had endeared herself to all, rich and poor alike, and they all hoped to join in the celebration.

Although there are portions of Luisita's life that are sketchy at best, when it comes to her wedding day, there is an abundance of information. Any wedding in Atotonilco el Alto brought about a break in the daily schedule of hard work in the fields, a time to relax, socialize, and enjoy family and friends. The wedding of the eldest daughter of the *hacendado* to the distinguished and respected Doctor Pascual Rojas was unparalleled in every way. The de la Peñas had the financial resources that made this wedding a day the whole town remembered for a long, long time.

Thankfully, many details of Pascual and Luisita's wedding day have survived the passing of decades. Luisita wore a sprig of orange blossoms in her hair as her carriage drove to the plaza. A carpet of flowers lined the street up to the door of the church. Pascual, dressed in an impeccable black suit, waited at the door of the church. He extended his arm to his bride as they walked slowly down the aisle together, according to the custom of the day.

Soft, midmorning sunlight shone upon the people. White flowers were everywhere. A complete orchestra was hired for the occasion; this included two kettle drums and multiple trumpets to accompany the wedding march. The repertoire included the favorites of the time and was more romantic than devotional. The church music reforms of Pope Pius X were to come several decades later.

The nuptial Mass and exchange of wedding vows followed, and the traditional shower of rice fell upon the newlyweds as they left the church. A soft breeze carried the joyful ringing of the bells across the plaza and beyond, into the town. The reception celebration following the ceremony lasted well into the afternoon. Luisita and Pascual took their time and greeted everyone personally. They both understood how far people had traveled by foot to attend their wedding. For many people, it was a hardship to travel to Atotonilco. The couple also realized that they would have to retrace their long journey back through Los Altos again later that day. The banquet with live music and dancing continued into the late afternoon, when the newlyweds finally slipped away for their honeymoon. Some biographies say that the honeymoon began that same day, and others say that it was delayed.

According to Hector de la Peña, Mother Luisita's nephew, who described his aunt's wedding in *A Biography of My Aunt: Mother Luisita*, the newlyweds began their honeymoon on horseback, riding the fifty-eight miles to Guadalajara, stopping along the way at small towns where they spent the nights and visited whatever local attractions the places provided. It is easy to picture the two of them beginning their honeymoon trip galloping across the countryside. Jalisco is known for its fine horses, and Pascual and Luisita were accomplished riders.

Although the Spanish conquerors had prohibited the native people in Mexico from owning horses, it did not take long for the Spaniards to learn that cattle raising required the use of horses. By the 1800s, wealthy plantation owners such as the de la Peña and Rojas families wore decorated versions of the distinctive *charro* clothing, and the intricate decoration of their horses displayed their status in the community. Even today, many of the traditional Jalisciense folk dances mimic horses prancing, galloping, and trotting. It is beautiful to watch.

Pascual had lived in Guadalajara for twelve years before his marriage to Luisita. He had received his higher education, which included medical school, in Guadalajara, so he knew that city well. For several years, he had lived in the neighborhood known as the Santuario, and during his final years of study, he resided in the neighborhood known as the Sagrario. Both neighborhoods were named for the nearby churches. When he completed his medical studies, internship, and other final requirements, Pascual returned to his hometown of Atotonilco. He had been back there for only four years before his marriage.

On their honeymoon, Luisita and Pascual toured Guadalajara leisurely, visiting the various attractions, including the Mariachi Plaza. Mexico's famed mariachi music is said to have begun in their state of Jalisco, and Guadalajara's mariachis even today are still considered the cream of the crop. After enjoying the attractions in Guadalajara, the couple boarded a stagecoach for the next part of their trip, the almost three-hundred-mile journey to Mexico City. To travel by stagecoach was a sign of wealth in those days, as was the length of their extended honeymoon. Luisita and Pascual journeyed along the newly paved road that stretched all the way from Ciudad Juarez in northern Mexico to Mexico City. The long, dusty, bumpy days of stagecoach travel held one monotonous scene after another as they crossed the central plateau.

The trip from Guadalajara to Mexico City at that time was both costly and risky. The road harbored robbers and revolutionary patrols who were still protesting "the War of the Reform," a civil war that had taken place in that area from 1858 to 1860, only twenty years earlier. Reminders of the violent battles, bloodshed, and revenge could still be seen on the road. One of these was the tree where conservative army general Leonardo Márquez ordered the hanging of Melchor Ocampo, the radical, liberal, fiercely anticlerical Mexican lawyer, scientist, and politician. After the war, the new 1859 Laws of the Reform, as they were called, stated that church property, except for places of worship, was to be confiscated without compensation, monasteries were to be suppressed, cemeteries were to be nationalized, and civil marriage was to be instituted.

Pascual and Luisita passed through San Juan de los Lagos, Lagos de Moreno, León, Celaya, Querétaro, and Tepeji del Río in the state of Hidalgo. Just outside Mexico City, they passed through the suburb known today as Satelite. Some called Mexico City "the Holy City of the New World." At the time the newlyweds were traveling on their honeymoon journey, there were at least seventy churches in the capital; fourteen were local parish churches in Mexico City. In addition, twenty-three churches belonged to religious orders, such as the Dominicans, Franciscans, Augustinians, Order of Mercy, and Carmelites. Twenty of these churches belonged to nuns, along with several chapels and public oratories. So many art treasures had been lavished upon the churches that they resembled elegant museums.

During the 1800s, Mexico City was distinguished for its scientific and literary institutions. Among those of higher learning were the University of Mexico (the oldest university in the Americas), the College of Mining, the seminaries of San Gregorio and Los Infantes, and the Academy of Fine Arts, to name a few. Luisita preferred to visit religious sites, and Pascual chose museums and other places dedicated to the advancement of science and the humanities. Unfortunately, the War of the Reform had destroyed many works of art in the name of progress, and only their memory lingered like ghosts trapped within the now "progressive" lecture halls and classrooms.

Mexico City offered Luisita and Pascual a variety of experiences to choose from: theaters, concert halls, museums, gardens, and parks. The Viga was among the very best and most popular parks at the time of their honeymoon. Tourists as well as locals took outings to the wharf and enjoyed boat rides on the canal or along the exquisite floating gardens of Xochimilco.

The Alameda, the lovely park west of the historical center of Mexico City, began as an Aztec marketplace. Created in 1592, it is the oldest public park in the Americas and is a popular tourist attraction. Along these streets, Luisita and Pascual found scattered booths where vendors sold fruit, cold drinks, sweets, and clothing typical of the area. The newlyweds were accompanied by the ringing of church bells that summoned people to prayer throughout the morning hours.

For fifteen-year-old Luisita, who had grown up in an agricultural milieu, her entire honeymoon presented a complete change of scene for her. Pascual, an ardent lover of the arts, took Luisita to the national galleries, museums, and parks. She, who enjoyed music and loved to sing and dance, was escorted by her husband to many concerts and operas. Because of their high social standing, the couple received many invitations from family friends to dinner parties and other social engagements.

Among all of Pascual and Luisita's honeymoon experiences, one stands out—the day Luisita asked to visit the convent of the Conceptionist nuns. When Pascual escorted Luisita to the convent, she was completely at ease talking with the Mother Superior. At one point, enjoying the beauty of the prayerful convent atmosphere, she turned and told Pascual to leave her there. There are different renditions to the story of what followed, but they all agree that

Pascual, with the Mother Superior's help, persuaded Luisita that her place was with her husband. When the couple left, that door closed behind them. In God's good time, another convent door would open for Luisita, but not until many years had passed.

By the time their extended honeymoon was over, husband and wife had come to know each other better and had learned how deeply each one cared for the welfare of the most impoverished of Mexico's people, those who had no education, no health care, and no religious formation. Basically, these people had no rights. In fact, when Doctor Rojas was offered a very good position in Mexico City, he did not accept it. He preferred to work in his own town where there was a greater need for a doctor.

The couple finally returned to their two-story Atotonilco home. It featured excellent views of San Miguel Arcángel Church. The view from the back of the house offered a panorama of the surrounding hills and countryside. Luisita began to settle down to her new life. After some time had passed, and with tears in her eyes, Luisita finally blurted out to Pascual, "I want to go to my mother!" Doctor Rojas, mature physician that he was, agreed that she should go and visit her mother. In a short time, the visits grew more and more infrequent, until one day Luisita no longer needed them. Her husband's unfailing gentleness and compassion, which she praised highly until the end of her days, endeared him to her. As time passed, Luisita became known for her gracious hospitality toward everyone as she grew gracefully into her new role as Señora de Rojas.

Luisita, an organizer by nature, developed a schedule for her new life as Señora de Rojas. Her day began at five in the morning as she prayed in her bedroom, kneeling before the crucifix Pascual had given her as a present.[30] She attended the early morning Mass and received Holy Communion as often as the Church permitted. As time went on, Pascual also attended daily Mass. She planned so that the servants could also attend Mass later in the morning. Several details about their daily routines are known. Although the couple had many servants, Luisita insisted that she wanted to prepare Pascual's breakfast of lime juice, a variety of fruit, and a steaming cup of chocolate. At nine, Pascual studied his medical journals and books. He was a good doctor and continued his specialized studies throughout his life. During the remainder of the morning, he made house calls.

Luisita stayed at home and kept to her schedule. Although others did the housework, it was Luisita's practice after breakfast each day to wash and dry their breakfast dishes. Afterward, she worked on her embroidery. At some point, spiritual reading was added to the staff's daily schedule. Each person brought some relaxing work to do as Mother Luisita read aloud to them, usually biographies of saints whose lives were described in *The Christian Year*. *The Life of Saint Jane Frances de Chantal* was her favorite. She also read sections from the popular *Catechism of Perseverance* by Abbot Jean-Joseph Gaume. Agapita had read excerpts from these books to Luisita when she was a child. *Catechism* is a historical, doctrinal, and moral study of the Catholic religion, still available in an updated edition.

At eleven o'clock, Luisita went outside for some sunshine. Her husband, who worried about her frail health, had prescribed this daily routine, and she followed his recommendation to the letter. Pascual also gave her a harmonica and asked her to learn a tune

[30] Author's visit to the Galería de Madre Luisita, Generalate of the Carmelitas del Sagrado Corazón, Guadalajara, Mexico, July 2016.

for him, telling her that it would help increase her lung capacity and strengthen her breathing. She was determined to master "Tres Saucitos," one of the most popular songs of the day, on her new harmonica. She finally perfected it, to his great surprise. Another natural remedy Pascual prescribed for his wife to build up her frail body was an order for beefsteaks to be set before her at breakfast. Eating these thick beefsteaks, and especially at breakfast, was a sacrifice for Luisita, but she did it to please Pascual.

Lunch with Pascual was next on her schedule, followed by the customary siesta. Pascual had told Luisita at the beginning of their marriage that he needed twenty minutes' rest each day. While he rested, Luisita remained at his side, reading a good book, and awakened him when it was time to get up. In the afternoon, she visited the sick and brought them nourishing food. When her visits included her property called Valle of Guadalupe, or Guadalupe Valley, she organized processions with the ranchers to pray for rain during times of drought.

After they had been married awhile, Luisita visited the sick with her husband in the afternoons. The townsfolk looked up to this special couple and began to call them their "Protectors of Atotonilco." And they were beginning to call Luisita "the heart and soul of Atotonilco."[31]

As the months passed, Pascual gradually became aware of a new restlessness within his soul. Luisita had noticed this also, and during the quiet evenings at home, she would sometimes turn the conversation to one of the spiritual books she was reading.

[31] Personal remembrance of Mother Mary of the Eucharist Nuñez Hernandez.

Sometimes Pascual would read these as well. Although he was accustomed to reading his medical journals, he discovered that at this stage in his life, he was being called to a deeper personal prayer. Pascual came to embrace his Catholic Faith more fully and to take his spiritual life more seriously.

Pascual and Luisita had settled into a comfortable and happy life together. They complemented each other. His medical practice was flourishing, and their social calendar was filled with dinners and other social events with family and friends. Their married life together was peaceful, and things were going well.

In the late afternoons, Luisita liked to sit quietly by the window and pray. Sometimes when her husband arrived home earlier than usual, and the servants did not notify her that he was home, Pascual would enter the house and come upon a peaceful scene in the living room: Luisita sitting by the window in complete silence, eyes closed and deep in prayer. He would quietly and respectfully leave her alone to pray.

Something new was about to happen, dawning on the horizon, and the couple was now ready.

Chapter 4

Healing

Luisita, since God has not willed to give us a
family, the poor shall be our children.[32]

The money God has given us to bring about this work is like
the blood of Christ. It must serve to redeem the world.[33]

—Pascual Rojas, M.D.

Gusts of swirling dirt billowed across El Camino Real as mule driv-
ers coaxed the sure-footed animals along the dusty road. Slumped
across the back of one of the mules was an elderly woman who was
barely alive. The muleteers had discovered her lying in a ditch by
the side of the road; she was sick, abandoned, and entirely helpless.
They had picked her up and placed her on one of the animals to
transport her to the next town, Atotonilco. When they arrived
there, they left her in the town prison because there was not one
place that would accept her.

The Castañeda family was the first to come and visit her. Then
the Romo family arrived and took her to their home. Doctor

[32] Personal remembrance of Mother Margarita Maria of the Sacred
Heart Hernandez.
[33] Caravacci, *Loving Kindness*, 56.

Pascual Rojas arrived and evaluated her. They gave her some nourishment and called a priest to give her the Last Rites of the Church before she died. This pivotal incident was the catalyst of the next stage in Luisita's life. After the woman's death, Luisita said that the situation of the destitute was deplorable, and it was clear that there was an urgent need for someone to care for them in their afflictions.

Señorita Carmen Gutiérrez, an Atotonilco governess, suggested to Luisita that they gather a group of women and establish a charity organization. Father Celso Sánchez Aldana, pastor of San Miguel Arcángel, wholeheartedly approved the project and chose the name of the group: the Conference of Saint Vincent de Paul, under the patronage of the Sacred Heart of Jesus. The first meeting was held on October 9, 1891, and the Conference was canonically established on November 15 of that year. Luisita was elected as the first president, but the pastor presided at meetings. From that day on, committees were formed to bring food and comfort to people in need. Catechism lessons were combined with women's visits to the people living in the humble barrios of Atotonilco.

It did not take the women long to realize that they needed more than their newly formed charity committees to address the problem. They needed a place for the seriously ill to stay while receiving treatment. Doctors would go only to the homes of sick patients who could pay for their services. Over the years, Pascual had wanted to establish a house of charity for the sick. Since it was impossible for the members of the Conference of Saint Vincent de Paul to take care of the patients in their own homes, Pascual decided to join with the Conference to establish his hospital for those who could not afford medical care. The time was right. Luisita had been elected president, and the pastor was in full agreement.

The minutes of the Conference of Saint Vincent de Paul state that Señora A. V. De González, Señorita Carmen Gutiérrez, and Señor Juan P. Shagún, a lawyer, were assigned to ask Don Pascual Reinaga if he would donate a house to be turned into a hospital. He gladly agreed on the condition that there would always be at least one sick person being cared for in it. Pascual immediately obtained funding and began to remodel the house.

The minutes go on to state that the first furniture was bought with a donation made by Señora Antonia S. F. De Carrillo. Other furniture was purchased with contributions collected among the neighbors. One woman sold her pocket watch and gave the money as her donation. Although a good number of the townpeople were lethargic and indifferent to the project, the energetic response of the others more than compensated for it.

Pascual and Luisita gave of themselves as well. They were no longer satisfied with a peaceful life for just the two of them: both wanted children to complete their lives, and they prayed novenas asking God to give them children. As they prayed for this intention and no babies came, they slowly concluded that it was not God's will for them to have their own family. With deep conviction, Pascual told his wife, "Luisita, since God has not willed to give us a family, the poor shall be our children."[34] From that moment on, they dedicated their lives to the realization of this mission, investing their time and fortune with ever greater earnestness and zeal.

On January 6, 1892, a month before their tenth wedding anniversary and only two months after the establishment of the Conference of Saint Vincent de Paul, the little Hospital of the Sacred Heart was solemnly blessed in the presence of almost all

[34] Sister Mary Jeanne Coderre, "Mother Luisita: The Marriage Years," *Carmelite Sisters Newsletter* 1, no. 3 (2003): 2.

the townspeople. Hard work together with the unstoppable energy of Luisita, Pascual, and the members of the Conference made this little hospital possible.

Today there is a bronze plaque engraved with the words Doctor Rojas addressed to all those attending the ceremony that cold January day: "The money God has given us to bring about this work is like the blood of Christ. It must serve to redeem the world." Carmen Gutiérrez and Doctor Pascual Rojas asked friends, neighbors, and parishioners of San Miguel Arcángel if they would make a monthly pledge to support the new hospital. Many people did, and Doctor Rojas became known as "the father of the poor."

Their first patient was a woman whose predicament stemmed from moral difficulties rather than physical ailments. She became a symbol of the hospital's mission to bring healing to both body and soul. She became one of the hospital's first volunteers.

Once Doctor Pascual Rojas had obtained Don Reinaga's donation of a one-room house to be used as a hospital, he saw that it needed serious repairs. These were done gradually.

Pascual and Luisita celebrated their tenth wedding anniversary on February 9, 1892. Luisita had accepted married life with all its responsibilities. Pascual, who loved Luisita so deeply, now lived his Catholic Faith more profoundly. Luisita, who had been so introspective, lost some of her shyness and learned to deal with the various personalities and temperaments of people, a skill that would be essential in the life of her future religious community.

Even before the establishment of the Conference of Saint Vincent de Paul and the little Hospital of the Sacred Heart, Pascual and Luisita had made it their special mission to care for the needs of the indigent. Pascual donated his services as a physician. Luisita provided them with food, clothing, and other indispensable items. Above all, she offered them kindness and affection. Marcario Rojas, Pascual's brother and a pharmacist, helped by filling prescriptions free of charge.

When Luisita accompanied her husband on his visits to the sick, one of the servants accompanied them, carrying a basket with items for the poor. Pascual would prudently place a "gift" under the pillow of the sick person or into the hands of a relative to help the person take care of some other need. His care was not confined to the physical ailments of his patients but extended to their financial or moral issues. Now the couple's lives did not revolve around the social activities of the privileged class but focused more on their home, their church, their hospital, and their visits to the sick.

The hospital always needed funds. The generous donations of the townsfolk were no longer sufficient. Pascual got the idea to host a bullfight as a fundraiser. The de la Peña home was directly across the street from Atotonilco's bullring. Bullfighting, which had come to Mexico from Spain, was to 1880s Mexico what baseball is to the United States today: a national pastime. Rural areas such as Atotonilco did not have access to the great matadors of Mexico, but the townspeople loved bullfights, so Pascual's announcement that he planned to host the national sport in Atotonilco to raise funds to aid the suffering poor was met with cheers.

The town was filled with expectation. People understood that the bullfight would serve a dual purpose: to bring joy to the people and to raise funds for the poor. Pascual was able to contract a special *corrida de toros* (bullfight) that included lively pre-show entertainment like circus acts. His promotional advertisement read: ¡A gozar! ¡A gozar, pueblo de Atotonilco! ¡Vengan todos a la corrida de toros! (Enjoy! Enjoy, people of Atotonilco! Everyone come to the bullfight!)

The day arrived. The seats around the arena filled quickly. Years ago, Doña Luisa had forbidden Luisita to attend bullfights. Perhaps now Luisita would see one of the reasons why her mother did not want her child to go. It was cruel, fierce, and bloodthirsty, with a matador brandishing his red cape and his sword poised for inflicting the mortal wound into the noble, massive bull. Now, at long last, Luisita had her opportunity to view this "sport," not as a little girl with a new yellow dress but as a mature, principled woman alongside her husband.

Even the pre-show had its cruel side. The biography *A Zaga de Su Huella* describes some of the gory details. Jaime de la Cruz, O.C.D., writes that bullfights are a serious business in Mexico. He explains how some people believe that the bullfight is a spiritual metaphor and that excuses the bloody drama.

Not everyone agrees.

What thoughts went through Luisita's mind and heart as she watched the spectacle? History has not recorded them. Nevertheless, a brief oral history that has survived the decades discloses that something unexpected happened during that bullfight. It does not reveal the cause, only the consequence. Did one of the bulls break loose? Or was an intoxicated person the reason for the commotion? Tequila flowed freely during these events. In any case, the story that has come down through the years reveals that someone was very badly injured. The matador?

Luisita asked her husband, "But, Pascualito, what of the responsibilities and the souls?"

"What about their souls?"

Souls.

This powerful word marked the dawning of the next stage in Luisita's life.

And Pascual never organized another bullfight.

∞

Luisita's father, Don Epigmenio, was dead. The year was 1895, and the little Hospital of the Sacred Heart was in its fourth year. Many people had been treated there since its opening on that cold January day in 1892. The women learned how to nurse and care for the sick; this was 100 percent better than the previous health care of the indigent, for whom nothing had ever been done. Luisita had learned much from her husband in her years working alongside him, and she took her place, too, as a nurse on a rotating schedule with the other women. One of the first photos we have of Mother Luisita shows her with this group of ladies, some children, and a recovered patient around a statue of Saint Vincent de Paul.

While Luisita was still grieving the death of her father, tragedy descended upon her home. On Ash Wednesday 1896, Pascual became very ill and traveled to Guadalajara for surgery. Her sister Mariquita was living at her ranch near Guadalajara, and Luisita asked her if she would help them find a house in the city where she and Pascual could stay after the operation. Mariquita found one centrally located on Calle Galeana. Luisita and Pascual quickly moved there.

Doctor Arce performed the delicate operation. It was not successful. In the days before antibiotics, infections claimed many lives, especially following surgery. Both Luisita and Pascual knew that his case was terminal. After the operation, Luisita sat by his bed and helped him prepare for his death. She led him through a retreat using a book on the Spiritual Exercises of Saint Ignatius. She also read to him from other spiritual books. He received the Last Sacraments. His death certificate states that the cause of death was a severe urinary tract infection.

An important conversation has come down through the years, and although some of the details vary, its essence can be easily gleaned. Here are three variations of what happened. Mother Margarita Maria of the Sacred Heart relates that "Pascual, holding a crucifix as he was dying, told his wife, 'He [Christ] will be your husband when I die.' "[35]

William Queen writes, "Pascual on the brink of eternity took her hand in his and said, with a smile radiant with reverence and devotion: 'Luisita, there is no need for me to ask you what you will do after I am gone.' "[36] He knew that she longed to enter the convent someday.

Helenita Colbert writes:

> One afternoon while Luisita was sitting beside his bed, he reached over and took her hand in his and smiled at her, a smile of deep reverence, affection and gratitude. Then he said, "There is no need for me to ask you what you will do after I am gone." She did not interrupt but waited for him to continue. He closed his eyes and seemed a long way off, as if he were reminiscing. Then he said quietly, "Do you remember when we were on our honeymoon, and I promised you that if you would come back to Atotonilco with me I would let you return to the convent? Very soon now I am going to keep that promise."[37]

On Good Friday, April 3, 1896, at six in the evening, Pascual Rojas gave his soul to God in peace and tranquility. Several moments after his death, Luisita walked quietly into the adjoining room and made a vow of chastity before the crucifix that Pascual had given her as a gift. This vow was received by his nephew, Friar

[35] Personal remembrance of Mother Margarita Maria Hernandez.
[36] Queen, *The Doctor's Widow*, 39.
[37] Colbert, *The Flower of Guadalajara*, 8.

Nicholas of the Child Jesus Fernández Santoscoy, O.S.F., who had accompanied his uncle during his final days. After pronouncing her vow, she came back to the room where Pascual's body lay and remained there for hours, praying and resting beside his body.

"I have never seen a preparation for death so perfect as that of Doctor Rojas," declared the pastor of San Miguel Arcángel, Father Celso Sánchez Aldana.[38]

At eleven o'clock on that same Friday night, Heliodoro de la Peña, another of Pascual's nephews, and Esteban Barga, a lawyer from Guadalajara, as well as Doctor Salvador Fernandez, a doctor from Guadalajara, knocked on the door of Ignacio Vallejo, a judge. Pascual's death was then inscribed in the Municipal Register of Deaths, and the judge signed the document that allowed Pascual's body to be transported to Atotonilco for burial.

Early April 4, 1896, Holy Saturday, a train began the sixty-eight-mile journey from Guadalajara to La Barca, Jalisco, with the body of Pascual in a special compartment used for the transport of coffins. Luisita boarded a separate compartment to accompany her husband's body to their hometown. When the train stopped at La Barca, Pascual's body was removed from the train and then transported by a horse-drawn funeral wagon to Atotonilco with Luisita following closely behind for the thirty-four-mile final journey from La Barca to Atotonilco.

Father Aldana, his altar servers, and nearly three thousand people met them as they neared the town. At an improvised altar, right there in the street, the pastor welcomed the body. The townspeople intoned the responses to the various prayers. Then everyone processed to the church, where the funeral rites were celebrated by Father Aldana with great solemnity. Meanwhile,

---

[38] Caravacci, *Loving Kindness*, 58.

Heliodoro presented to the judge in Atotonilco the documents from Guadalajara that authorized the transferring of Pascual's body to be buried in Atotonilco. The people formed a procession to the municipal cemetery, where Pascal's body was laid to rest. In the memorial book for the fourth centenary of the foundation of Atotonilco, a picture of Doctor Pascual Rojas is accompanied by the following lines, which summarize his life as one of the "Distinguished Sons of the Town."

> The townspeople remember him
> with admiration and affection
> for the favors he rendered
> to the poor.[39]

After the burial, when Luisita announced that she would return to her beautiful home, Doña Luisa turned to her and said, "I have let all your help go, Luisita, because you are going to stay here with me. If you wish, you can have your own maid, but you are not going to live alone. You are coming home with me."

---

[39] *Memorial Book of the 400th Anniversary of the Founding of Atotonilco* (Atotonilco, Jalisco, 1951).

Part 2

The Mexican Revolution (1896–1921)

Widow to Foundress

I was walking down the school corridor when the mother of one of my sixth-grade students walked up and said that she had something to tell me. An atmosphere of unrest had settled in our little town. Everyone was on edge, restless, apprehensive. I honestly don't recall now exactly what caused it.

Out of the blue, the mother looked me squarely in the eye and said, "Sister, I decided something last night. I made the decision that if anything catastrophic happens – a great earthquake, war, whatever – I'm going to come here to the school. It's the only place I feel that my family would be safe."

– Author

Chapter 5

The Widow with a Basket

Before his death, the doctor had said to his wife,
"Luisita, everything I have, I leave for your work."[40]

On Holy Saturday evening in 1896, a horse and buggy traveled slowly along one of Atotonilco's narrow cobblestone avenues. A subdued Luisita, dressed austerely in traditional mourning attire, was in the buggy. Her husband was not at her side this evening, nor would he ever be again. After fourteen years of marriage and after Pascual's burial, she was now traveling back to her childhood home to live again with her mother, who was also recently widowed.

It had been a long weekend. Pascual's final agony and death on Good Friday: the late-night knocking on the door of the magistrate to get the required signature to take the body back to Atotonilco for burial; the somber train ride to La Barca and the seemingly endless journey following his horse-drawn funeral wagon along the dusty roads between La Barca and Atotonilco; and, finally, the funeral rites and procession to the municipal cemetery, where he was buried on that Holy Saturday. After the funeral, her required period of mourning began.

[40] Personal remembrance of Sister Paulina of Jesus Flores.

Grieving the death of a spouse was taken very seriously in Mexico at the end of the nineteenth century. A widow was not supposed to enter society for twelve months. No lady or gentleman could attend social events while grieving. Servants wore black armbands when there had been a death in the household. To this day, in traditional regions of Mexico, widows maintain the custom of wearing black for the rest of their lives.[41]

Later that day, when Doña Luisa overheard Luisita say that she was determined to surpass even the strict mourning protocol followed in Mexico at that time, she became worried that Luisita would harm her health. That evening, Doña Luisa slipped into Luisita's bedroom and quietly took away from her daughter's wardrobe the black nightgown that was "symbolic of the widow's grief that knows no slumber."[42]

The next morning, Luisita went into seclusion and invited her dear friend and goddaughter Francisca Rivera, or "Pachita," to accompany her in her sorrow. Pachita had grown up alongside her and remained a close friend throughout the years. She still worked as a domestic in the de la Peña family home. It is because of Pachita that some details of Luisita's widowhood are known today. Luisita and Pachita moved into a back area of the de la Peña home that overlooked the garden. The room was more like a hall, and it was there that the two women came together each day for prayer, penance, and charitable services. During her mourning period, although Luisita remained president of the Conference of Saint Vincent de Paul, she remained in her mother's home.

---

[41] Marian Horvack, Ph.D., "Catholic Funeral Etiquette, Part 3: The Mourning Period," Tradition in Action, August 6, 2008, https://www.traditioninaction.org/Cultural/A048cpCivility_Funeral_3.htm.

[42] Queen, *The Doctor's Widow*, 40.

The two women followed a strict schedule, and when Luisita did not have enough time during the day to complete all her prayers, she would slip away to pray during the night or in the early morning hours. Her younger sisters, young ladies still residing at home, would hide and watch her as she performed her acts of penance or prayed aloud in front of her crucifix. They watched as she had her hair cut short and asked that a wig be made of it for a statue of Jesus of Nazareth. Luisita's sisters called this room the "Capuchin Monastery," a name that was quite significant, and the reality even more so because the area resembled a cloistered convent.

Every evening, Luisita put her watch under the pillow, and at four in the morning, she got up quietly and knelt before the crucifix on her bedside table, the crucifix that Pascual had given her. She and Pachita set time aside daily for spiritual reading. They would find a quiet place outside or would read in their rooms.

During this time, Luisita implemented Pascual's instructions regarding his estate as he had asked. Before his death, he had said to his wife, "Luisita, everything I have, I leave for your work." Luisita saw to it that her husband's personal belongings and clothing went to poor seminarians. The value of his library and his stock portfolio were given to the poor. The only items she kept for herself were the crucifix he had given her and his statue of Saint Pascual in adoration before the Most Blessed Sacrament. Sometime later, she asked for his doctor's bag. She removed everything else from their home and distributed it all between the church and the hospital.

After putting everything in order, Luisita applied for entrance to the Monastery of the Visitation Nuns in Morelia, Michoacán. Saint Jane Frances de Chantal, her favorite saint, who had co-founded the Visitation Order along with Saint Francis de Sales, had also been widowed. Saint Jane Francis de Chantal had made a vow of chastity and entered the monastery following the death of her husband, and Luisita had always experienced an affinity with her. Luisita's application to the monastery was not accepted, however, because the nuns felt that she did not have the strength to meet the demands of their life.

So Luisita resumed her life in her childhood home. Although twenty-nine years old and a mature woman, she was still the daughter of the strong-willed Doña Luisa, who was aware that Luisita's health was failing, a consequence of her long fasts, vigils, penances, and extended isolation in the semidark room. Her mother insisted that her daughter see a physician and brought Luisita to his office to be evaluated. His prescription was for mother and daughter to get away for a while and take a vacation. The doctor told them that Luisita should spend time in the countryside and breathe in the fresh air and exercise regularly. Doña Luisa and Luisita did just that.

Among the places they visited, they vacationed for several days at Cuyutlán. It was a quiet little beach town about twenty-five miles south of Manzanillo with endless sable beaches, swaying palms, and gentle waves. It was during those vacation days at Cuyutlán that Luisita met Señor Domingo Hinojosa, a distinguished gentleman who was staying at their hotel and who noticed her deep spirit of recollection. He later told some friends, "I have met a widow from Atotonilco, a saint."[43]

Her vacation changed Luisita's frame of mind. People living on the outlying haciendas began to see her walking once again through the town and countryside. They called her "the widow with the basket" because she always carried a basket of food, medicine, and

---

[43] Caravacci, *Loving Kindness*, 65.

other necessities for those in need. She would often bring a servant carrying another basket of things to give to the poor.

Don Juan Godinez, who was a small boy at that time, witnessed Luisita leaving her home in the early morning hours, sometimes walking and at other times riding a donkey. Donkeys were more sure-footed than horses in the nooks and crannies of Los Altos. She searched for the sick, and Juan said that she always seemed to know where to find them.[44]

He recalled that after greeting each person lovingly and giving everyone present a catechism lesson, Luisita offered them whatever she carried with her: food, some natural medicine, or a sheepskin to be used as a mattress. After this, she took care of whatever each household needed. "One must approach the sick like beggars, with a plea," Luisita used to tell one of the servants when he expressed to her that she was too preoccupied with the poor. This was different from the commonly used and somewhat patronizing term *charity work*.

In the afternoon, after visiting the sick who lived in huts scattered throughout the hillside, Luisita sat down to rest, read, or crochet. She would bring along some strong rope and would often make a swing to hang on a sturdy tree branch and then call the children over to join her and push them back and forth, to their utter delight. After this, there was a time for prayer followed by dinner. She offered advice when asked and showed prudence when answering their personal questions.

Workers gathered at the hacienda to join Luisita for the recitation of the Rosary. They used to meet in the shade of one of the trees and present their bouquets of wildflowers as their gift to the Blessed Virgin. "Every flower is like a Hail Mary to the Blessed

[44] Caravacci, *Loving Kindness*, 60.

Virgin," Luisita told them as she received the humble gifts for the Most Holy Virgin. After praying the Rosary, she prayed for the needs of the people present that day. The *campesinos* went back to their homes and returned the next day, even though they were tired after their long workday.

Memories of Luisita's exquisite kindness and compassion remained in the hearts of those who knew her:

"Her kindness, her loving ways, her understanding, and, in general, the image of goodness reflected in her person, remain in my mind."

"We observed kindness, charity, equanimity, and that intimacy with God which formed the saint in her."

"I would unburden myself with her because I always found in her kindness and the balm which cured my afflictions."[45]

The same can be said of her trust in God and His divine providence that began in her childhood and continued throughout her married life and widowhood. She would always say, "God will provide." She visited the sick, and even when she was not able to do as much for them as she would like, one thing was certain—she always left them with hope.

Ever since Pascual's death, Luisita had mulled over what type of memorial should be constructed in his memory. She wanted to build something big and beautiful, something that would last. At first, she decided on a monument in the holy ground of the cemetery or at the hospital, the best that money could buy. It would be designed by the finest European artists, something worthy of

---

[45] Personal remembrances of Mother Luisita selected at random by the author.

Pascual. That is, until Luisita spoke of her plans with her pastor, Father Sánchez Aldana. When she told him her ambitious idea, he did not agree. Would it not be a better choice for his widow to erect a living tribute in his memory that would serve the poor, whom he had loved so dearly? Why not build a chapel for the hospital that the two of them had founded together?

Luisita agreed with her pastor, and the result is Atotonilco's inspirational Calvary Chapel. It still stands today as the masterpiece Luisita dreamed it would be, created by the finest artisans, among them the noted Italian architect Adamo Boari and Jalisco's master painter José Vizcarra. Today, the motherhouse entrance includes a wrought-iron front gate with the words *Dad a los pobres*, meaning "Give to the poor," emblazoned across its archway.

As president of the Conference of Saint Vincent de Paul, Luisita continued to oversee the growth of the hospital with great interest. In 1894, two years before Pascual's death, the hospital had been extended. It now featured two reception rooms and two patient rooms, one for men and one for women, one surgery room, a pharmacy, a kitchen, a lounge, and an ample patio. All this was paid for by Luisita's sister, Concepcíon de la Peña.

Under Luisita's direction following her husband's death, a second wing was added to the hospital. Luisita hoped that at some future date it would provide living quarters for religious sisters who would work there. Calvary Chapel was built next. Construction began in 1900 and was completed in 1903. Luisita placed the cornerstone.

Father José Refugio Huerta, a long-time friend of Luisita, began a school for girls that was dedicated to the Sacred Heart of Jesus in 1899. He had spent his meager savings on this project. With many sacrifices, he had supported the school and maintained its high standard of education until 1903, when it became necessary to move the school to another location.

One of Luisita's greatest ideals was to make education available to those children who had never received any instruction. She offered Father Huerta some rooms in the new addition to the hospital. He was happy to accept her offer, and the school was moved and remained under his direction until he was transferred to another parish toward the end of the same year. Luisita and the women who assisted her continued with classes, and in November 1905, they took over full responsibility at the school.

When Calvary Chapel was completed, Luisita's thoughts turned once again to a life of consecration to God as a religious sister. Her family had prayed the fifteen decades of the Rosary daily as she was growing up because her mother was devoted to Our Lady of Mount Carmel. Luisita also had a great devotion to Our Lady of Mount Carmel and thought about applying for entrance to an order of cloistered Carmelite nuns. [46]

God had been drawing Luisita closer to Him in an ever-deeper friendship. From her earliest days with Agapita, she understood His deep, abiding presence within her. The spirituality of Saint Teresa of Jesus resonated within her. Luisita had loved God and spoke with Him often, either vocally or silently in her heart. She needed to come to a decision. Should she apply to enter the Monastery of Saint Teresa in Guadalajara and become a Discalced Carmelite nun?

Luisita sought the advice of Father Sánchez Aldana, who knew her so well. He was her pastor at the time of the establishment of the Conference of Saint Vincent de Paul. He had counseled her to build a chapel in memory of Pascual, and he now encouraged

---

[46] *Cloistered* refers to religious orders whose members strictly separate themselves from the affairs of the external world. The term is synonymous with *enclosed*. In the Catholic Church, the enclosure of nuns is regulated by the *Code of Canon Law*, either the Latin code or the Oriental code, and also by the constitutions of the specific order.

her to enter the Monastery of Saint Teresa. The remembrances of some of the original sisters state that she also asked her special friends, the poor and the needy of Atotonilco, what they thought about her leaving them, and they helped her decide. It is not known how they counseled her, but she applied for entrance to the cloistered Carmelite Monastery of Saint Teresa.

On March 3, 1904, at almost thirty-eight years of age, Luisita entered the cloistered Carmelite nuns at the Monastery of Saint Teresa in Guadalajara as a postulant. Soon after, on Monday of Holy Week that same year, she began her novitiate[47] and took the name Sister Maria Dolores of the Blessed Sacrament.

Luisita's presence in their monastery was refreshing to the nuns. As they observed how she lived out Carmel's path of profound prayer in their monastery, they came to realize that the spirit of Carmel resided deep within her. Her soul drank deeply from the wellsprings of Carmelite spirituality available to her within the monastery. Several nuns remembered that her superiors noticed Luisita's piety, her love for the Most Blessed Sacrament, her gentleness in all things, and her enthusiasm in desiring to advance in the life of divine contemplation.

The nuns quickly realized that Luisita definitely had a Carmelite vocation but not as a nun in their monastery. She could not eat

---

[47] When a woman enters the convent, she begins as a postulant in the initial stage of formation, called "postulancy." The duration of this stage differs among religious communities. Most communities have a postulancy of six months to a year. In Luisita's time, the period of postulancy was shorter. The next step is known as the novitiate, when the postulant receives a new name and the religious habit and is known as a novice. The novitiate lasts a minimum of one year and is followed by the profession of vows.

their food and was not able to observe their mandatory fasting or their penances. Luisita's health did not adjust to their rigorous lifestyle. During her three months in the monastery, she had several long conversations about this with the prioress, Mother María Refugio Josefa of St. Albert.

At the same time, back in Atotonilco, the people were hoping that Luisita would return. A group of women from the Conference of Saint Vincent de Paul tried to carry on the work of running the hospital. Despite their best efforts, supplies were wasted, and the patients suffered from lack of expert attention. The building itself was falling into disrepair. During the three months that Luisita was not at the helm, the women came to realize the vital role she had played in the early success of the Hospital of the Sacred Heart. They needed her to return so that the hospital could survive.[48]

Consequently, these women made a visit to the archbishop of Guadalajara with a plea for Luisita's return, and he listened to them. Archbishop José de Jesus Ortiz, who had been a successful lawyer in his native Chihuahua before entering the seminary, was noted for his wisdom and piety.

In addition to her conversations with Father Sánchez Aldana, Luisita consulted with Archbishop Ortiz several times during her three months in the monastery. She told him that she used to "dream," although she was not sure whether awake or asleep, that a multitude of the sick and children were waiting for her and calling out to her to return to her works of mercy. He listened and continued to guide Luisita toward a decision.

A second "dream" of Luisita's also had to do with children. One day when she did not appear in the refectory at mealtime, the superior sent one of the nuns to look for her, and she eventually

---

[48] Queen, *The Doctor's Widow*, 44.

found her praying in the chapel. When questioned, Luisita answered that she had fallen into a kind of sleep and had seen schools, orphanages, and all the things for which she was responsible. She could hear the voices of children who said to her, "You will be saved, but what about us?"[49]

Years later, when her sister Mariquita was asked to share her remembrances of Mother Luisita with the author of *A Zaga de Su Huella*, she noted that Mother Luisita had told her about another time she had "fallen asleep." Luisita had said, "Once when I was at Santa Teresa's Monastery, the convent I entered to become a Carmelite, after receiving Holy Communion, I seemed to have fallen asleep. But was I really asleep? They came and questioned me, and I responded that I didn't know what had happened to me; then, I added that I saw myself with the same Carmelite habit but in the hospital, in the schools, in the orphanages, amid them all, and they were speaking with me."[50]

Sister Maria Dolores and the archbishop had extended conversations during Luisita's time at the monastery. His further collaboration with the pastor in Atotonilco helped the archbishop to realize that God was calling Luisita away from the monastery. He advised her to leave Carmel in order to continue her work in Atotonilco.

So, on June 26, 1904, Sister Maria Dolores of the Blessed Sacrament removed her Carmelite habit, reclaimed her baptismal name of Luisa, and returned to her hometown of Atotonilco. She resumed her service to the people once more with the blessing of the archbishop, her pastor, and the nuns at the monastery.

---

[49] Personal remembrance of Sister Carmen Celina of the Child Jesus De La Torre.

[50] Personal remembrance of Maria de la Peña de Arambula, Mother Luisita's niece.

Chapter 6

Prayers and Presence

If this work is pleasing to God, the number of members
will increase. If not, it will be dissolved.[51]

— Father Arcadio Medrano

A holy silence lingers throughout monasteries. In its mysterious way, this silence impacts the world profoundly, something that monks and nuns find difficult to explain to those who are not called to their unique way of life. "Be still and know that I am God" (Ps. 46:10). Be still. And in that quiet, that stillness, prayers rise to Heaven on behalf of our world. Carmelites refer to this prayerful silence through the story of the prophet Elijah waiting in the cave for God. God was not found in the rumbling earthquake, the burning fire, or powerful wind gusts.

A great and strong wind rent the mountains, and broke in pieces the rocks before the LORD, but the LORD was not in the wind; and after the wind an earthquake, but the LORD was not in the earthquake; and after the earthquake a fire, but the LORD was not in the fire; and after the fire a still

---

[51] Personal remembrances of Sister Piedad of Jesus Arquieta, O.C.D.

small voice. And when Elijah heard it, he wrapped his face in his mantle and went out and stood at the entrance of the cave. (1 Kings 19:11–13)

It was in sacred, fruitful silence that God spoke gently to Elijah, and that is how He continues to speak to us today.

∞

When Luisita departed from the Monastery of Saint Teresa in June 1904, she did not leave that mystical silence behind her. It had become a part of her as much as the Carmelite spirituality it expressed. The deeper her prayer, the closer she came to God, the greater her compassion for the poor and the sick.

An extraordinary presence of God emanated from the silence of Luisita's soul. Sister Mary of San Pedro, a Sister of Perpetual Adoration, shared that as a young girl she had once met Mother Luisita walking toward her along a road in Mexico. As she drew closer to Mother Luisita, she tangibly experienced the presence of God within and surrounding Mother Luisita. She said that she had wanted to kneel and prostrate herself right there on the dirt road to acknowledge this sacred Presence emanating from Mother Luisita, but deciding it wasn't appropriate, she continued walking. She never forgot the experience.[52]

One of Mother Luisita's nieces, Conchita, the daughter of her youngest sister, Lupita Ugarte de la Peña, trying to express her aunt's tender compassion, struggled to find the right words. Finally, frustrated that she could not express herself the way she wanted, tears flowed spontaneously, and she put her hand over

---

[52] As told by Sister Mary of San Pedro, A.A.S.C., to Sister Mary Jeanne Coderre, O.C.D., at the San Francisco Monastery of Perpetual Adoration, 2003.

her heart and said, "Oh, if only you could have seen, as I did, her eyes change when she saw someone in need. Her face softened and her whole being reached out in love and compassion to help in any way she could." And then Conchita simply shook her head, sighed, and said, "Ah, I guess it's something you just have to see. Words don't work to express this."[53]

Four months after her return to Atotonilco, Luisita and Guadalupe Ruiz, a member of the Conference of Saint Vincent de Paul, spoke with Father Medrano, the new pastor of San Miguel Arcángel. Luisita had consulted with him while in the monastery. The two women told him about their hope of establishing a religious community to help the poor in Atotonilco. He told them to pray together with our Blessed Mother and ask God to reveal His will for them.

Later, when Father Medrano attended a retreat in Guadalajara, he spoke to Archbishop Ortiz about Luisita and the women who had come to join her at the hospital. He brought the archbishop's positive response back to the little group. Only two months after his initial meeting with Luisita, and six months after Luisita's departure from the Monastery of Saint Teresa, Father Medrano confirmed the birth of her new community on December 24, 1904.

On Christmas Day, at six o'clock in the evening, Father Medrano welcomed and received the first members of the new little community: Luisa de la Peña, Guadalupe Ruiz, Paula Ibarra, Maura Castellanos, Mónica Angulo, and Maria del Refugio Pérez. *Rostro de Bondad: Biografía de la madre María Luisa de la Peña Navarro* (The

---

[53] Author's interview with Conchita Jorba, Mother's Luisita's niece, Duarte, California, 1999.

face of goodness: biography of Mother Maria Luisa de la Peña Navarro), the definitive biography of Mother Luisita, calls them the "six hopefuls." In a simple but solemn ceremony, Father Medrano told the women, "If this work is pleasing to God, the number of members will increase. If not, it will be dissolved."[54]

He told the five women to call Luisita by the new title of Sister Superior and for them to address each other as Sister. He asked them to follow as closely as possible the way of life as lived in monasteries. They would also actively care for the poor, the sick, the uneducated, and especially the children, basing their way of life on the ebb and flow of work and prayer in monasteries. The delicate balance of this flow would still need to be worked out as Mother Luisita continued to grow in her understanding of the founding charism God had entrusted to her.

The historical record of their entrance ceremony contains some details. A litany was prayed, with each petition concluding with the same pleading response: "Intercede for us before the Lord, you holy virgins, you holy widows." Father Medrano gave the little group regulations regarding their common life together with a rule of life as strict as that of monasteries and yet not cloistered. Although the sisters would not go out on any business, they would care for the sick in the first wing of their hospital and for children in the school in the other wing. They would have a chapel for prayer.

With their pastor's words still in their minds and hearts, the new community focused on their goals of helping the poor, the sick, the abandoned, and orphaned children and establishing schools. These goals, however, would not be reached all at once. They would all be attained, but only incrementally.

---

[54] Personal remembrances of Sister Piedad of Jesus Arquieta, O.C.D.

Carlos Hector de la Peña, in *A Biography of My Beloved Aunt, Mother Luisita*, wrote that he discovered "a notebook of remembrances by Mother Luisita herself, with the following lines: 'Society was not pleased that these young women had united together in community. Immediately, the devil stirred up a tempestuous fury against the pastor and these aspirants to the religious life. The members of the Conference of St. Vincent de Paul were even making efforts to establish another hospital.' "[55]

Some people in the town proclaimed that it was not reasonable to lock oneself up in a hospital and to venture out only to teach children and to nurse patients. Some of the relatives of these first sisters looked negatively at the new community because the women not only lived in extraordinary poverty but were also surrounded by moral problems brought about by the desperation of the hopeless. Because of this idle talk, Father Medrano suffered slander and false interpretation and was reassigned to Tepatitlán, and Father Arnulfo Jiménez became the new pastor of San Miguel Arcángel.

Carlos Hector de la Peña also provided the following information from the early history of the community regarding what happened after Father Medrano's transfer. "The new pastor and Mother Foundress had entirely different concepts and viewpoints regarding the formation of the community. Difficulties increased day by day."[56]

It was difficult for Luisita to give in to the wishes of her pastor because they were contradictory to what she felt God was asking of her. Father Jiménez wanted the sisters to have less time in

[55] Carlos Hector de la Peña, *A Biography of My Beloved Aunt*, trans. Sister Mary Gonzaga Martinez, O.C.D. (Alhambra, CA: Carmelite Sisters' Printing, 2005), 16.

[56] De la Peña, *A Biography of My Beloved Aunt*, 17.

the convent and more time providing services to people. While he wanted them to mix more with the people, Luisita wanted to retain the beauty of the powerful, contemplative silence that enveloped the scheduled times of prayer as the hub to which all other aspects of their lives were directed. Father Jiménez wanted the work to take priority.

Mother Luisita obeyed, but her obedience came at a cost. She redoubled her efforts to provide a solid spirit of recollection, prayer, and silence for the sisters. This inner battle took its toll. Her already fragile health, beset with illness since childhood, collapsed. She became weak and was ill for several months.

On June 14, 1905, on the Feast of Corpus Christi, Archbishop Ortiz visited Mother Luisita and her community for the first time. He gave his approval to their efforts thus far. The new pastor, Father Arnolfo Jiménez, told the sisters they would now begin daily adoration of the Blessed Sacrament by taking shifts from six in the morning until six in the evening. When the number of sisters increased, he changed the hours. Their adoration would begin at four in the morning and conclude at ten at night. This was in addition to their services provided to the poor.

One year after the six sisters had come together, they made a one-year promise to observe obedience, chastity, and poverty and to care for the sick and for the children. Father Jiménez received the sisters' promises in the presence of the Blessed Sacrament and gave them each a gray uniform and cloak with a white collar, a cincture, and a crucifix. The sisters had worn simple black dresses up to this point. Father Jiménez directed the little group to address Luisita with the title *Mother* and gave them a new schedule and new customs. Some of these changes still went against Mother Luisita's personal ideals. They were contrary to her way of thinking, especially the changes to the cloistered aspect of their way of life.

The teaching sisters were now required to attend the formal, public ceremonies at the school during examination time, and the nurses were required to make home visits. Because of such stipulations, Mother felt that the prayerful recollection she desired for her community would disappear, but she did not resist. Father Jiménez enforced the new regulations. She obeyed.

One day, Mother Luisita asked her spiritual daughters, "What is happening? Something happens when I close my eyes. Our capes change color and become white. This happens to me all the time, even when I am not looking at our capes!"[57] She used the term *daughters* often when talking to or about the women in her community. In fact, the whole town was already calling her Mother Luisita.

About this time, the sisters made a retreat directed by Father Macario Velázquez. During these early years, Father Velázquez began to have a greater role in the spiritual direction of Mother Luisita and her community. Not long afterward, Archbishop Ortiz sent Mother Luisita the constitutions of the "Servants of the Poor." Primary documents seem to indicate that this community was the Sister Servants of the Blessed Sacrament, although that is debatable, according to Mother Luisita's definitive biography. There is speculation in the definitive biography that "Servants of the Poor" was an early name given to Mother Luisita's new community, but the author concludes that it was only one theory. The identity of the "Servants of the Poor" remains unknown today.

At the same time, the archbishop sent the sisters the ceremonial of the Visitation nuns. The ceremonial is a collection of the body of ceremonies or rites used by the Catholic nuns. Using them as a model, the archbishop asked Mother Luisita to begin formulating

---

[57] De la Cruz, *A Zaga de Su Huella*, 87.

her own constitutions. Each year, he sent a Jesuit priest who provided the Spiritual Exercises of Saint Ignatius of Loyola for their spiritual formation. "Father Izaguirre was the first Jesuit that the archbishop sent to the sisters to give the retreat conferences." Father Izaguirre ordered Mother Luisita to write her desires regarding the community, adding with his customary good humor that "there was no turning back now."[58]

Not one of the women was a licensed teacher, yet they taught. Not one sister among that original group was a nurse, and yet they nursed to the best of their abilities. The people they served were illiterate, undernourished, poor, sometimes to the point of misery, and without religious instruction. It was quite a challenge that confronted these dedicated women as they worked among the people most in need. And they met the challenge joyfully and successfully.

Even though the sisters were teaching and nursing, their handwritten remembrances refer mostly to God and the spiritual dimension of their lives. They wrote about teaching the Ten Commandments to children and parents and how they prepared them to receive the sacraments, guiding them in their growth in virtue and helping them learn to pray from the heart. The sisters wrote of the special Masses that were held on the First Fridays of nine consecutive months in honor of the Sacred Heart of Jesus. The students and the hospital patients who were physically able attended these Masses.

The children used to sneak into the chapel when they knew Mother Luisita was there because they were intrigued by the change that would come over her as she prayed. They watched her face become radiant. She appeared to be deeply absorbed in contemplation,

---

[58] De la Peña, *A Biography of My Beloved Aunt*, 17.

and a glow shone on her countenance as she knelt with her back perfectly straight, and her eyes focused on the tabernacle.[59]

Eyewitnesses to this phenomenon over the years, including both sisters and laity, have spoken about this change in Mother Luisita's countenance—so much so that it has been preserved through the oral tradition of the community.

"I saw her in the chapel, always happy and with a radiant face when she was in the chapel."[60]

"She was so totally and prayerfully fervent that her face even used to become radiant when she was at prayer."[61]

"She was a person of prayer. As I saw it, she loved to be by the Tabernacle, while at the same time she was ignited by the fire in her which consumes all apostolic souls, which is the glory of God and the salvation of souls."[62]

The women yearned to share their joyful relationship with God so others would also come to have a closer relationship with Him. Above everything else, the sisters helped people live their faith through trust in God. They emphasized devotion to their heavenly Father and the Sacred Heart of Jesus in the Blessed Sacrament and loving trust in our Blessed Mother. And, as can be seen from their

---

[59] The tabernacle is a liturgical furnishing used to house the Eucharist outside of Mass. This provides a location where the Eucharist can be kept for the adoration of the faithful and for later use (e.g., distribution to the sick). It also helps prevent the profanation of the Eucharist. Thus the law requires: "The tabernacle in which the Eucharist is regularly reserved is to be immovable, made of solid or opaque material, and locked so that the danger of profanation may be entirely avoided." *Code of Canon Law*, canon 938 §3.

[60] Personal remembrance of Sister Ines of Jesus.

[61] Personal remembrance of Sister Josefina of the Child Jesus Bacerra.

[62] Personal remembrance of Sister Clara of Our Lady of Guadalupe Padilla.

remembrances, their love and devotion to the Holy Eucharist was paramount. Mother Luisita often used the expression "the love of the Sacred Heart of Jesus in the Blessed Sacrament."

Mother Luisita's devotion to the Eucharist was profound. Apart from the scheduled times of prayer, she would make at least one hour of adoration before the Most Blessed Sacrament each day. On the special Eucharistic feasts, such as Holy Thursday and Corpus Christi, she was very enthusiastic. She wanted the best flowers and altar linens they could provide on these feast days. She also asked one of the sisters to play hymns on the organ during the special days when the Blessed Sacrament remained exposed on the altar.

It is interesting to note something else that was not written down in these early entries but is known from the personal memories of the sisters—the more mundane tasks of the daily life of nursing the indigent: the squalor of their dwellings, the stench of disease, the rot that accompanies lack of medical care, and the repugnance that arises when in the presence of wanton immorality. Those who were destitute were often exposed to deplorable moral situations and even to physical danger. And so were the sisters who attended them.

Among the personal remembrances of Sister Maria of San José is her memory of Mother Luisita searching the children's hair to discover and remove lice. Together with her sisters, Mother Luisita helped to relieve the ravages of smallpox, measles, typhus, and cholera, for which the people had no immunity. Before antibiotics were discovered, an untreated sore that became infected could cause death.

The homes of the poor lacked hygiene. Families slept on the dirt floors on their *petates*, thin sleeping mats made of dried palms. Mother Luisita gave away her own bed linens and clothing when people told her of their needs.

∽

In May 1907, because of her continued poor health, Mother Luisita traveled to Guadalajara, where she remained for two months. During that time, she visited the archbishop and discussed matters related to the hospital, the school, and living quarters for the sisters. He was very interested. She talked to the archbishop about making her will and began the preliminary steps.

By 1909, there were twenty-two members in Mother Luisita's community. The people had given the community a name: the Sisters of Atotonilco. Of the twenty-two who entered, only three had left because of poor health. So, when Mother Luisita met again with Archbishop Ortiz, he offered to give her community a rule of life to follow. He said it would be based on the mission of the community: to make reparation to the Blessed Sacrament, to spread God's love, and to attend to the needs of the sick and the instruction of children. The archbishop agreed with Mother Luisita's thinking that the sisters should not go out of the house, as Father Jiménez had insisted. Although he gave forceful reasons for his thinking, he respected the opinion of the pastor, who wanted the sisters "out and about."

In March 1909, Mother Luisita received the Holy Rule promised by the archbishop. He gave her complete freedom to voice her opinion and to add or delete whatever she deemed convenient according to the circumstances of the community. The cloistered element of their contemplative-apostolic life was reestablished in this Rule. In accordance with the wishes of the archbishop, the sisters no longer left the house. At that time, many communities followed this type of arrangement, which was called "semicloistered." Jaime de la Cruz, O.C.D., in *A Zaga de Su Huella*, gives a good explanation of the semicloistered concept of religious life. The term was used until the Second Vatican Council.

During the next few years, Archbishop Ortiz closely observed the new community. Information in the definitive biography of Mother Luisita opens a window into the archbishop's relationship with the sisters. He was glad that the women entering came highly recommended. He was satisfied with the community's service to the poor, according to a letter of February 1907. Beginning in January 1909, he guided the requests of pastors who wanted the sisters to make foundations in their parishes. A few years later, in 1911, he sent the sisters books that would model them after a Carmelite religious—Saint Thérèse of the Child Jesus and the Holy Face. Archbishop Ortiz did not realize that God's plan for Mother Luisita was to be the foundress of a new, active Carmelite community for women.[63] Because of this, Archbishop Ortiz guided Mother Luisita's community toward annexation with another community.

There was a relationship of mutual understanding, affectionate respect, admiration, and interest between the archbishop and Mother Luisita. He was aware of his responsibility regarding this new community in the Catholic Church that he represented as archbishop. Mother Luisita, for her part, remained faithful to God's will as shown in the mediation of her superiors.[64]

During these years, Mother Luisita implemented a series of much-needed improvements at the hospital. The sisters remember the installation of electricity and the breaking of ground in 1909

---

[63] Fray José de Jesus Orozco Mosqueda, O.C.D., *Rostro de Bondad: Biografía de la madre María Luisa de la Peña Navarro* (Guadalajara: Amate Editorial, 2021), 70.

[64] Orozco Mosqueda, *Rostro de Bondad*, 71.

for a new hall financed by Mother Luisita's sister Concepción de la Peña. On May 30, 1909, Sister Maria del Rosario (Paula Ibarra) entered eternity, the first sister of the community to die.

Rostro de Bondad reveals details regarding the astuteness of Mother Luisita in planning ahead for the future of her community. The author describes how she had already begun the formalities to ensure the legacy of her community through the Archdiocese of Guadalajara in 1907. Below is the 1909 partial summary of her will and a letter that included some accompanying notes from the archdiocese. The notes cautioned her not to forget to name an heir to her property. They point out that the will mentioned only the name of the executors but did not include the word *heir*. This was a very important omission that Mother Luisita subsequently corrected. Because the Laws of Reform were still in full force, religious had to appoint laypersons — not institutions or consecrated persons, such as nuns—as heirs because of the danger of losing possession of their assets. Otherwise, these properties could go into the wrong hands.

At this time, Mother Luisita wrote an important letter that she stipulated should be read by future archbishops of Guadalajara and superiors of her community, explaining the reason why she had made the donation to the Archdiocese of Guadalajara. The interest of the donation was to be used explicitly for the "Hospital House of the Sacred Heart of Jesus," the good of the poor, and the teaching of the children of Atotonilco. The amount of her 1907 donation to the archdiocese was forty thousand pesos. Only the interest incurred could be used, and the capital was to be kept intact. The distribution of interest would be done in the manner described in the letter. A copy of the letter was given to Archbishop Ortiz and to Mother Luisita's sister Concepción, who, before civil law, was named as universal heir to Mother Luisita's assets in her will. She left Conchita all the necessary instructions regarding her "true" will.[65]

During these six years of putting down the roots of their new little community, an ominous thunder had already sounded in the distance, barely audible at first, but its intensity increased until all of Mexico shook with a terrible dread. The sisters did not know that their six years of untiring labor was bordering on an almost complete collapse.

The distant thunder of the epic Mexican Revolution increased in volume until its crescendo drowned out everything else.

---

[65] Orozco Mosqueda, *Rostro de Bondad*, 71.

Chapter 7

Revolution

*At this time, the history of our community comes to a
pause. Blended with the life of our unforgettable Mother
Luisita, it will reappear luxuriant and vigorous after four
years of trial to begin the third epoch of the Institute.*[66]

—Remembrances of the Original Carmelite Sisters

By 1910, Mexico began to shake with the passionate intensity of
its oppressed people, who cried out, demanding their rights. Amid
continuing bloodbaths perpetrated by power-hungry men who vied
for control of the government, the Mexican people arose in anger.
Like a squeaky wheel or a dripping faucet, it had been something
to put up with—but only for so long. Then, one day, the cry finally
escaped: *"Enough!" "No more!"* The gathering storm that had begun
with sprinkles and small showers was gearing up for the torrential
downpour that shaped the next part of Mother Luisita's life.

It was a revolution.

The revolutionaries believed that the Catholic Church had
too much power, owned too much land, and wielded too much

[66] Personal remembrances of Sister Piedad of Jesus Arquieta, O.C.D.

influence. They were suspicious of Catholics and did not trust them. These revolutionary leaders vowed to overthrow not only the government but the Catholic Church as well. And that would include Mexico's Catholic Sisters.

People were afraid.

There were three main reasons for the revolution: Porfirio Diáz's dictatorship-like rule for more than thirty years, the continued exploitation and poor treatment of workers, and the great disproportion between rich and poor. The multilayered "caste system" created by the Spaniards kept the *campesinos* entrapped in great poverty with absolutely no chance of advancement. The natural right of basic justice was denied them, and that is always a catalyst for uprisings. According to its constitution, Mexico was a representative, democratic federal republic. By 1910, there was no democracy and only one "official" party, which monopolized the power.

Revolution broke out in 1910. President Porfirio Díaz was ousted. Francisco Madero was elected president, but then uprisings broke out in different parts of the country; these were led by Venustiano Carranza, Álvaro Obregón, Pancho Villa, and Emiliano Zapata. These divergent uprisings, when seen as a whole, are called the Mexican Revolution. It was bloody. It was ruthless. It unleashed its fury especially toward wealthy landowners and targeted the Catholic Church.

What happened to Mother Luisita's community during this time? Where were they? How did they survive? Finding the answers to these questions revealed a hidden, dark facet of the revolution: the atrocities committed against Catholic sisters by the revolutionaries. Research provided very few answers. There are books on the Mexican Revolution, but on the topic of what happened to Catholic nuns during the Revolution, history was silent.

Finally, three years after the the revolution was over, Mother Maria Elias of the Blessed Sacrament Thierry, a Discalced Carmelite nun from the monastery in Querétaro, was called to testify before Congress.

Mother Maria Elias testified in Washington, D.C. on Thursday, April 29, 1920, before the United States Subcommittee on Foreign Relations. Her testimony, one of the few resources available on this delicate topic of what happened to Catholic sisters during the revolution, answered the questions and provided the missing historical background of Mother Luisita's life during the ten-year Mexican Revolution.

Mother Maria Elias's testimony before the Congressional committee told it "like it was" — disgustingly raw and filled with repulsive and often sacrilegious atrocities. She had been an eyewitness to and a victim of the revolution's abuse of priests and religious. Her witness gives historical background to the chain of events that turned upside down Mother Luisita's world as well as the lives of all Mexican Catholics — priests, religious, and laity. Her words articulated the very real dangers that impacted the lives of all religious communities during the revolution, including Mother Luisita's group of newly founded sisters.

United States Senate, Subcommittee on Foreign Relations, Washington, D.C. Testimony taken at Washington, D.C., April 29, 1920, by Francis J. Kearful, Esq., U.S. Assistant District Attorney, Department of Justice of the United States in pursuance of an order of the subcommittee of the Committee on Foreign Relations of the Senate.

MR. KEARFUL. I understand the natural disinclination you would have to relate incidents of this kind, and so I will ask you if you wrote a letter addressed to the Archbishop of New Orleans?

MOTHER MARIA ELIAS OF THE BLESSED SACRAMENT, O.C.D.
Yes, sir, I did.

MR. KEARFUL. November 4, 1914?

MOTHER MARIA ELIAS. Yes, sir.

MR. KEARFUL. Did you write that letter in English or in Spanish?

MOTHER MARIA ELIAS. I wrote it in Spanish.

MR. KEARFUL. I have here what proposes to be a translation in English, and I will read that portion of it and just ask you whether the statements in that letter are correct.

MOTHER MARIA ELIAS. Yes, sir.

MR. KEARFUL (*quoting from the letter*).

Since Francisco Madero declared war on Porfirio Díaz until the present day, we have not had a moment of peace. Following Madero's example, many others have arisen, some worse than others, and have attacked on all sides, every State in the Republic is the victim of horrible outrages.

The Catholic Church is attacked by the revolutionaries. They have closed the churches and prohibited the sacraments to the extent of shooting any priest who dares to hear confession or to administer the sacraments. The confessionals and some images of the saints have been burned in the public squares to the accompaniment of bands of music and impious speeches.

They have profaned the churches, entering them on horseback, smashing the images, treading the relics underfoot, throwing the Hosts about on the floor and even giving them to the horses to eat with the fodder.

In some churches, the Carrancistas themselves have pretended to say Mass and have seated themselves to hear the confessions of a multitude of people.

Dressed as priests, they have heard the confessions of sick people and then in derision have revealed what they had heard in the confession. They seized our great convent of the Carmelites in Querétaro. The colleges of the Reverend Jesuit Fathers and many others were destroyed. The property of the church has been seized and some of the ecclesiastical archives have been burned.

All the communities of nuns have been expelled from the entire Republic, being given but one-half hour to leave and not allowed to take with them a change of clothes, and, in many cases, not even a breviary to pray.

Many sisters were taken to the barracks and police stations, where their vows of chastity were in great danger. The furnishings of the Catholic schools and colleges have been stolen. Immorality has increased to such a degree that they have profaned not only virgins, but have violated nuns, carrying them away by force where they now suffer horribly.

To the great suffering of my soul, I have seen in Mexico the sad and lamentable fate of many sisters who have been victims of the unbridled passions of the soldiers. I found many bewailing their misfortune that they were about to become mothers, some in their own homes, others in maternity hospitals. Others unable to flee from despair have surrendered to a life of evil until, filled with desperation and shame, they have complained against God, declaring that He has abandoned them.

I have seen many sisters of different orders, dressed in the latest style, showing themselves on the balconies, losing the little spirituality remaining to them, and singing and playing the piano all day, saying that it is only a camouflage to hide the fact that they are nuns for fear that they be carried away by Carrancistas or Zapatistas, or Villistas, etc. Some priests, deserving of confidence, have told me that in a hospital near (I will give you the name in confidence) there are 51 sisters who had been seized by the soldiers, of whom 45 are about to become mothers, although they have religious vocations and are bound by vows. In Mexico and in the Hospital de Jesús there are others in the same condition. The Carrancistas deny this, saying that they went with them voluntarily because they were held in the convents by force.

In Mexico, I have seen others whom they have compelled by force to enlist in the Red Cross, and under this pretext holding them as slaves to serve them as though they were their own women, and if many look after the sick there are also others who have lost their chastity. In general, many young girls, after having been forced to live with them, have been thrown out, and many have been killed in the streets as though they were animals.

Do you remember that you wrote that letter?
MOTHER MARIA ELIAS. Yes, sir.
MR. KEARFUL. And is it all true?
MOTHER MARIA ELIAS. Yes, sir.

∽

Back to Mother Luisita. A mere two months before the revolution began, Archbishop Ortiz informed Mother Luisita that he wanted her sisters to merge into another community, the Sisters of Perpetual Adoration. Three days later, he confirmed this decision in a note to Mother Luisita, stating that the Sisters of Perpetual Adoration willingly agreed to annex the little group from Atotonilco to their community. Although obedience to the archbishop's request impacted Mother Luisita's health, she obeyed.

On September 18, 1910, because Mother Luisita was ill, Sister Consuelo of the Divine Eucharist Diaz spoke with the superior of the Sisters of Perpetual Adoration about the annexation. Shortly after, because of their vow of obedience, the sisters were ready to transition into the community of the Adoratrices, as the Sisters of Perpetual Adoration were known. Mother Luisita and her little community braced themselves to say their final goodbyes to their beloved family, friends, and hometown. Months passed as they awaited the arrival of the official document from Rome that authorized their transition.

On June 19, 1912, however, everything came to a standstill when Archbishop Ortiz died. The official document from Rome that arrived soon after the archbishop's death had authorized him to finalize the annexation of Mother Luisita's little group to the Sisters of Perpetual Adoration. This document was no longer valid because of the archbishop's untimely death. A new one would be needed to authorize the new archbishop to continue with the annexation.

The sisters waited. When Archbishop Francisco Orozco y Jiménez (hereafter called Archbishop Orozco) arrived in Guadalajara, Mother Luisita traveled there to explain to him the restless uncertainty within her sisters, not knowing what would come next. The new archbishop prayed for enlightenment as he tried to determine the best solution for them. He finally decided that they should join a different community and chose the Sister Servants of the Blessed Sacrament. Their motherhouse was in Zapotlán, Jalisco, about eighty-five miles southwest of Atotonilco and within the Archdiocese of Guadalajara.

Mother Luisita's former pastor, Father Arcadio Medrano, who had helped her so much when she transitioned from the Carmelite monastery back to Atotonilco in 1904, wrote to her at this crucial time in her community. An excerpt of the letter reveals his love and esteem for Mother Luisita and her sisters. The letter is treasured today by the sisters and preserved in the community archives of the Carmelitas del Sagrado Corazón.

May 15, 1913

... Do not fear. For a long time, you have been serving the Lord and have asked Him to let you know His will. It has been made manifest to you very clearly, and now, "Down to work." He will lead you with much care and great love because He cannot fail in His promises. So, blindly and with utter confidence, you should place yourselves in the hands of God. Neither the house, nor the habit, this or that Order, should attract you. Only what God wants.

What I told all the founders together in that little garden, I repeat now and shall always repeat it, "May this community, which is God's Garden, be formed with the end to please God and to become holy.... I have never been disturbed about the future of that little convent. I placed it in the hands of God, and God has guided it wherever He has pleased. Blessed be the Lord, Who answers our prayers although we are so miserable. May He be praised for ever for so many graces poured upon all of you. Some of you are already in heaven, others are taking care of the sick, others working in the school, and all are serving God. What else could we desire?

The Lord has filled you with blessings during the eight years you have lived with Him. He has loved you as small lambs are loved and spoiled by the shepherd. May He be blessed a thousand times for His love and protection upon you. Wherever obedience places you, there God is with you.[67]

Dissolving her community and joining the Sister Servants was difficult for Mother Luisita. Her suffering was not caused by poor treatment or anything of that nature. Rather, it was because she had worked so long, intensely laying the cornerstone and building up her new community. Although this change deeply troubled her, she surrendered in faith to what she firmly believed to be God's will. She voiced again to her sisters one of the phrases that has come to characterize her and her spirituality, an expression that she uttered time and time again: "¡Adelante! Onward! God will provide!"

Records of the Sister Servants of the Blessed Sacrament provide information about the annexation of the Atotonilco Sisters to their community.[68] Entries from that year state that on May 7, 1913, Archbishop Orozco asked the superior general of the Sister Servants, Mother Teresa del Rosario, S.J.S., and Sister Catherine of the Child Jesus, S.J.S., the local superior of the Sister Servants' Guadalajara convent, to attend a meeting in Guadalajara. The Atotonilco Sisters who were at the meeting were Mother Luisita and Sister Consuelo of the Eucharist.

---

[67] Caravacci, *Loving Kindness*, 83.
[68] Orozco Mosqueda, *Rostro de Bondad*, 73ff. summarized.

Archbishop Orozco and Mother Luisita had recently created the conditions of the annexation together, and the Sister Servants were surprised when they learned why they were called to the meeting. With the sisters in leadership of both communities present, Archbishop Orozco ordered Mother Luisita to give her community over to the Sister Servants.

As stated in the definitive biography of Mother Luisita, the following assets were available at the time of the aggregation. The assets included twenty-one staff members, the dowries of five sisters, and a fairly large estate that consisted of Calvary Chapel, a chaplain's home, and two other main areas: the sisters' residence and the hospital, which included the school. The hospital area would not be included in the aggregation because the Sister Servants did not offer health care. They would, however, take over the school.

Mr. Ramón Garibay was present as the archdiocesan financial representative of the capital that Mother Luisita had donated to the Archdiocese of Guadalajara back in 1907. She had stipulated at the time of her donation that the interest incurred would go solely toward the school and the hospital. Now, new terms for this donation, as well as other important factors concerning the aggregation of the two communities, needed to be agreed upon at the meeting. Interest incurred from the forty-thousand-peso donation would be redistributed as follows: interest incurred from thirty thousand pesos would now go to the community of the Sister Servants of the Blessed Sacrament; interest from the remaining ten thousand pesos would continue to go to the needs of the hospital. Mother Luisita's brother Salvador was named to receive the interest on behalf of the hospital.

The following day, Ms. Luisa de la Peña, as she was called in the document, in a humble and respectful letter, expressed to Father Silviano Carrillo, founder of the Sister Servants, her desire for the aggregation of the two communities. When the founder accepted her request, the archbishop commissioned him to move forward and finalize the annexation and admission of the new members.

It all happened quickly.

Only two days after the initial meeting with the archbishop, Ms. Luisa de la Peña and Sister Consuelo of the Eucharist left Guadalajara together with two of the Sister Servants, Sister Teresa and Sister Catherine of the Child Jesus, to tell the news of the annexation to the sisters in Atotonilco.

When they all arrived together, the Atotonilco community was puzzled. What had happened? Their petition to join the Sisters of Perpetual Adoration had already been signed, submitted, and accepted. How did these other sisters come into the picture? The Sisters of Atotonilco knew very little about the community of Sister Servants. This was news indeed!

They wept.

At this point, Archbishop Orozco realized that the aggregation would be helped along if Father Carrillo would go to Atotonilco to communicate the vision and mission of his community to the sisters. Father Carrillo left his parish in the town of Ciudad Guzmán, Jalisco, and arrived in Atotonilco in May 1913. The sisters were waiting for him.

Father Carrillo resided at San Miguel Arcángel's rectory during his stay as he helped the two communities understand the annexation more fully. On the day he arrived, he visited the school right away and was pleased with what he saw. In the afternoon, he spoke to the Sisters of Atotonilco about the Sister Servants' community. He told them that he witnessed their goodwill toward the aggregation and that he wanted each sister to feel perfectly free to explain to him simply and spontaneously whatever each felt inspired to do; that is, to join or not to join the Community of Sister Servants of the Blessed Sacrament.

When Father Carrillo was satisfied that the Atotonilco Sisters understood the purpose of his community, he asked them to have confidence in him as he spoke to each one privately. After that, he proceeded with the definitive arrangements of their admission.

Soon after, new agreements were reached concerning the funds needed to complete the annexation process. These included the requirement of a dowry for each sister who had asked to join the Sister Servants. Mother Luisita paid for the dowries.

Twenty Sisters of Atotonilco applied. One other sister who wanted to remain in nursing was given assistance in finding another community that provided health care. All applicants were admitted, but only nineteen of them began their postulancy on May 22, 1913, because Sister María de San José had been asked to remain temporarily at the hospital to continue assisting the sick while the hospital was being reorganized.

The theme of beginning over recurs at this point in Mother Luisita's life: years of building up followed by deconstruction that revealed new dimensions of God's plan for the little band of Carmelites that developed slowly. Repeatedly. It must have been very difficult for her.

She did not whimper.

She did not complain.

In faith, she began again.

Scripture says, "Behold, I am doing a new thing; now it springs forth" (Isa. 43:19). These sacred words would be fulfilled repeatedly during Mother Luisita's life. Her faith-led obedience guided her wherever the Lord called, time and time again, as the following chapters will reveal.

The aggregation ceremony took place on the solemnity of Corpus Christi, May 22, 1913. Because the long dresses they were already wearing were similar to those of the Sister Servants, the Sisters of Atotonilco received only the black cape and medal of their new community on that day.

Years before, Mother Luisita had established the Honor Guard of the Love of Jesus in the Most Blessed Sacrament in order to encourage good conduct among the students. The Honor Guard, wearing an array of white dresses, red ribbons, medals, and badges, now took part in the annexation ceremony as they scattered flowers along the path during the procession of the Most Blessed Sacrament. Everything seemed the same, but it was so different. The new black mantles of the Atotonilco Sisters stood out even more in the midst of so many white dresses.

The day of departure arrived two weeks later, at the end of May, when, as new members in the Sister Servants' community, they began to leave in groups on different days for Zapotlán, where they would adjust to the new rules and customs at the motherhouse of the Sister Servants. Because they were allowed to keep the same religious names and the title *Sister* as postulants, Luisita was admitted as Sister Luisa.

In early June, several Sister Servants arrived in Atotonilco to take charge of the school. Challenges soon arose because Mother Luisita's sisters had been formed with a different "spirit" than theirs. Some of the sisters in both communities found the transition problematic for this reason. When these difficulties became known, arrangements were made so that Sister Luisa, with the approval of the Sister Servants, could travel to Guadalajara for an appointment with Archbishop Orozco.

Consequently, on June 18, 1913, Sister Luisa "interrupted her retreat" to travel to Guadalajara for an appointment with the archbishop because "she was not at peace." She was accompanied by the local superior at the Sister Servants' motherhouse, Sister Margarita Maria Alacoque. The result of that interview was that Sister Luisa returned to the motherhouse three days later—changed, calm, and happy—and continued her spiritual retreat.

On July 1, 1913, Archbishop Orozco went to Atotonilco to adjust the financial agreement between the two communities because there was insufficient income for the support of the house there. One of these new arrangements was that the pastor would help them with a contribution of twenty pesos a month.

At that time, Sister María de San José Espinosa, who had stayed in Atotonilco attending the sick while the hospital was reorganized, also received the habit of the Sister Servants.

Finally, on July 22, Mother Luisita departed from her beloved Atotonilco, leaving her most treasured ideals behind. Accompanied by the seven remaining sisters who had delayed their departure because of classes, Sister Luisa, a new postulant, could be heard whispering quietly, "My hope is in God" as she squared her shoulders to begin over once again.

Her spiritual notes revealed her deep feelings about this change. One week after she joined the Sister Servants, Sister Luisa wrote:

July 30, 1913

I was told that up until this time I had been pleasing only myself and that now I am pleasing God; that the deeds I had performed up until now were merely my own deeds, and that now they are God's. I was also told that if I humble myself, God will exalt me, and that I can gain more merit here sweeping a room through obedience than if I were somewhere else doing great deeds. Now God is my all. Humanly speaking, I have nothing.

July 31, 1913

I shouldn't be a coward. Rather, I should avail myself of every opportunity within my present circumstances to become a saint by offering myself as a holocaust and victim, even if this would mean becoming a martyr of obedience.

Other entries during her first month in Zapotlán reflected her very human feelings. "I will pay no attention as to whether the habit fits me well or poorly, and neither will I pay attention to the way the sisters are wearing their habits. I know that I like flattery." "I will practice humility by only giving my opinion if it is asked of me. I will keep silence."[69]

Documents in the Sister Servants' archives show that Ms. Luisa de la Peña received the habit of her new community as well as her new name of Sister Juana Francisca de Chantal of the Blessed Sacrament on September 24, 1913, the feast of Our Lady of Mercy. Her mother attended this ceremony. Only twelve of the Atotonilco Sisters who had transferred received the habit that day. They all settled into the novitiate routine over the next nine months, trying to learn the customs of the new community.

The distant thunder was closer now. It wasn't long before Father Carrillo wrote to Mother Teresa del Rosario, the superior general of the Sister Servants, and gave her guidelines to follow if

---

[69] Sister Timothy Marie Kennedy, O.C.D., ed., *In Love's Safekeeping: The Letters and Spiritual Writings of Mother María Luisa Josefa of the Most Blessed Sacrament*, vol. 2, *Spiritual Notes* (Alhambra, CA: Carmelite Sisters' Printing, 1999), 922–923.

and when the revolutionaries came to Zapotlán. In March 1914, he wrote:

> Daughter:
> Blessed be God! I am sending you Sister Catherine's letter so you can know what is going on in Guadalajara. I have just heard from several people of the great persecution against priests there.
> The storm is coming. Let us bless God and resolve to accept whatever comes; if it is martyrdom that heaven will send us, let us bless God a thousand times if we are chosen to suffer. I authorize you to go ahead and do whatever you deem the best thing to do; because many times you won't have enough time to consult me. Place the sisters in the homes of persons you can trust. Seek refuge with them. Trust in God and take courage.
> Silviano Carrillo

In Guadalajara, priests and religious were already homeless and living on the streets after being thrown out of their cloisters and religious houses. Some had been jailed. Others had fled or gone into hiding.

This was the exact time referenced in the detailed testimony of Mother Elias regarding what happened to priests and nuns during the Mexican Revolution.

Not long after, the Sister Servants were warned to leave quickly because they could be thrown out of their convent in Zapotlán that very night. The revolutionary forces did not show up that night, but three days later, at ten o'clock in the morning, Colonel Aurelio Sepulveda and his companions seized the convent. The novices of Zapotlán, including Sister Juana Francisca de Chantal, finished their novitiate year of probation scattered here and there in various hiding places, mostly in homes of respected people, hidden away from the revolutionaries and their assaults.

Sister Juana Francisca's hiding place was in the home of Don Juan Domingo Hinojosa, the gentleman she had met eighteen years before at the beach in Cuyutlán while on vacation with her mother after Pascual's death. He was the gentleman who had said upon meeting her that he had met a widow from Atotonilco, a saint.

Sister Carmen Josefa, his niece who would enter Mother Luisita's community years later, recalled details about that time. She said that she was still a young girl when Sister Juana Francisca was hiding with them in her uncle Juan Domingo's home. She shared the following:

By the time the sisters had to leave their convents to live in the houses of lay people, my uncle, as well as his family, had already become prominent citizens of the town. The Sister Servants' main convent was in the town where he lived, so they sent their novices to hide in his home. It was there that I met the little holy widow about whom my uncle had spoken. He called her "*la santita*" (the little saint). We, the girls in the family, were taking sewing classes with the Sister Servants when I first saw Sister Juana Francisca. The Sister Servants told me that she showed a high degree of sanctity, and that they had developed a deep affection and respect for her, calling her by the nickname *Chantalita*.

At that time, we had an oratory, a prayer room, in our home. The room next to it was unoccupied, and my cousins, who were still very young, told us, "Girls, come to the room next to the oratory so that you can see Sister Juana Francisca when she receives Holy Communion!" The boys were altar servers and had told us that they were impressed with the glow on her face when she received Communion.[70]

When it came time to profess her vows as a Sister Servant, Sister Juana Francisca requested another appointment with Archbishop Orozco. On October 12, 1914, Sister Margarita Maria Alacoqué of the Sister Servants again accompanied her to Guadalajara. They remained there eighteen days. After that, Sister Juana Francisca applied for her profession of vows as a Sister Servant of the Blessed Sacrament.

During her retreat before Sister Juana Francisca professed her vows, she wrote the following in her spiritual notes:

February 24, 1915

How good God is! On the eve of these holy exercises, I received the conviction that Our Lord wanted to talk to me about them Himself. This was a great consolation for me and helped me in my solitude and seclusion here.

Because of the gratitude I felt toward God and my willingness to listen to Him, I was thinking that if He were going to talk to us, He hadn't provided any human means to do it. For we were in such a situation that it appeared as though we lacked everything in the spiritual realm, and even on the human level I didn't feel any attraction or support. My desire was to find Him, to follow Him, and to please Him on whatever path He would lead me because I want to earnestly do His holy will and to abandon myself totally into His hands.[71]

---

[70] Personal remembrance of Sister Carmen Josefa of the Sacred Heart Vergera.

[71] Kennedy, *In Love's Safekeeping*, vol. 2, 928.

Sister Carmen Josefa shared some details about the day Sister Juana Francisca professed her vows: "Sister Juana Francisca and four other novices professed their vows of poverty, chastity, and obedience while still hiding in my uncle's home on March 2, 1915. The ceremony was completely private, not even the boys attended. There were no flowers, only the stubs of some candles."

Mother Teresa del Rosario, one of the original nine sisters to enter Father Carrillo's new community in 1904, was the community's first superior, and the local superior while the sisters were hiding there. She recognized Sister Juana Francisca's profound spirit of prayer and recollection and recommended that she be given the responsibility of directress of prayer.

"Sister Juana Francisca carried out very humble duties as she worked in the kitchen, did the housecleaning, and toiled in the orchard. She rose early and began to make tortillas at six in the morning using wood from a eucalyptus tree that gave off suffocating fumes and copious smoke, extremely irritating to her eyes. She had never done that kind of work."[72]

Times were hard in Zapotlán during the Mexican Revolution. Among their many sufferings, one of the most difficult was hunger. Mother Luisita suffered along with everyone else. Her sister Mariquita said that when Mother Luisita was with the Sister Servants, she asked Mariquita, "Why didn't you come by?"

Mariquita answered, "We, Lupita and I, were making bread."

"Why didn't you bring me some of it?"

Mariquita added, "Later we found out that the sisters did not have any food. My mother took a variety of groceries and even some of the twisted candy that Mother Luisita enjoyed. She liked sweets very much."

[72] Author's interview with a Sister Servant of the Blessed Sacrament, at a teacher conference in 1994.

It is through Sister Juana Francisca's spiritual notes that her hidden, inner anguish and total trust in God is revealed. She wrote, "In this terrible state of my soul, I will seek to be faithful to my good God and not to part from Him.... Union with God is like when a drop of water gets absorbed into the ocean and becomes part of it, or when wax taken from different honeycombs is totally melted and then fused into one. That is the way that union with God takes place."[73]

In another entry, she states, "Whatever today's world contains will never be sufficient for a soul that was created for heaven. What answer are we supposed to give to our senses when they try to drag us down toward those miserable pleasures that the earth is offering? The answer is this—I was born for greater things. I cannot be happy with so little."[74] This was the first time she used the expression by which she is remembered almost one hundred years later, "For greater things you were born."

The chronicles of the Sister Servants reveal that during the sisters' stay in his home, Mr. Hinojosa and his son were threatened and persecuted by the revolutionaries. Everyone in the house was evicted. By God's grace, the ten sisters and three orphans who were sheltered there were taken in by "a good neighbor of ours, wife of the manager of the Bank of Jalisco, Mr. Vincente Castellanos, who offered his house, which guaranteed their safety."

In March 1915, strong uninterrupted bombings created terrible panic. Soon after the bombings, the little money they had to live on became worthless in the eyes of the new regime, and the Sister Servants had to ask for charitable donations in order to

[73] Kennedy, *In Love's Safekeeping*, vol. 2, 938.
[74] Kennedy, *In Love's Safekeeping*, vol. 2, 935-936.

survive until the financial situation became more stable and their currency was accepted again.

Sister Juana Francisca had professed her first vows in 1915 and renewed them yearly. The Sister Servants had accepted her as a humble, happy person who had never done hard manual work. They admired her for the effort that she made in her various duties. None of them realized the terrible suffering piercing her soul.

Chapter 8

¡Adelante! Onward!

The Lion Sleepeth.[75]

—Inscription over the tomb of Archbishop Francisco
Orozco y Jiménez in the Cathedral of Guadalajara

Mother Luisita and Archbishop Francisco Orozco y Jiménez are candidates for sainthood in the Catholic Church. Though of completely different temperaments, the two had a kind of spiritual kinship in which they worked together and shared in the sufferings of living out the gospel of Jesus Christ during extreme religious persecution. Both were caught up in the aftermath of the anticlerical articles against the Church. Mother Luisita was called by God to establish a new community of sisters in the Catholic Church during the rule of a godless government. Archbishop Orozco was called by God to help her, especially in facilitating the approval of the Catholic Church and the acceptance of the Carmelite Order despite the hurdles and endless opposition of those in political power.

This chapter offers a deeper look into Archbishop Orozco's life and his crucial role in the establishment and development of

---

[75] Author's visit to the Cathedral of Our Lady of Aránzazu, Guadalajara, Mexico, 1998.

Mother Luisita's community as well as an understanding of how and why devotion to the Sacred Heart of Jesus was integral to their spirituality. Bishops are shepherds of their dioceses and have the responsibility of overseeing the lives of their flocks. Mother Luisita had the responsibility of overseeing the lives of those under her care as well as the sisters in her community.

Since the 1600s, the majestic spires of Guadalajara's regal cathedral have called out to passersby, beckoning them to step inside for a while and drink in the comforting presence of that holy place overlooking the bustling city. Built in the Romanesque architectural style of the Spanish Renaissance, it is the main church of the Archdiocese of Guadalajara, established during the colonial era, and the church of the archbishop.

Archbishop Orozco's tomb, located in a side niche of Guadalajara's cathedral, was created as a fitting memorial to this great man. A magnificent marble lion dominates the memorial directly above Archbishop Orozco's tomb. It was patterned after the original famed Swiss Lion of Lucerne, hewn out of the face of a mountain in Switzerland in 1821 to honor the memory of the eight hundred Swiss Guards who were massacred during the French Revolution while protecting the French king. The Lucerne Lion was carved entirely in stone and "measures a staggering thirty-three feet in length and is twenty feet in height. The lion lies in his lair in the perpendicular face of a low cliff in Lucerne, Switzerland. His size is colossal, his attitude is noble. His head is bowed, a broken spear is sticking in his shoulder, his protecting paw rests upon the lilies of France."[76]

---

[76] See "The Nest of the Cuckoo-Clock," chap. 26 in Mark Twain, *A Tramp Abroad* (Hartford, CT: American Publishing Company,

This magnificent sculpture was the model for a similar lion created in marble to guard Archbishop Orozco's tomb in the Guadalajara cathedral. The evocative sculpture honors the memory of Archbishop Orozco, outstanding champion of religious freedom, as it guards his grave despite its mortal wound. The following inscription welcomes the visitors who come to pay their respects.

The Lion Sleepeth.

A fitting epitaph.

Why?

Archbishop Orozco was a lion. Like John the Baptist, he was a voice crying out. He cried out for the rights of the Mexican people and for their freedom to worship. His zealous strength protected and rallied his people during the religious persecution of the Mexican Revolution. He played a major role during the rapid sequence of historical events taking place throughout the republic. In fact, one of the first things he did as archbishop of Guadalajara was to help Mother Luisita and her sisters merge with the Sister Servants of the Blessed Sacrament in Zapotlán.

Archbishop Orozco was highly esteemed by the people. They trusted him. As shepherd, together with the other bishops, he increased preparation in his archdiocese for the battles that he knew would surely come, spiritual as well as physical. Perhaps the most important preparation was the bishops' decision to consecrate their country publicly to the Sacred Heart of Jesus, as Pope Leo XIII had asked, and, together as a nation, to beg God's protection upon their beloved Mexico. This consecration was directly related to the revolution that they saw looming on the horizon.

1880), 259, Project Gutenberg, https://gutenberg.org/files/119/119-h/119-h.htm#p259.

In his 1899 encyclical *Annum Sacrum* (Holy Year), Pope Leo XIII urged consecration to the Sacred Heart of Jesus as a means of bringing peace and restoring right order to the world. Bishops in several countries began consecrating their countries to the Sacred Heart. It did not happen all at once throughout the world, but over a period of years, many countries made this consecration.

In 1911, the bishops of Mexico also resolved to ask for permission to consecrate Mexico to the Sacred Heart of Jesus. They wanted to entrust their suffering country to Him, asking His blessing. The times were too unstable to carry out their plan right away, however, because uprisings were exploding throughout Mexico.

Two years later, Archbishop José Mora y del Río of Mexico City sent Pope Pius X the bishops' petition to consecrate Mexico to the Sacred Heart of Jesus. The pope gave his wholehearted approval and agreed to the bishops' additional proposal to enhance the traditional image with something new: insignias of royalty—the crown and the scepter—to be placed at Jesus' feet in the sacred image. To Catholics, the Kingship of Christ is supreme. The title *Cristo Rey* (Christ the King) would soon have monumental historical significance throughout Mexico.

The pope wrote to the bishops, "For a long time now, We have experienced great concern for your nation and your affairs, disturbed by grave unrest, and we well know that in order to preserve and sustain the health and peace of the people, it is necessary to lead them to this safe harbor of salvation ... the Sacred Heart of Christ His Son."[77]

---

[77] "Consagración de México a Cristo Rey," Hispanismo.org, https://hispanismo.org/hispanoamerica/15527-consagracion-de-mexico-cristo-rey.html. In the past, when a pope spoke or wrote about himself, he used the "royal We"—e.g., "We declare" or "We

The date assigned for the consecration of Mexico was the solemnity of Epiphany, Tuesday, January 6, 1914. It was decided that the following Sunday, the faithful were to make pilgrimages to the cathedral church in their dioceses, and the consecration would be made before the traditional image of the Sacred Heart of Jesus as King, but with the added scepter and crown, and emblazoned with the words of His title: *Christ the King.*

As soon as the bishops received the approval of Pope Pius X, they came together to plan the celebration. The main proclamation would be in the metropolitan cathedral in Mexico City. Pastors would do the same in their local churches. Archbishop Orozco had major difficulties with the Guadalajara government officials when he applied for permission to organize the January 11 procession. Governor López Portillo y Rojas adamantly refused to give permission for the pilgrimage because no religious activity, including pilgrimages and processions, was allowed in Mexico.

Pilgrimages were still against the law.

On January 8, 1914, the governor had a change of heart and gave permission for the "march" to take place in a smaller, modified, quiet manner, with a brief procession. The "march" had been curtailed to almost nothing. It would no longer begin, as they had planned, at the Church of Our Lady of Guadalupe, popularly known as the Sanctuary, and continue down several streets as it processed toward the cathedral, about nine blocks away. Rather, the governor ordered that it would have to begin in the plaza adjacent to the church and proceed the short distance into it.

As soon as the governor's permission for a smaller procession was received, Archbishop Orozco extended an invitation to all

---

decided"—meaning that the pope speaks not just for himself but as the Vicar of Christ on earth.

the people to attend. A notice of the procession was placed in the editorial section of the January edition of the Guadalajara newspaper, *La Nación*:

> It is necessary to proclaim Jesus Christ for our King, publicly. And we will do this in an impressive demonstration. We invite you, Mexican Catholics, to be part of the great public demonstration that is being prepared in the name of God and for His honor. Come all with flags, and above all with courage. Let the world know that we are not ashamed of God; peace, well-being, honor will reign in this chosen people, in this town dedicated to the Blessed Virgin Mary.

On the day of the procession, when the governor realized that thousands upon thousands of people were lined up along the original longer route, he got nervous, and at the last minute, he withdrew his permission and cancelled the "march." When the archbishop was notified about the last-minute cancellation, he sent to the governor a delegation of distinguished wealthy women who met with both the governor and the state attorney and pleaded with them to allow the procession to continue. The governor finally gave in. He stipulated, however, that only women, who were classified as noncitizens, could take part in the march; in that way, the march would have no political significance.

When the assembled groups found out that only women could participate, all of them — men, women, and children — began to process anyway. Not knowing what else to do with this spirited group of thousands of Catholics, Archbishop Orozco joined the end of the line, and soon the other bishops and priests joined him.

The Guadalajara procession was well organized. There were almost one hundred groups of people taking part who were arranged efficiently into social, religious, and occupational clusters.

As the throng of people walked along the original longer route, they passed the federal government building, the state government building, the military hospital, the University of Guadalajara, and several other significant sites.

The "march" continued without incident, but when the throng reached the San Francisco Gardens, they saw a group of liberal party activists. Some of the people in the procession began to shout, "Death to the Liberals" and sang the religious hymn "Corazón Santo" (Sacred Heart). Soon all the marchers were singing the hymn enthusiastically. Government troops tried to close off streets before the crowd reached them, but to no avail. Finally, when the procession concluded about nine o'clock in the evening, the archbishop, dressed in pontifical white and gold, intoned the Te Deum and blessed the crowd within the cathedral.

Governor Portillo y Rojas was enraged. The whole thing had turned into a political-religious demonstration. Archbishop Orozco had followed the governor's guidelines, but the people in the procession did not. Soon after this incident, the government expelled the Mexican bishops from the country. Before Archbishop Orozco left, Archbishop Mora y Ríos of Mexico City asked to see him. He then commissioned Archbishop Orozco to travel immediately to Rome and brief Pope Pius X on everything that was happening in Mexico. Governor Portillo y Rojas was removed from office soon after in punishment for having allowed the march to take place.

Archbishop Orozco stayed in Rome for two years, from 1914 to 1916. During that time, he became good friends with Father Francis Clement Kelley, the priest who had helped Mother Maria Elias, whose testimony before Congress is related in chapter 7. He was a guardian angel to her after she escaped Mexico during the revolution. Years later, he also financially assisted a plethora of Catholic refugees fleeing the religious persecution in Mexico during the Cristiada of the 1920s. After becoming the bishop of Oklahoma City, he wrote the now classic *Blood-Drenched Altars: A Catholic Commentary on the History of Mexico* in 1935. He continued to remain a close friend of Archbishop Orozco.

In 1916, Archbishop Orozco asked the pope to give him permission to return to Mexico. He reasoned that it was time for him to minister to his people secretly while hiding from the revolutionaries. The Holy Father agreed on the condition that he go first to Archbishop Mora y Ríos to ask for his blessing on this new venture. This he did and then quietly carried out his work in disguise again, under a different name, moving frequently to different locations to avoid capture.

The revolutionaries tried to remove all components of Catholicism from Mexico. All Catholic bishops, except for the bishop in Cuernavaca, were forced to leave. A schism attempt followed. A person named Monsignor Riendo arrived in Mexico City on an alleged mission of the Holy See. A cable from Rome soon arrived that said he was not a part of the Catholic hierarchy. The travesty stopped.

In the period from 1914 to 1918, many priests and religious were imprisoned or killed. Religious sisters were evicted from their convents and many of them subjected to vile outrages by the soldiers. Churches, sacred images, and sacred vessels were desecrated. Masses were discontinued. Catholic colleges in the republic were closed, and church property was confiscated. Mother Luisita and her sisters remained relatively safe with the Sister Servants.

∞

The next period of Archbishop Orozco's life, and Sister Juana Francesca's as well, followed the February 5, 1917, signing of the new constitution, although fighting continued long into the next decade. Following Archbishop Orozco's return from exile, he inspected the situation in Atotonilco and found the school functioning as well as could be expected in those turbulent days, but the hospital was once more in trouble. He communicated again with Sister Juana Francisca. She, in turn, shared the struggles she had been facing in trying to adapt to the charism of the Sister Servants, which did not include health care. She felt an inner restlessness.

Although she had already professed vows as a Sister Servant, Archbishop Orozco advised her to make a retreat to discern whether to leave or stay in that community. The archbishop told her that he would send a Jesuit priest to assist her in discerning God's will using the discernment principles of the Spiritual Exercises of Saint Ignatius. At the conclusion of the retreat, she voiced her desire to return to Atotonilco. The archbishop agreed and gave her his blessing.

Monsignor Manuel Alvarado, the vicar-general of the Archdiocese of Guadalajara, who administered the archdiocese while the archbishop was in hiding, gave Sister Juana Francisca the official authorization to separate from the Sister Servants together with any sisters who would choose to leave with her.

Four years earlier, on May 22, 1913, on the solemnity of Corpus Christi, the merging of the two communities had been authorized. Significantly, again on May 22, 1917, the separation of the two communities was authorized. Sister Juana Francisca began immediately to make the arrangements for her departure. She would find a different world awaiting her. Mexican priests and nuns were homeless, with nowhere to go. Displaced people now, with their convents and monasteries pillaged, burned, or converted into government buildings, they received little financial support, for others had also lost everything during the revolution.

Why?

The new Mexican constitution's prejudicial articles, approved in February 1917, targeted the Catholic Church in general and her clergy and sisters in particular, leaving them unsupported and ostracized by the government yet again.

When Mexico won its independence from Spain in 1821, its first constitution established Catholicism as the official and only religion. Article 3 stated that "the religion of the Mexican nation is and will permanently be the Roman Catholic apostolic religion. The nation protects her [the Catholic Church] with wise and just laws and prohibits the exercise of any other religion."

But not for long.

Another constitution was enacted thirty years later and marked the beginning of the Mexican government's anticlerical legislation. Later, when Porfirio Díaz became president, he chose to overlook some of these anti-Catholic articles and only barely enforced the others. That made the Porfiriata era of Mexican history, which lasted thirty-four years, a relatively peaceful time for Catholics.

When the 1917 constitution was enacted, it, too, was hostile not only to all religious faiths but to the Catholic Church in particular. It retained the previous anti-Catholic articles and added more. This anticlericalism allowed no clerical garb outside churches, mandated state control of all Church matters, outlawed religious orders and foreign-born priests, and denied all priests the right to vote.[78]

When Mother Luisita opted to return to Atotonilco following her four years with the Sister Servants, she was reentering what

---

[78] Federal Constitution of the United Mexican States (1824), University of Texas at Austin, Tarlton Law Library's Jamail Center for Legal Research, last updated January 29, 2020, https://tarlton.law. utexas.edu/c.php?g=813224.

had come to be known as the bloodiest, most destructive century in human history, the twentieth century. The world had changed during their four years with the Sister Servants, and so had the sisters. Of the nineteen sisters who had joined the Sister Servants with Mother Luisita, only three of them returned to Atotonilco with her: Sisters Maria de la Luz de San Luis Gonzaga, Manuela de la Inmaculada, and Gertrudis del Corazón de Maria. Two others, Sisters Magdalena de la Inmaculada and Carmen of the Sacred Heart, had previously left the Sister Servants of the Blessed Sacrament and were already living in Atotonilco. They had been asked by the pastor to get the hospital and convent ready for Mother Luisita's return.

On May 22, 1917, Luisa de la Peña and her three companions began their return journey back to Atotonilco.

"*¡Adelante!* Onward! God will provide!"

Part 3

Religious Persecution Years
(1921-1927)

*The Beginning of Religious Persecution
to Refugees in the United States*

Sisters, by your witness of trust in God, by doing your work with serenity and joy, seeking God's holy will in everything and by sharing the life and teachings of Mother Luisita, you can bring people to trust in God again.

This is our great task at this moment: to help our brothers and sisters to know that the world is in the gentle Hands of our loving Father, and that even in hardship and sorrow, our Father's designs are for love, and He hears our prayers and guides our lives.

—Archbishop José Gomez of Los Angeles, 2021

Chapter 9

Soul of Atotonilco

Pray and expect.[79]

—Mother Luisita, spiritual notes

As Mother Luisita was returning to Atotonilco, in another section of Jalisco a Mexican vaquero (cowboy) galloped across Jalisco's spreading hills, sitting in his carved leather saddle and shaded by his sombrero.

He was an imposter.

Unrecognizable in one of his disguises, Archbishop Orozco was still hiding from the revolutionaries. Under assumed aliases and moving frequently to avoid capture, he was as proficient on horseback and wearing a sword as he was in ascending the altar steps to begin Mass in his cathedral or in corresponding with Mother Luisita through his vicar-general.

Even though the revolution had supposedly ended, the Mexican bishops could not believe the extent of the chokehold placed on them by the strengthening of the anticlerical measures of 1857. Together, they wrote a pastoral letter protesting this curtailing

---

[79] Kennedy, *In Love's Safekeeping*, vol. 2, 929.

of religious liberty. Their protest was approved by the Vatican's apostolic delegate to Mexico.

It took more than a month to obtain all of the bishops' signatures because fourteen had already been exiled from the republic and were now living in El Paso, Texas. Archbishop Orozco's signature was not included because his current location was unknown even to the bishops. He had shrewdly found ways to communicate with them as often as he could. He wrote his own pastoral letter to his flock in Guadalajara, a strongly worded message that was read to the congregations during Mass in specified churches on June 4, 1917. His plan was to introduce the letter to these selected churches and from there to have it distributed to as many people as possible in his archdiocese.

Manuel Diéguez, the new governor of Jalisco, had been in office only three days when he learned of Archbishop Orozco's stinging letter. He retaliated by ordering the state attorney to close all the churches in which the letter had been read and to arrest the priests in those churches on charges of rebellion. Twenty-four priests were arrested and jailed,[80] but they could not find Archbishop Orozco.

Ever since 1914, the archbishop's palace had been used as both the mayor's office and the city jail. The twenty-four priests continued their protest from this jail. Fines were set at two hundred pesos per priest. Mexican law stated that fines could not be higher than one week's wages, so the priests asked the authorities to change the fines to follow Mexican law. When their appeal was denied, they all refused to pay and served their full fifteen-day sentence.

---

[80] Robert Curley, *Citizens and Believers: Religion and Politics in Revolutionary Jalisco* (Albuquerque: University of New Mexico Press, 2018), 146.

∞

How much outside news had Mother Luisita received during the four years she was gone in Zapotlán? Did she hear reports of the priests in jail or the archbishop's letter that was read in their churches? How secluded had the sisters been during their four years as Sister Servants? Even though the sisters needed to hide in private homes in Zapotlán, wearing lay clothes as a precaution between 1914 and 1917, Zapotlán's troubles were not as violent as those in Guadalajara. Mother Luisita's definitive biography states that, although removed from the Guadalajara area, they were well aware of the atrocities committed by the revolutionaries, including the abuse, exile, and death of priests and consecrated religious women.

None of Mother Luisita's personal notes during those years in Zapotlán mentioned the political sphere, and there are no documents or surviving oral history that give her reaction or perspective regarding politics during the revolution. As with Saint Thomas More, her protection lay in her complete silence and prayer. No accusations based on politics could be made against her.

On the day of their departure from the Sister Servants, Father Arnulfo Jiménez, their pastor in Atotonilco, met Mother Luisita and her three companions in Guadalajara and accompanied them during the sixty-eight-mile train ride to La Barca, where a stagecoach awaited them. Doctor Joaquín Acevez, a friend of Mother Luisita, had offered hospitality to them on their way back to Atotonilco at his El Tarengo hacienda, about twelve miles from La Barca. The sisters arrived at the hacienda around three in the afternoon and lunched there.

Following their lunch, Mother Luisita and her companions stopped for a few moments in the hacienda's chapel and then completed the last fourteen miles to Atotonilco by stagecoach.

At five thirty that same afternoon, they finally approached the outskirts of Atotonilco. News of Mother Luisita's arrival had already reached the townspeople, who were gathered together to welcome her back. Their respect and love for Mother Luisita had not diminished since she had left them. She remained "the soul of Atotonilco."

Thirteen years had elapsed since that December 24 when six women had been accepted as a fledgling community by Father Medrano, their pastor at that time. The number of women was back to six because Sister Carmen of the Sacred Heart and Sister Magdalena had remained in Atotonilco, where they had worked in the hospital instead of moving to Zapotlán, and they rejoined Mother Luisita and her three companions. All the other sisters had opted to remain with the Sister Servants.

As soon as Sister Magdalena had been notified by the pastor of Mother Luisita's return, she went to the hospital to try to put it back in order. The Sister Servants had taken excellent care of the school during their four-year stay in Atotonilco, but the condition of the hospital was a different story—unorganized and lacking supplies and qualified personnel. Its deterioration was obvious. A caustic germicide that had been used to disinfect the area from a recent epidemic nearly ruined everything it touched. Moreover, only two pious ladies, Señorita Pomposa de Loza and Señorita Evarista Vazquez, were left to care for the hospital as best they could.

Sister Magdalena was able to acquire some donated furniture, dishes, and food to welcome her four dear friends with a better-looking hospital and a hearty, delicious dinner.

The sisters evaluated the situation at the hospital right away. All six women pitched in to reestablish some order, and one month later the hospital was ready to take in patients. Even though the sisters did their best in caring for the sick, it was a massive undertaking for only six people. It was not long, however, before they followed a daily schedule that included Holy Mass, meditation, and their assigned times for their service in the hospital. Soon, the six grew to thirteen.

They continued their practice of setting aside one day each month for prayer as a Day of Recollection. Here is the October Day of Recollection entry from Mother Luisita's spiritual notes.

October 20, 1917, Day of Recollection

I see my soul as filled with faults, and I lack the fruit which should flow from my prayer. I am careless in the examination [of conscience]. There is a total weakness in my soul. At least I have willed to do well, but I do not overcome myself regarding the way I treat others, nor do I overcome my pride regarding spiritual things. My conduct is filled with an exaggerated superficial dissipation of my energy. Perhaps all of this is the result of too much self-love.

Mother Luisita's thoughts kept turning to the patients' families, especially their children, many of whom lived in great poverty. Her heart went out to them, and she was determined to find a way to help them. As a result, the School of the Spelling Book was established in one section of the hospital in 1918. The girls were divided into small groups and attended classes every afternoon from Monday through Friday. Mother Luisita herself gave reading and writing lessons.

One by one, Mother Luisita saw the needs, and she tried her best to alleviate them as best as she could. Whenever she was with the girls, she would always take them to the chapel to visit Jesus in the Blessed Sacrament, "so He would form their little hearts," as she would say.

Unleashing Hope

Sister Maria Ana of the Holy Family recalled the following:

Mother Luisita looked upon every person suffering from poverty with great respect and affection saying, "They are the image of God." She took them all to heart—the rich, the poor, men, women, and children alike. We called her the soul of our little town of Atotonilco. She always demonstrated her gratitude to the poor for their gifts. One day, one of the young girls from the school brought her flowers and candy for her feast day. The flowers had already withered, but Mother Luisita showed her gratitude as if it had been the greatest gift ever given to her.[81]

President Porfirio Díaz had been lenient in the implementation of some of the anticlerical laws. Under his thirty-four-year administration, parish priests, lay associations, and new religious congregations had been able to establish primary schools in their areas. These schools included catechism classes. According to the custom of the time, boys and girls attended separate schools. As the years passed, schools became more regulated by the government. Catholics were now prohibited from engaging in any primary education at all.

This was the climate in Atotonilco el Alto when Mother Luisita returned. In spite of it all, she provided health care and educational classes to those in need of her help. How amazing that, in her quiet, steadfast way, she was able to continue each day to try to help wherever she could, as she saw to the many details of those years of beginning again. The echoes of persecution continued. The Church was still suffering, religious education was illegal, and she continued moving forward. She just prudently carried on.

---

[81] Personal remembrance of Sister Maria Ana of the Holy Family Ramirez Gutierrez.

With the first donations from those first small classes, Mother Luisita purchased small capes and crucifixes on chains for the sisters to wear as a sign of their consecration to God. Their new uniform included a black pleated dress and a black translucent veil held in the back with a little strap. The cape had a white collar.

The year 1918 saw the outbreak of the deadly Spanish flu pandemic. Three waves of the pandemic were identified in Mexico: the first during the spring of 1918, followed by the second wave in the fall, and the third wave in the winter of 1919–1920. Fortunately, the Los Altos region of Mexico was not among those most seriously hit, although it had many cases.

Mother Luisita joined the other sisters in caring for these flu patients, nursing the most repugnant cases herself despite her own frail health and the high possibility of contagion. When the third wave was nearly over, a January 1920 newspaper cited "half a million dead" and that "the disease had been more deadly than the weapons of the Mexican Revolution."[82]

Years later, in an interview, one of Mother Luisita's nephews, Henry Ugarte, shared that Ramón Ugarte, his father and Mother Luisita's brother-in-law, had told him that the primary means of learning any news during the early 1900s was through the pulpit. He remembered his parents telling him that the priests had a system of learning the news, and in this way the news was circulated. Henry's father told him that the government targeted the priests so it could control the news that reached the smaller towns.[83] Radio broadcasts in Mexico began a few years later, but it took several

---

[82] "100 Years after the Pandemic That Killed 300,000 Mexicans," *Puerta Vallarta Daily News*, September 1, 2018, https://www.vallartadaily. com/100-years-after-the-pandemic-that-killed-300000-Mexicans/.

[83] Author's interview with Mother Luisita's nephew Henry Ugarte, Alhambra, California, 1998.

more years before the radio transmissions were heard in outlying rural areas such as Atotonilco.

In July 1918, the state legislature in Jalisco mandated that all priests register with the government and obtain permission before holding any religious services. This law placed the Catholic Church directly under the control of the state. Refusing to abide by the unjust law, the priests in Jalisco chose to respond with passive resistance. They withdrew from all their churches until the government removed its order. The people, denied access to their sacraments, supported the Church. Catholics in Jalisco responded actively by organizing an economic boycott. All churches and many businesses in Jalisco were closed in August 1918. Because of this boycott, the state legislature finally canceled the decree, and priests and laymen ended their strike in March 1919.

And Mother Luisita? She wanted to do something for poor orphan girls who wandered about with no place to go. Some lived in nearby caves. They needed help. They needed food and shelter, education and health care. They needed someone who would acknowledge their dignity as human beings, love them, care for them, and give them a good upbringing. But what could she do? Her hands were tied since she had very little money on hand to help them and no way of acquiring more. She asked the other sisters to join her in asking God to show them His will regarding the little homeless girls. In answer to their prayers, several benefactors stepped up to help out with this new project.

The first benefactor was the pastor of San Miguel Arcángel, Father Macario Velázquez, who contributed a very substantial sum. Other benefactors were Señora Secundina Rodriguez, and Señoritas Maria Vázquez and Maria Sánchez. With their help, an orphanage was established on January 19, 1919. At first there were only two orphans, but six more girls soon joined them. Mother

Luisita placed the orphanage under the patronage of Our Lady Help of Christians. Living spaces were rearranged. The sisters began to occupy the middle section of the hospital as their living quarters, and the area that they vacated became part of the new orphanage, as did the School of the Spelling Book.

Mother Luisita possessed natural prudence and great aptitude in dealing with people. She was the same toward everyone, regardless of their status in Mexican society. At a time when class distinctions were strictly observed, she managed to keep the wealthy and the poor in the school and the orphanage united as one family.

Before long, people began bringing clothing and other necessities for the girls. A kitchenette was arranged, and wooden boxes became a storage area for their tableware. Beds and chairs were constructed out of boards, and thin mattresses were woven out of palms.

Two caring doctors, Martín del Campo and José Mercado, offered their services free to the girls and donated needed medication. Even with the contributions toward the orphans' support, at times the girls had nothing to eat. Sister Carmen of the Sacred Heart cried when she saw them so hungry. She would get up early in the morning and go to the orchard behind the orphanage to pick up any fruit that had fallen from the trees during the night so they would have something to fill their stomachs.

Mother Luisita greatly loved her orphans, and they, in turn, grew to love her. They liked to gather around her whenever she spoke to them. She took it upon herself to be the one who checked their heads to remove "the little bugs" (lice), as she called them. Because she wanted the girls to learn how to support themselves, as time went on, Mother Luisita was able to purchase a stocking-making machine and fabric so they could learn how to make stockings. She also saw that other trades were taught in order to prepare them for the time when they would leave the orphanage. In this respect, she was ahead of the times.

∞

A lot happened during 1919 and 1920, times of joy, growth, uncertainties, and trials for the fledgling community. The number of sisters increased. Archbishop Orozco finally emerged from his hideout. In 1919, Mother Luisita established a Sunday school that was held in the orchard behind their buildings or in one of the rooms inside the orphanage. Father Almaquio Rodríguez taught the religion classes there. Other classes, such as painting, bone lace, embroidery, wood drawing, and art, were given by professional laypersons. Some ladies from the town also took advantage of these classes.

Mother Luisita wanted the sisters to learn all these skills as well. She gave them vocal lessons using a small organ. They met frequently in the garden for a change of scenery and some fresh air. These times in the garden inspired many of the natural images she frequently used in her conversations with the sisters and the girls.

Let us not be just teachers. Rather, let us be souls of prayer. Just what are we going to give the young girls? Let us not be like canals. A canal empties itself and is left dry. Rather, let us be like fountains which are always giving.[84]

Fix your gaze on heaven, not on earthly things, which all pass away like a breath, leaving behind nothing but remorse and sadness like smoke, which disappears with only reality remaining.[85]

[84] Personal remembrance of Mother Socorro of the Holy Spirit Cholico Rodriguez.
[85] Kennedy, In Love's Safekeeping, vol. 2, letter 626, 891.

Atotonilco el Alto, in Jalisco, Mexico, is the hometown of Mother Luisita and the birthplace of her Carmelite community. It is nestled against the Los Altos highlands in northeastern Jalisco, where violent battles of the Cristiada of the 1920s took place.

Aerial view of San Miguel Arcángel Church in Atotonilco el Alto, Jalisco, Mexico.

Sister Joseph Louise Padilla, O.C.D., stands in front of the Church of San Miguel Arcángel in Atotonilco. This was the parish church of the de la Peña family. Mother Luisita received the Sacraments of Baptism, Confirmation, and Matrimony in this church.

Baptismal font in San Miguel Arcángel Church, where Luisita was baptized a few days after her birth because of her frail health.

View of the interior courtyard of the motherhouse of the Carmelitas del Sagrado Corazón in Atotonilco looking toward the small gold dome chapel that contains Mother Luisita's remains. The blue dome of Calvary Chapel can be seen in the background.

Interior view of Calvary Chapel, Atotonilco el Alto, Jalisco. This is the memorial chapel built by Mother Luisita to honor the memory of Doctor Pascual Rojas.

Left: painting of Mother Luisita in 1879 at thirteen years of age. Right: photo of Mother Luisita in 1904 at thirty-eight years of age in the Carmelite habit of the Discalced Carmelite Monastery of Saint Teresa in Guadalajara.

Left: passport photo of Mother Luisita as a refugee fleeing persecution in Mexico taken in 1927 when she was sixty years of age. Right: Mother Luisita in 1936, only a year before her death.

This de la Peña family photo was taken in 1896 after the deaths of Epigmenio de la Peña, Mother Luisita's father, in 1895 and Pascual Rojas, her husband, in 1896. Mother Luisita is seated in the middle row at the left and her mother is seated next to her.

Left: Luisa de la Peña Navarro (1844–1922), Luisita's mother.
Right: Epigmenio de la Peña (1831–1895), Luisita's father.

Doctor Pascual Rojas, Luisita's husband from 1882
until his death in 1896.

Left: Archbishop Francisco Orozco y Jiménez of Guadalajara, who,
together with Mother Luisita, established the Carmelite Sisters of the
Third Order of Guadalajara; right, Bishop John J. Cantwell of Los Angeles,
who welcomed the three refugees, Mother Luisita, Sister Margarita Maria
Hernandez, and Sister Teresa Navarro, to the United States in June 1927.

Mother Luisita, seated with her arms around the children, together with her first companions and some patients at the Hospital of the Sacred Heart in Atotonilco after she returned from the Monastery of Saint Teresa in Guadalajara.

Photo of Mother Luisita (second row from the bottom, with the number 6 on her habit) taken after her community was merged into the community of Sister Servants of the Blessed Sacrament.

One of the earliest photos of the Carmelite Sisters of the Third Order of Guadalajara. Approved in 1921, the community could not receive new members until 1922. The first three postulants of the new community can be seen in upper right of the photo.

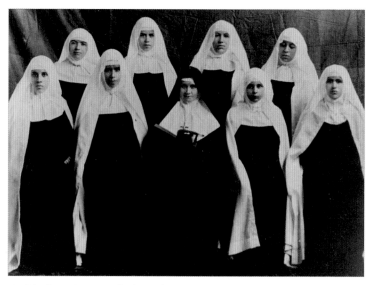

Archbishop Orozco asked Mother Isabel Rioseco, R.F.R. (center in black habit), to be the first directress of novices of the Carmelite Sisters in 1923. She stayed one year to help with their initial formation.

Undated photo of Mother Luisita.

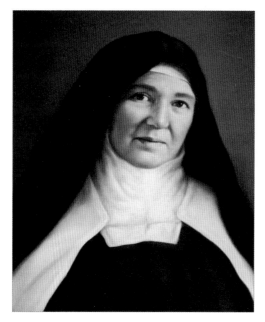

Undated painting of Mother Luisita.

Mother Luisita and Mother Margarita Maria Hernandez, 1936.

Father Leroy Callahan helped the three Carmelite refugees when they arrived in Los Angeles. He helped them find a home parish and assisted them when they began Santa Teresita Sanatorium in Duarte, California. He was the archdiocesan liaison with Mexican refugees during the Cristiada.

Father Francis P. Ott welcomed the Carmelite refugees to his parish, Holy Innocents in Long Beach, California, in 1927. He assisted them in every possible way, and when he was transferred to Saint Patrick's Church in Los Angeles in 1928, the Carmelite Sisters moved there also.

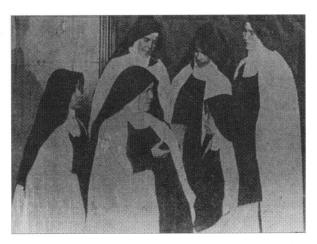

Photo of the Carmelite refugees taken by the San Francisco Catholic newspaper the *Monitor* in 1928 while they were in Oakland, California, before their move to Saint Mary's College, Moraga, California. Mother Luisita is seated in the center with her hand extended.

Photo taken from library microfiche from the *Monitor*'s May 1928 article featuring the Carmelite refugees. Mother Luisita is pictured here with Margaret Mary Williams, the daughter of Frank Williams, who wrote the articles on the "Exiles of the Little Flower," as he called them.

This January 1930 photo of Mother Luisita was taken after she returned to Mexico from the United States following the signing of the peace agreement between the Catholic Church and the Mexican government.

One of the original "cottages" in 1930 at Santa Teresita in Duarte, where the Carmelite Sisters cared for young girls with tuberculosis.

Archbishop Orozco, with Mother Luisita (at left of Archbishop Orozco) in the mid-1930s.

Archbishop Orozco (center), Mother Luisita (right), and other Sisters at Santa Teresita in the 1930s.

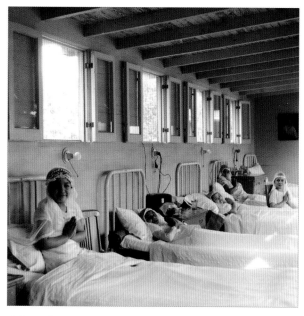

Tuberculosis patients at Santa Teresita on their First Communion day. This photo shows the interior of one of the original cottages.

Mother Teresita Angela, C.S.C., presents bound copies of the original letters of Mother Luisita to Mother Vincent Marie, O.C.D., in 1995.

Mother Luisita's two communities discuss her writings at the motherhouse in Atotonilco in 1995.

Mother Luisita's two communities peruse the archives at the motherhouse in Alhambra, California, in 1995.

Mother Teresita Angela, C.S.C., and Mother Vincent Marie Finnegan, O.C.D., present the Offertory gifts during Mass in the Sisters' choir at the motherhouse of the Carmelite Sisters of the Most Sacred Heart of Los Angeles in 1995. Father Paul Sustayta is the celebrant.

Council members of Mother Luisita's two communities pose for a photo together at Santa Teresita in Duarte, California, in 1995.

Father Carlos Martinez, O.C.D. (right), with Mother Luisita's two communities (in front of grille) and Discalced Carmelite nuns in Mexico City (behind grille) in 2016. The Carmelite Sisters had hiked up Tepeyac Hill, where Our Lady of Guadalupe had appeared to Juan Diego, to reach this monastery near the top of the hill.

Sisters from Mother Luisita's two communities break bread together in 2016 at the motherhouse of the Carmelitas del Sagrado Corazón.

This doctor's bag had belonged to Doctor Pascual Rojas. Mother Luisita kept her correspondence in it during the religious persecution in Mexico.

The Blessed Sacrament was hidden in this desk during the religious persecution in Mexico. A candle was placed on top when the Blessed Sacrament was present.

The bound volumes of the letters of Mother Luisita are kept in a special museum cabinet to prevent deterioration.

This trunk contains some clothing from Luisita and Pascual's fourteen-year marriage, from 1882 to 1896, the year Pascual died. The gold letters on the front originally were *P* and *R* for *Pascual Rojas*. Luisita painted over parts of each letter so that they read *L* and *P*, for *Luisita* and *Pascual*.

When Mother Luisita was told to merge her community into the community of the Sister Servants of the Blessed Sacrament, the Sisters there, recognizing her holiness, saved her hair and returned it to the Carmelitas del Sagrado Corazón at the beginning of the process of Mother Luisita's canonization.

The final resting place of Mother Luisita is in this urn in a memorial chapel adjacent to Calvary Chapel. Each of the eight sides of this handwrought bronze urn shows an aspect of her Teresian Carmelite charism.

Words on the scroll: "Our Lord in the Blessed Sacrament wants to be your Confidant." (Mother Luisita)

"May the Sacred Heart of Jesus be your refuge." (Mother Luisita)

"Work endlessly on the behalf of children and the sick, and in your conversations lead them to love the Most Blessed Sacrament and Our Most Holy Mother." (Mother Luisita)

Words on the scroll: "How beautiful it is to be in the hands of God, searching His Divine Gaze." (Mother Luisita)

Words on the scroll: "My food is to do
the will of my Father." (see John 4:34)

Photo showing the actual size of the beautifully wrought
urn. Standing next to the urn is Sister Joseph Louise Padilla,
O.C.D. (she is four feet, eleven inches tall).

Don't worry and don't allow yourself to drown in a drop of water. You're all right. You are all right.[86]

One day when Mother Luisita saw the girls crying from hunger, she sent them to the chapel to ask Saint Vincent de Paul to send them some bread. Soon after, Sister Luz came by with a gift of bread from a benefactor who had just arrived. From that time on, the girls always had enough bread.

Realizing how much the girls missed their families, the sisters tried their best to fill the void in those little hearts yearning for their mothers' love. Every night, Mother Luisita gave each girl a personal blessing and some words of encouragement. When they got sick, she nursed them.

One day when the archbishop was visiting them, he suddenly told the sisters with apparent calmness, "Stay here doing good, but the day you do not want to do it anymore, you may return to your homes." It seemed as if he no longer wanted to give them any hope at all that their community would be approved by the Catholic Church. His words pierced Mother Luisita's heart. When the archbishop left, she went to her cell and cried profusely.[87]

Mother Luisita carried on as she brought to reality the restless urgings in her heart all these years—to care for the poor, the sick, and orphans and to educate children. Everything would have been complete were it not for the still-pending official approval of her community by the Catholic Church and the archbishop's directive to stop receiving new postulants.

---

[86] Kennedy, *In Love's Safekeeping*, vol. 1, letter 206.

[87] In monastic terms, a *cell* is the personal, private bedroom of a monk or a nun.

She obeyed, although there was a waiting line of applicants to enter her community.

In time, Mother Luisita came to understand that her calling was far greater than merely to care for the sick and to teach children. This impulse of grace had consistently remained within her soul over the years as her community was being formed. It would ultimately find fulfillment in a Carmelite way of life that united contemplative prayer and active service.

The affiliation with the Third Order Carmelites came about when Archbishop Orozco returned to Atotonilco on his way to the town of San Francisco de Asís shortly after the day Mother Luisita had cried. He spoke in a different tone. "The Holy Father does not want more Orders. Affiliate with a Third Order." How different from his tone during his last visit. No documentation was found of the reason for this change.

In those days, religious orders were divided into three categories: The First Order comprised the friars. The Second Order was for cloistered nuns. The Third Order included everyone else and was subdivided into two groups: (1) priests and friars and (2) sisters. There was also the Third Order Secular for laity, whether single, married, or widowed.

After discussing their options among themselves, the sisters told Mother Luisita that they would join the Third Order Franciscans. They submitted their application to aggregate with the Franciscan Order, but Sister Teresa of Jesus continued to talk about a community of Third Order Carmelites in Mexico City and the Carmelite Sisters of Charity of Spain. She had investigated both communities before deciding to join Mother Luisita's new group. She thought they should join the Carmelites as Third Order Discalced Carmelites.

Many Discalced Carmelite monasteries of cloistered nuns were in existence throughout the world, but there were very few affiliated Carmelite groups who lived the Carmelite way of prayer together with an active apostolate. *Apostolate* comes from the word *apostle*, which is derived from the Greek and means "messenger" or "one who is sent." *Apostolate* is defined as the "office, duties, or mission of an apostle" and includes the concept of being "called and sent in the name of Christ by the Church."[88]

When Mother Luisita heard Sister Teresa of Jesus Navarro continue to speak about Third Order Discalced Carmelite communities, something resonated deep within her heart—something that fulfilled the stirrings within her, that ever-present intuitive understanding that there was something else, something new, something more, drawing her onward; a spiritual desire that had yet to be fulfilled, though she did not know when or how. That is, until now. She understood immediately. This was it. Third Order Carmelites. Yes!

Although the sisters had already decided to petition to become affiliated with the Franciscans, Mother Luisita mentioned to the archbishop another possibility—joining the Carmelite Order. The sisters presented the idea to him through a tableau depicting their future if they were to become Carmelites. *Rostro de Bondad* gives a vivid description of the sisters' tableau. A large, nearly life-size picture of the archbishop was hung on the wall. From the picture, material like a veil flowed down to the lower part of the tableau onto three figures: a young girl dressed as a Carmelite, a schoolgirl holding a globe in her hands, and a young boy holding some gauze.

---

[88] Today, the word *ministry* is used more often than *apostolate*; but Mother Luisita called the sisters in her community "apostles," and she used the word *apostolate*, as does this biography.

At the end of the gauze was a sick man on one side and an orphan girl on the opposite side. The archbishop understood and liked the idea so much that he revoked the first petition and asked the sisters to make a new petition, this time to the Carmelite Order.

Before leaving, he visited their hospital and told them, "I want you to know that I am going to send your application to Rome. It is very difficult, this step to the Eternal City. We will see what the will of God is regarding your community."[89]

On September 7, 1920, the archbishop sent the sisters' request for affiliation with the Carmelite Order. This document can be found in the archives of the Congregation of the Carmelite Sisters of the Sacred Heart of Mexico and is recorded in the Book of Government (appendix B).[90]

At this time, Mother Luisita had received the constitutions of the Third Order Carmelite Sisters of Saint Teresa, founded in 1903, who were established in the Santa Julia colony of Tacuba, Mexico City. She placed their constitutions near the tabernacle in their chapel and asked all the sisters to pray that they would obtain permission to start living their Carmelite life according to those constitutions.

On December 9, 1920, Mother Luisita took those constitutions to Guadalajara to give them to the archbishop. When she arrived at the archbishop's office, she was led right away into a private parlor. When Archbishop Orozco walked in with a document in his hand, he said, "Mother Luisita, I have great joy for you! Carmelites! Carmelites!"

He gave her the document, adding, "Savor it, Mother, and tell your dear sisters."

---

[89] Personal remembrance of Sister Refugio of Jesus Navarro.
[90] Orozco Mosqueda, *Rostro de Bondad*, 121.

On her knees and filled with emotion, Mother said, "Your Excellency, what can we do for you in return?"

"Pray for me," he replied. "I want to personally establish that foundation." After she read through the document, he asked her to leave it with him so that the Carmelite superiors of the Archdiocese of Guadalajara could sign it as well. Mother Luisita remained in Guadalajara for a month and a half, locating brown material to purchase for their Carmelite habits. She also ran a variety of errands, as she always did when in Guadalajara, including a visit with the Discalced Carmelite nuns of Saint Teresa.

Meanwhile, the Sisters of Atotonilco continued to wait, carrying on despite their uncertainty about their community's future. Mother Luisita had been gone since December 9, and January was almost over. They had received no word from her. It had been a long seven weeks of trying to learn the virtue of patience.

Finally, the day arrived when the sisters heard the bell at the main door ringing. Hoping it was Mother Luisita, they all ran to the door. In a calm voice, she said, "Come, come" and took them into the chapel. She prayed a while before the Blessed Sacrament and then led them to the orchard in their backyard, where she gave them the news—"Carmelites! Carmelites!"—and shared the details of her visit with the archbishop.

Material for the Carmelite habits began to arrive. With each delivery, more bolts of material were carried into the convent. A doll dressed in the Carmelite habit came. In those days, the nuns used dolls to show the proportions of the different parts of the Carmelite habit to be sewn. The ceremonial of the Carmelite Sisters of the Monastery of Saint Teresa also arrived.

February 2, 1921, marked a huge milestone in the life of Mother Luisita and her community. That was the day that they began to follow the Carmelite Rule with their official title of Carmelite

Sisters of the Third Order of Guadalajara. In the Catholic Church, it is a significant feast day and over the centuries has held various names: the Purification of the Blessed Virgin Mary, the Presentation of the Child Jesus in the Temple, and Candlemas. It falls on the fortieth day after the birth of Christ, in commemoration of Mary's obedience to the Jewish law that stipulated that new mothers must follow the prescribed ritual of purification after giving birth to a son. It is also the day on which the Church commemorates the Presentation of the Child Jesus in the Temple. Mary and Joseph followed the Jewish law that required the presentation of every firstborn male child to God in the Temple.

Early that morning, the traditional song that begins, "Praised be Jesus Christ, and His Virgin Mother. Come to prayer, sisters. Come to praise the Lord," was intoned by a sister as she rang the rising bell. Later that day, Father Macario Velázquez offered a Mass of Thanksgiving. The official signed document of affiliation to the Carmelite Order arrived that afternoon. Although Mother Luisita had originally included the word *cloistered* in the community's title until that time, the original document clearly stated that the community was accepted into the Carmelite Order with the name Discalced Carmelite Sisters of the Third Order of Guadalajara (see appendix B).

The sisters began to sew the habits that the archbishop would formally present to them on their Investiture or Clothing Day in a private ceremony. Mother Luisita began arrangements with the archbishop regarding an appropriate day for the ceremony and the priest who would preside at the Clothing Ceremony and celebrate Holy Mass.

One item Mother Luisita still needed to work out was how to acquire the traditional white bridal gowns that each sister would wear during the Clothing Ceremony. In those days in the Carmelite tradition, each sister would walk up to the altar wearing a simple bridal gown, receive her new name from the archbishop or his representative, and then leave the chapel in order to change into the Carmelite habit that would be given to her.

How to borrow so many gowns during these challenging times was a dilemma. Where would she get them? They decided to ask friends and relatives if they could borrow their bridal gowns. Of course, none of the gowns fit any of the sisters, but they gladly accepted them and soon had an assortment to choose from and to use as samples when they sewed theirs. That was their original plan.

On February 27, 1921, Mother Luisita wrote to the vicar-general of religious, Father Abundio Anaya, and asked that the required time of postulancy be dispensed because the sisters had already spent so many years together in community in Atotonilco. She asked to "begin our novitiate now." She pleaded with him to allow the original six sisters who had come together in 1904 to receive the Carmelite habit on the ninth and tenth of March.

The answer came right away. Father Velázquez of San Miguel was authorized to go ahead with the required canonical examination of the six sisters prior to their becoming novices and to give them their holy habits. Father Anaya replied: "I have your last letter. Go ahead and do the Spiritual Exercises as you wish, and I will promptly let you know what day I will be able to meet you there and receive your vows. I will also explain to you more fully the dispensation that is allowing you to profess your vows right away."

The community continued to prepare with fidelity and fervor, living the season of Lent with greater intensity because the ceremony of receiving the habit and profession of vows as Carmelites would be done after Lent.

On April 1, 1921, Friday of Easter week, Father Anaya arrived at approximately ten thirty in the morning and rang the doorbell.

He asked that all the sisters meet him in their convent parlor. After greeting them in Latin, "Venite et videte opera Domine," which is "Come and see the works of the Lord," he let them know that today would be their Clothing Day. He was delegated to preside at the ceremony as the authorized representative of the archbishop.

He went on to tell them that the private ceremony would begin soon and asked if they could be ready in half an hour. Had they heard correctly? In just thirty minutes? How would they ever get ready in time? During the previous week, Holy Week, Mother Luisita had urged them to spend the sacred week in prayerful silence, remaining recollected in God's presence during their daily activities to prepare themselves spiritually for the reception of the habit and the profession of vows. She never realized that it would come so soon.

Mother Luisita tried to take in what Father Anaya had just said. Today? She hid her astonished embarrassment as best she could but refused to let this turn of events dampen the joy of what was finally to happen after all these years. Maintaining her serenity, and unruffled by the way the day was unfolding, she directed the sisters to help find all the things that were needed for the ceremony.

Before they left, Mother Luisita announced that only she and six others would receive habits that day. She had wanted the ceremony to take place on July 15, the vigil of Our Lady of Mount Carmel. That would have left them enough time to sew the bridal gowns and the Carmelite habits. No documentation was found that shows the reason why Father Anaya arrived so unexpectedly and so early that April morning.

In a state of shock, a few sisters flew to the chapel to prepare the altar. The others, along with Mother Luisita, donned the bridal gowns that they had borrowed. No matter what they looked like or how they fit, each sister put one on. For the bridal veil, they quickly arranged some small pieces of curtain material, made of a mesh cotton fabric, and since there was not enough of it, they completed their veils by donning some of the tabernacle veils from the chapel. Thus attired, the new brides of the Lord were now prepared for their Clothing Day. It must have been quite a sight to behold—unique and very humbling.

They waited at the back of the chapel for the entrance procession to begin. At eleven o'clock, Mother Luisita, wearing her bridal gown and carrying a lighted candle, advanced slowly toward the altar. Father Daniel Arias, one of the priests from San Miguel Arcángel parish, intoned "O Gloriosa Virginum!" The community then processed into the main chapel, each carrying a lighted candle. Following his homily, Father Anaya invested Mother Luisita in the Carmelite habit. Following the Carmelite ritual, she prostrated herself on the sanctuary floor and the sisters scattered flower petals upon her as she lay there. When she arose with her characteristic dignity and sweetness, her face was radiant with joy.

The investiture of the six sisters followed immediately. Poor dear ones! Their bridal attire was a sight to behold! It was a relief that it was a totally private ceremony. Father Arias could not hold back his amusement and chuckled to himself.

Sister Socorro of the Holy Spirit recalled:

> I can still see Mother Luisita with that spirit of recollection, with that spirit of faith, humility and submission to the disposition of the superiors, with such modesty and wearing the dress that did not belong to her and, of course, did not fit properly. For their crowns, the other sisters borrowed some of the artificial orange blossoms that they used to pin onto the tabernacle veils, and that was just the way it was, as these new brides of Christ prepared to receive their new name and their Carmelite habit.

During the ceremony, Mother Luisita officially received the name Maria Luisa Josefa of the Most Blessed Sacrament, adding Josefa because of her devotion to this patron saint of Carmel.

As the ceremony was ending, Father Anaya made another surprise announcement. He informed the group of sisters that at five in the afternoon on that day, Mother Luisita was going to pronounce her vows first, followed by the other six sisters. Father Anaya then intoned the hymn of praise, Te Deum Laudamus, and the Clothing Ceremony ended. It seemed that the six-month period of novitiate was also waived for these six sisters.

April 1, 1921, held surprise after surprise for them. They began preparations for their next ceremony, hardly believing what was happening as they got ready as best they could for the profession of first vows. This time it would be a public ceremony. Their relatives and friends would be permitted to attend. The invitation was sent by word of mouth throughout the town.

Years later, Sister Maria Socorro remembered that

as soon as the chapel doors were opened, the people entered. The hour arrived and the ceremony began. Organ music accompanied the special hymns for the ceremony. Everything was joyful. First, our Mother Luisita professed her vows. And, so it happened, that for the first time, amid all this joy, we heard Mother pronounce her vows with her religious name of Maria Luisa Josefa of the Most Blessed Sacrament. Everything was done according to the ceremonial of the Discalced Carmelite Nuns of Saint Teresa's Monastery. The other sisters proceeded to make their profession of vows according to the same ceremonial: "I, Sister N., make my profession and vow obedience, chastity, and poverty to God, and to the Blessed Virgin Mary of Mount

Carmel, and to our Reverend Mother Superior and her successors, according to the Primitive Rule of the Order of Discalced Carmelites and our constitutions."

At this time, the sisters were following the primitive rule that was in use at the Monastery of Saint Teresa, where Mother Luisita had been a novice for three months.

Sister Maria Socorro continued her remembrance of that day:

The following day, each sister received her Carmelite veil in another private ceremony, called the Imposition of the Veil. It took place with all solemnity. The people and relatives of the sisters kept going back and forth, bringing baskets of food. Gifts kept pouring in.

During the Imposition of the Veil ceremony, something curious happened. Father Arias asked Tomás, the community's faithful volunteer, to ring the sanctuary altar bells. Misunderstanding, he ran to the bell tower of the church and rang the large church bells enthusiastically. All the people came running, wondering what was going on, and so the church doors were opened, and the Imposition of the Veil Ceremony was no longer private. When the people saw Mother and the sisters fully clothed in the Carmelite habit, they cried.[91]

It was still against the law to wear religious habits in public.

Three weeks later, on April 22, with their pastor, Father Velásquez, presiding, the first elections of the new community were held, and Mother Luisita was elected superior general. She was fifty-five years old.

---

[91] Personal remembrance of Mother Socorro of the Holy Spirit Cholico Rodriguez.

Mother Luisita wanted to accept right away the young women who had been waiting to join the community, but when she mentioned it to the archbishop, he did not agree and told her not to accept any more candidates until the original sisters had learned to live according to the Carmelite constitutions. He said, "How are you going to teach others what you yourselves do not know?" With this reason resolutely in his mind, he canceled the entrance of the young women. The community continued their study of the constitutions, Carmelite history, and Carmelite spirituality even more diligently. The archbishop had kept the constitutions of the Third Order Carmelites of Mexico City that Mother Luisita had given him, so they studied those of the Discalced Carmelite nuns in Guadalajara.

On July 15, the rest of the sisters received their habits, and on the following day, the solemnity of Our Lady of Mount Carmel, they, too, professed their vows. The other sisters had borrowed a painting of Our Lady of Mount Carmel and had decorated it by adding clouds. Kneeling in front of Mother Luisita one by one, each sister then placed her hands in Mother Luisita's hands and professed her vows.

At that time, in both the ancient orders and the newly founded congregations, there existed a distinction between the sisters: sisters of the black veil and sisters of the white veil. The first group were the choir sisters who prayed the Divine Office, while those of the white veil, known as lay sisters, took care of the household tasks. That is not to say that they did not go to the choir at all, but they had fewer choir obligations. This distinction among sisters disappeared with the Second Vatican Council. There is no longer any distinction.

Mother Luisita had a beautiful, lifelong devotion to the Blessed Virgin Mary. Her love for her was gentle and easy to imitate. She would always pray the Rosary at the beginning of her travels. Before becoming a religious sister, she called the workers on the hacienda each evening for prayer, which included the recitation of the Rosary. It was Mother Luisita's love of our Blessed Lady that led her to the Carmelite Order, with its stellar devotion to Mary. Mother Luisita invited her sisters to deepen and strengthen their love of Mary, as can be seen in her letters:

> Since this month (October) is dedicated to the holy rosary, I would like you sisters to pray all fifteen decades for the needs of the Community. The rosary, it seems to me, has infinite value.[92]

> Love the Blessed Virgin with all your soul. Make her the confidant of all your troubles.[93]

> May the Immaculate Conception be the star that leads you to heaven; may she be your model and your consolation in this valley of tears.[94]

With prayer and contemplation as their main goal, the new Carmelites deepened their friendship with God through prayer and study. Following the Carmelite Rule and adapting it to support their various services among the people, they studied the works of Saint John of the Cross and Saint Teresa of Ávila. This Teresian Carmelite charism of Mother Luisita's Carmelites would continue to develop during her life.

Their new community was finally a reality, and life began to take on a regular routine.

---

[92] Kennedy, *In Love's Safekeeping*, vol. 1, letter 128, 245.
[93] Kennedy, *In Love's Safekeeping*, vol. 1, letter 59, 140.
[94] Kennedy, *In Love's Safekeeping*, vol. 2, letter 420, 706.

Chapter 10

The Way of Carmel

For me, nothing is lacking. I have found the fullness
of happiness in my Carmelite vocation.

—Mother Luisita

Mother Luisita was now Mother Maria Luisa Josefa of the Most
Blessed Sacrament, foundress of the Carmelite Sisters of the Third
Order of Guadalajara. She and the members of her community
were accepted in the Catholic Church as bona fide Carmelite
Sisters. But what does that mean? What exactly is a Carmelite?

The Carmelite Order began during the 1200s with a group
of men who began living on Mount Carmel, which had been the
home of the great prophet Elijah. These men wanted lives of prayer
and solitude that would lead to a profoundly personal experience
of God. They chose Mount Carmel's Fountain of Elijah as the site
for their hermitage and eventually became known as the Brothers
of the Blessed Virgin Mary of Mount Carmel. This was the foundation of the spiritual charism of the Carmelite Order.

The Carmelite nuns were officially established in Italy in 1452,
and their monasteries quickly spread throughout Europe. Beginning in 1562, Saint Teresa of Jesus established seventeen Discalced

Carmelite monasteries, in which the nuns lived the austere Carmelite Rule. One of these original seventeen monasteries was San José de Caravaca de la Cruz in the province of Murcia, Spain, which later formed a new Carmelite monastery in Puebla, Mexico. In time, six Carmelite nuns set out from the Puebla monastery to establish the Carmel of Saint Teresa in Guadalajara, where Mother Luisita had lived the Teresian Carmelite charism from March until June 1904.

∞

Father Pedro had originally arrived in Mexico in 1899 to help the Mexican Carmelites. He had met with many Discalced Carmelite nuns in Mexico City. He had also guided several new Carmelite congregations, including the Carmelite Missionaries of Santa Teresa in Mexico City. It was Father Pedro who had given Mother Luisita a copy of their constitutions.

During the three months that Mother Luisita lived in the Carmel of Saint Teresa in 1904, Father Pedro Heriz of Saint Elias, vicar provincial of the Discalced Carmelites of Catalonia, Spain, was visiting Guadalajara. As a general definitor of the order, he had been authorized to oversee all the Carmelite communities in Mexico. Not long after Mother Luisita left the Monastery of Saint Teresa, "Father Pedrito," as Mother Luisita called him, was again in Jalisco. With his wise and prudent spiritual direction, he helped her and the five women who had joined her during the beginning days of the little community of women.

During the Revolution, monasteries were confiscated by the government. Thanks be to God, they were not destroyed. Not only did all the buildings survive after the revolution, but several new foundations had been established by the nuns who returned to them, and the monasteries now flourished once again.

After the Mexican Revolution, there were very few priests left in Mexico. Many had fled, and the bishops had been exiled. Father Pedro had remained, and his help was vital to the fledgling community. Because of him, Mother Luisita's community was able to receive an authentic Teresian Carmelite formation. Father Pedro's guidance was sound. The sisters knew how blessed they were to have one of the few Carmelite priests left in Mexico as a friend who had the authority to help them. When the sisters became officially affiliated with the Carmelite Order, he directed the Carmelite formation of Mother Luisita's new community.[95]

In October 1921, Mother Luisita contracted a serious typhoid infection. As her condition worsened, she made her last will and testament. The sisters prayed intensely for her recovery. Some of them even walked on their knees up the chapel aisle (a custom still practiced in Mexico when asking God for something important) and into the sanctuary to beg the Lord to restore her to health. Every night, the sisters carried Saint Joseph's statue in a procession, asking his intercession on Mother's behalf before God. Each sister was told that she could make the same petition to her own favorite saint as well. After lingering at death's door, Mother Luisita finally recovered.

Mother Luisita felt that it was time for a Carmelite sister to become the principal of her school, but none had a teaching certificate from the government. Victoria Alatorre had been the principal

---

[95] Antonio Unzueta Echevarria, *Beato Pedro De San Elías: Biografía y Espistolario* (Vitoria-Gasteiz: Ediciones El Carmen, 2015), 86–94.

while the Sister Servants were there. After Mother Luisita had returned to Atotonilco, Lupe Escoto had accepted the position of principal from 1918 to 1921. The sisters recalled that they had worked in the school without any principal for about a year after becoming affiliated with the Carmelite Order.

It was toward the end of 1921 that Mother Luisita wrote to Father Pedro, who was residing in Durango, Mexico, and asked him if he would help them find a qualified principal, a teacher, and an organist for the school. She also asked him to pray for good vocations for the new community. The community began praying the devotional and lengthy Seven Sundays of Saint Joseph Novena for this intention.

At the beginning of 1922, Father Pedro responded to Mother's request and sent Maria Chavez Martinez and Carmen Heredia, two qualified, experienced teachers, to help in the school. These two women told Mother Luisita that they both wanted to join the community but could not until the archbishop authorized the entrance of new postulants. So, the two women taught in the school as they waited for Archbishop Orozco's permission, and the sisters continued to ask God to inspire the archbishop to authorize their acceptance of new members.

Toward the middle of May, Father José del Valle stopped by Atotonilco on his way to Guadalajara.[96] He was a native son of Los Altos, born in the Hacienda del Valle. He had known Mother Luisita since childhood and called her *tia*, or aunt. The two knew each other very well. He had been left an orphan at a young age, and Mother

---

[96] Father José de Jesus Angulo was the pastor of San Francisco de Asís. He was persecuted during the Cristiada, and he had to change his name to José del Valle when he became bishop of Tabasco in 1945.

Luisita's parents had taken him in and helped him financially with his studies in the seminary and again with his studies in Rome.

When he greeted Mother Luisita, she told him about the archbishop's refusal to give them permission to accept vocations. She asked Carmen Heredia to plead her case with Father del Valle and to ask him to intervene with Archbishop Orozco so that she and the others could enter. Promising that he would do all that he could, he left them.

A few days later, early in the morning of May 25, a telegram arrived from the Archdiocese of Guadalajara. It informed Mother Luisita that Archbishop Orozco had given permission to accept Carmen Heredia, Maria Chavez Martinez, and Maria del Rosario Fonseca, and they entered that very day—the first postulants of the Carmelite Sisters of the Third Order of Guadalajara. It was the solemnity of the Ascension.

At their Clothing Ceremony several months later, Carmen Heredia received the name Sister Elena of the Cross and the Holy Spirit. Maria Chavez Martinez received the name Sister Carmen of Jesus. Maria del Rosario Fonseca received the name Sister Isabel of Saint Pascual. Sister Isabel continued in nursing. Sister Carmen de Jesus was assigned as principal of the school as well as teaching the fifth and sixth grades. Sister Elena was a teacher and professional organist with a beautiful singing voice. Interestingly, she had also prayed the Seven Sundays of Saint Joseph Novena, asking for clarity in discerning which community she should enter. Not long after her novena, Father Pedro had directed her to Mother Luisita's new community.

During the next four years, Catholics in Jalisco were vigorously persecuted by the infamous José Guadalupe Zuno, who became the mayor of Guadalajara in 1922 and the governor of Jalisco in 1923. His administration was characterized by his relentless attacks on the Catholic Church. Simultaneously, the anger and indignation of the Catholic citizens of Jalisco, especially those in Guadalajara, were coming to a head. Catholic groups came together to discuss their options and to mobilize in different ways to ready themselves for whatever would come.

The year 1921 saw three bombings. The first bomb exploded in Archbishop Orozco's residence in April, causing considerable damage. It happened about ten days after the sisters had received their habit and professed their vows. It seemed to be a response by the government to the huge gathering of fervent Catholics who had come together to witness the crowning of the statue of Our Lady of Zapopan. Archbishop Orozco had not been able to go to Atotonilco to receive Mother Luisita's vows because he had presided at that crowning. Father Anaya had been delegated to take the archbishop's place for the sisters' Clothing and vow ceremonies.

A second bomb went off on June 4 at Archbishop Orozco's residence.

The third bombing was the much-publicized blast in the Basilica of Our Lady of Guadalupe in Mexico City. On the morning of November 18, a factory worker had quietly placed twenty-nine sticks of dynamite in a flower vase at the foot of the famous image of Our Lady of Guadalupe in Mexico City. The explosion burst the basilica's windows, smashed vases, and completely destroyed the marble altar. The large bronze cross near the image was bent twenty degrees. The windows of buildings hundreds of yards away were shattered. The image of Our Lady and the glass surrounding it, however, remained untouched.

Within a short time, about twenty thousand Mexicans protested. Businesses closed that day for a five-hour mourning period. The fact that the famous image was unharmed is considered by Catholics to be a miracle.

The lay Catholics of Guadalajara had already been preparing their response for just such an event. The Mexican Catholic Youth Association had formed a security team. The Knights of Columbus, the Catholic Ladies' Society, and many other Catholic groups banded together and had begun demonstrations. Four thousand people had marched in a peaceful demonstration in the city of Guadalajara. The Union of Catholic Worker Syndicates had signed a petition asking for the ousting of the chief of police. In the highlands of Jalisco, the town of San Julián had organized a demonstration.

In a short time, Guadalajara experienced three city councils, three mayors, and three state governors—and all the while Mother Luisita was arranging for Clothing and vow ceremonies in addition to administering the hospital and the orphanage. It became her standard response to keep quiet about the political intrigues and to continue doing what she was doing—to pray and work with all her heart and soul right where she was and leave the rest in God's hands. This became her hallmark. No matter what might be happening at a given time, she placed her trust absolutely in God and continued working quietly and steadily in her portion of the Lord's vineyard—the little town of Atotonilco—where she and her sisters could make a difference. She was a prayer warrior who was well aware of the fact that "more things are accomplished by prayer than this world dreams of."[97] Mother Luisita's role was as an intercessor before her God.

A letter to the mother of two of the sisters refers discreetly to the troubled times of religious persecution rising in Mexico. Mother Luisita replied to Maria de Jesus Chavez, "We have been praying for

---

[97] Alfred Lord Tennyson, "Morte d'Arthur," *Idylls of the King* (London: Edward Maxon, 1859), page unknown.

the intention you mentioned in your letter. May God remedy that immense need which is causing the Church in Durango so much suffering. My best regards to your beloved family. Affectionately yours in Christ from one who appreciates you in God and wishes for you to be a saint. Maria Luisa Josefa of the Blessed Sacrament, T.C.D."

∞

Mother Luisita knew the community needed a more specific Carmelite formation. In 1923, she asked Archbishop Orozco if he would provide them with a Carmelite directress of novices to assist them in their formation as Carmelites. Instead, he sent them one of the Franciscan Sisters of Our Lady of Refuge. Her name was Mother Isabel Rioseco, R.F.R. The community of Franciscan Sisters of Our Lady of Refuge was founded on May 7, 1897, in Guadalajara, by the Venerable María Librada del Sagrado Corazón de Jesús Orozco Santacruz, also from Los Altos.

Previously, Archbishop Orozco had called upon Mother Isabel to help in the formation of another new community, the Congregation of the Servants of the Most Holy Trinity and of the Poor, founded by Blessed Vicenta Chávez Orozco during the attacks against the Church in the late nineteenth and early twentieth centuries in Mexico. That community had been established as a religious institute in 1905 in Guadalajara.[98]

The Carmelite Sisters called her Mother Isabelita. Short, with a fair complexion and blue eyes, she was very active and had a good

---

[98] "Nuestra Historia," Religiosas Franciscanas de Nuestra Señora del Refugio, http://franciscanasdelrefugio.org/la-congregacion/historia/; "Nun in Mexico Celebrates 75th Anniversary of Her First Profession," Catholic News Agency, August 9, 2018, https://www.catholicnewsagency.com/news/nun-in-México-celebrates-75th-anniversary-of-her-first-profession-33346.

sense of observation; she was exact, neat, and, to the wonder of the sisters, walked noiselessly. Through God's grace and Mother Luisita's obedience, it worked out that a Franciscan was able to teach the community how to become Carmelites. She remained exactly one year, and the sisters remembered that she did her job well and grew to love the Carmelite Sisters.

On January 11, 1924, the constitutions of the Carmelite Sisters from Spain, founded by Saint Joaquina de Verdruna, arrived. The sisters already had the constitutions of the Carmelite Sisters in Mexico City and now had a blend of these two constitutions as their way of life. Mother Luisita continued to read and modify these two constitutions, and by the end of 1924, the Carmelite Sisters of the Third Order of Guadalajara had their own constitutions.

More women entered, and Mother Luisita was able to establish new foundations: Guadalajara in December 1922, San Francisco de Asís in Tepatitlán in September 1924, and Ocotlán in May 1926. She began her custom of bringing a tabernacle to each new foundation. When she sent her sisters to new areas, she insisted that each have a chapel with the Blessed Sacrament and that the sisters would work with the poor of that area.

Each of these locations had its own story to tell, overflowing with the setbacks and hardships that seemed to have accompanied every step that Mother Luisita took. In her quiet, steadfast way, she kept on helping those she saw in need, continuing to bring them hope and the opportunity to better their lives, physically and spiritually.

Their first new foundation was made in Guadalajara in 1922. Greater poverty could hardly be imagined. The best feature of the house was the orchard with its flowers and produce. The rest was improvised: beds made of boards that were supported by benches, a couple of chairs, a few cracked dishes, poor food, and overcrowded living conditions. A room was fixed up as an oratory and another room in the house was used as a schoolroom for poor children. "As long as your congregation works for the poor," Archbishop Orozco had told Mother Luisita, "it will be blessed by heaven."

When the archbishop came by to visit, however, he found out for himself how poorly the sisters were living. He observed first-hand how Mother Luisita was eating her frugal meal seated at the window. He noticed how she placed her plate on the windowsill, which served as her table. That same afternoon, he sent them some furniture, silverware, and dishes.

Saint Teresa of Ávila spent many years establishing new foundations. Her biographers marveled that she moved seamlessly between contemplative prayer and the solid practicality of daily living as she traveled from place to place. The same can be said of Mother Luisita. Remembrances of the first sisters in her community mention this amazing ability so apparent to those who knew Mother Luisita.

Mother Luisita used to say, "What about your soul? Is it taking little steps toward heaven, or is it flying up there?" It is interesting to note that she begins using the word *soul* about this time in her letters. In fact, she used the word *soul* a total of 416 times in her letters. She writes, "May the grace of the Holy Spirit be in your soul." Because the religious persecution was now imminent, raising its head like a serpent ready to strike, she began her letters asking the Holy Spirit to be within the soul of each person to whom she wrote.

In 1924, Father Guadalupe Miranda, pastor of the Church of the Immaculate Conception in Guadalajara, asked Mother Luisita if she would take over the administration of his parish school. The little house (her first foundation outside Atotonilco) was in his parish. After she agreed, the sisters moved their schoolchildren from their current rooms in the little house into the parish school building. The classrooms were soon full, and the school, like all the other schools, underwent the mandated incorporation into the Mexican Federation.

That same year, Mother Luisita wrote a letter to Archbishop Orozco. In it, she requested permission to open a school in Tepatitlán in Los Altos (see appendix B). This foundation took place at the parish of San Francisco de Asís on September 7, 1924. At ten o'clock that morning, a small band of Carmelite Sisters left Atotonilco astride little donkeys and wearing lay clothes. The winding path that led to the town of San Francisco de Asís took them along the edges of rocky slopes to where they would establish their next school. After traveling for many miles, they stopped under an oak tree to pray Vespers and Compline together under the clear, open sky of the Los Altos highlands.

After a short time of prayerful reflection, the sisters changed from lay clothes to their Carmelite habits and continued up the hill. When the group finally came close to the town, three vehicles decorated like floats approached them. The cars were from San Francisco de Asís. One of the cars showcased a stunning floral Carmelite shield created with fresh daisies, another carried a floral monogram of the Blessed Virgin, and the third was adorned with flowers.

The pastor of San Francisco, Father José de Jesus Angulo, rode in the first car, followed by Mother Luisita's brother-in-law, Ramón Ugarte, who was the town's mayor. Father Ignacio Velázquez, parish associate, was in the third car. When they arrived at a place called Stone Hill, a double honor guard of *charros* (the well-known horseback riders from Jalisco) awaited them and escorted the cars.

They all proceeded to the entrance of the town, where women and children were waiting, standing in perfect formation. Bells pealed. Father Velázquez, clapping enthusiastically, yelled, "Long live the benefactors of our town!" Townspeople applauded and shouted, "¡Viva!" Ramón Ugarte, seeing the road strewn with flowers, and recalling Christ's entrance into Jerusalem, commented, "Today is the triumphal entrance. Tomorrow, Good Friday will arrive."

The cars stopped in front of the church entrance, and bells continued to ring as the crowd cheered. The sisters followed the pastor into the church, and the Salve Regina was intoned. They continued to the rectory, where they stayed for eight days because their house was not yet ready. Mother Luisita named the foundation the Carmel of Saint Joseph.

At the end of the eight days, their house was blessed, and the sisters began living in it. Two rooms were used as dormitories. The corridor became their dining room and kitchen, with only simple curtains to divide the corridor into sections. They used three benches from the school as tables. They had their own well with very good water.

On May 14, 1926, the third foundation was established in Ocotlán. Since the sisters did not have state teaching credentials yet, they could not establish a school, so they immediately started with an academy, teaching religion, commercial art, dressmaking, arithmetic, and drawing. The Ocotlán academy looked promising.

One of the amazing things about Mother Luisita is the fact that she began her community at a time that was so precarious: when Catholic orphanages and schools and hospitals were against the law; when just to be a Catholic was against the law.

Even more, everything the sisters had done was once again bordering on collapse.

Chapter 11

Faith, Family, and Freedom

Today is the triumphal entrance; tomorrow, Good Friday will arrive.

—Ramón Ugarte, mayor of San Francisco de Asís
and brother-in-law of Mother Luisita

Storytellers have the important role of preserving and passing along historical memories to succeeding generations. With folklore and ballads, they provide a human touch to history, a release of the human spirit, an outpouring of immense joy or, in the case of Mexico's Cristiada, the pent-up emotions of dread, terror, and deep mourning. During and after the Cristiada, the role of the storyteller was critical in Mexico, because the government successfully hid for several decades the true story of the suppression of the Catholic Church and the murder of Catholics.

During the final decades of the twentieth century, however, the truth finally began emerging through books and articles that unveiled the hidden history of the Cristiada. About the same time, Cristeros, already advanced in years, were finally willing to be interviewed to let the world know their story—the story of the Mexican Cristiada of the 1920s. Mother Luisita and the first Carmelite Sisters were not only eyewitnesses to the horror but victims as well.

The rest of Mother Luisita's life took place during this time of varying degrees of religious persecution in Mexico. One of the purposes of this biography is to uncover this cover-up and give voice to the Catholics of Mexico, including the Carmelite Sisters, who had been silenced. They suffered this unjust, violent persecution with the "determined determination" described by Saint Teresa of Ávila. They steadfastly continued their worship of God and passed on Catholic values to the children. Many were killed. *Abuelas* and *abuelos* told their grandchildren what had happened to their family members who had gone missing or had been tortured or martyred for their belief in God during the Cristiada. They also shared stories of the heroism and holiness of the priests they knew who were killed solely for adhering to their Catholic Faith.

In the sacred atmosphere of their homes, children and grandchildren tried to patch together a memory quilt of what they had heard, hoping to make sense of what their elders were telling them about a time before they were born.

One way that Mexican men passed along their memories of the Cristiada to the next generations was the cowboy pilgrimage known as the *Guanajuato Cabalgata*, or Guanajuato Ride.

In the early twentieth century, Guanajuato, the Mexican state that is adjacent to Jalisco and hosts the magnificent Cristo Rey statue, was one of the richest and most beautiful cities in central Mexico because of its silver mines. The original monument in honor of Christ the King had been built in 1921 a few years after the Mexican Revolution. It was destroyed seven years later during the Cristiada. Because Guanajuato was an important center of Cristero resistance, in 1928 the government ordered an air raid to target the monument. After the bombing, although the statue of Christ the King was destroyed, the statue's heart and head were miraculously preserved.

The Mexican people's devotion was preserved as well. In 1950, Mexican Catholics built a bigger shrine and placed a larger statue of Cristo Rey on the Cerro del Cubilete, an 8,900-foot mountain in Guanajuato. Made of bronze, it is sixty-five feet tall and weighs eighty tons.

This statue allegedly marks the exact geographical center of Mexico, and for Mexican Catholics, the monument, situated in the heart of their country, symbolizes the central place that religion holds in their lives.

In 1956, a cowboy pilgrimage to this place so rich in symbolism and history began. Mexican men mounted their horses to join. From all over Mexico and beyond, these survivors of the Cristiada of the 1920s rode several days through the rugged Guanajuato terrain. As the decades passed, the yearly pilgrimage continues as sons and grandsons of the original Cristeros, as well as others, continue to participate in the yearly *Cabalgata* to the shrine of Cristo Rey.

During the pilgrimage, the original Cristeros sang the *corridos* of the Cristiada. *Corridos* are Mexican cowboy ballads that form a great part of Mexico's cultural and historical memory. The original Cristeros made the pilgrimage to embed personal memories of the Cristiada more firmly in their hearts and in the hearts of their descendants. They could not—they would not—let the story die. Today, cowboy pilgrims still come to worship God and to ask for blessings upon themselves and their families.

The solemnity of the Epiphany was the date originally chosen for the *Cabalgata* because it was on the Epiphany in 1914 that all of the bishops in Mexico, together with priests and laity, had consecrated Mexico to the Sacred Heart of Jesus. Recall that, at that time, they had added the crown and scepter to the traditional image of the Sacred Heart, proclaiming "*¡Viva Cristo Rey!*" (Long live Christ the King!) During the *Cabalgata*, the cowboys throw gifts of wrapped candies to children waiting with their mothers along the trails and rural roads. This signifies the Magi's journey to the Savior, Christ the King, bringing gifts for Epiphany.

During the pilgrimage, several of the riders held aloft the large, colorful flags of their hometowns. Others carried replicas of the banners of Our Lady of Guadalupe and Christ the King, like the ones the Cristeros carried. Pictures of the event are stunning. In a solemn ceremony, the riders received a special blessing during an outdoor Mass. Afterward, they rode up the mountain to venerate the famous statue of Christ the King and prayed for the special intentions they carried within their hearts during the procession. This ended the pilgrimage.

Every year since 1956, cowboys have continued to make this pilgrimage — even during the COVID pandemic of 2021, as this book was being written. Many pilgrimages from different areas are made now, and for some participants, the *Cabalgata* is no longer a religious event but more of a historical one.

Historians are still trying to decipher the sociopolitical religious intrigues of the Cristiada. From the point of view of Mother Luisita and her community, the Cristiada formed them into stronger women and reinforced their trust in God's providence. Their decision to carry on despite the government's threats helped define their new community as protectors of the Faith and advocates of the downtrodden. It brought out qualities in Mother Luisita that distinguished her as a *light of hope* during the darkness of the Cristiada.

The sisters battled mightily against this evil darkness. Their main means of spiritual warfare was their constant, faith-filled, trusting prayer. The sisters' remembrances describe their foundress as she knelt in the chapel before the Blessed Sacrament: back straight, head bowed, hands devoutly clasped, she was a "beggar" advocating for her people day and night.

The Cristiada brought to the forefront an important reminder —that the sisters' first and foremost apostolate as Carmelites was prayer. They watched as their foundress abided deeper and deeper in that quiet stillness that accompanies contemplative prayer. They, too, felt the inner nudging to spend more time with Our Lord in the Blessed Sacrament.

Mother Luisita used to call herself "the Blessed Sacrament's little beggar," because whenever there was an emergency, she would say, "Go ahead; I will go with Our Lord, so that everything will be all right." At random times during the day, they would find her on her knees before the Blessed Sacrament, with utmost composure and reverence. In all places, especially in the chapel, they observed her relationship with the One whom she loved. She would often say, "Sisters, let us love prayer and recollection in the midst of our work."[99]

This was a momentous time in the development of the specific Carmelite charism of Mother Luisita. With so much poverty surrounding them and the needs of the people so great, their hungry children with hands outstretched for food, what about the times of prayer so essential to Carmelites? The constitutions as lived by the cloistered nuns had been incorporated into Mother Luisita's Rule, but the nuns within their cloister walls did not work directly with people, ministering among them. The calling of the Discalced Carmelite nuns was to worship God within their cloister and to intercede for the whole world.

The prophetic gift of Carmel to the world is prayer flowing from a relationship with God that is authentically deep and personal—to stand always in the presence of the Living God as the prophet Elijah did.

[99] Personal remembrance of Sister Maria Ana of the Holy Family Ramirez Gutierrez.

I have been very jealous for the LORD, the God of hosts;
for the people of Israel have forsaken thy covenant, thrown
down thy altars, and slain thy prophets with the sword; and
I, even I only, am left; and they seek my life, to take it away.
(1 Kings 19:14)

History was repeating itself in 1920s Mexico. Elijah's words echoed
in the lives of Mother Luisita and her sisters during the Cristiada.
The atheistic government had forsaken God, destroyed altars, and
slain priests and was actively searching for the members of the de
la Peña family to take their land and money. Scattered in various
households in several towns, the sisters prayed daily in the most
unlikely environments. Mother and the sisters were vigilant and
ready for change at any moment; and as Mother would see the
need, she would reassign sisters to different families, so that each
of them could keep a low profile at all costs.

In this milieu, she attained clarity as to the spirit and mission
of her community. Like Elijah, the sisters stood in the presence of
the Living God and made known the personal love of the Living
God as they went about their daily work. From their lives of prayer
that flowed into service, they ministered physically and spiritually
to the people they accompanied. Many years after Mother Luisita's
death, Mother Margarita Maria of the Sacred Heart remembered
that she had said many times, "Let us not forget that the spirit of
Carmel is a spirit of continuous prayer and mortification.[100] May
our apostolate among the people be an overflow of our interior
life of prayer."[101]

---

[100] Mortification is the ascetical practice of subduing one's inordinate
(unrestrained or disorderly) desires.
[101] Personal remembrance of Mother Margarita Maria of the Sacred
Heart Hernandez.

Mother Luisita and her first sisters doggedly persevered through unstable, perilous periods in Mexican history that included revolutions, assassinations, a variety of coups that overthrew presidents, and a religious persecution that left friends and relatives dead. Her life and the lives of the sisters in her community cannot be told without placing them in this historical context. History shaped the path they followed in the development of their charism in their efforts to help the poor, the oppressed, and the demoralized.

Something happens when freedom is stripped away. One must dig deep into the very roots of one's soul and, in order to survive, take a stand according to conscience and before God. This kind of decision impacts one's response to injustice and the denial of basic human rights.

This part of Mother Luisita's life is about her choices and her decisions during the bloody persecution of Catholics in the 1920s and 1930s. A year before the community was affiliated with the Carmelite Order, President Venustiano Carranza had been assassinated during the Rebellion of Agua Prieta on May 21, 1920. Congress had appointed Adolfo de la Huerta as interim president of Mexico from June through November.

Álvaro Obregón was elected president in the federal elections of 1920. He tolerated the Catholic Church—to a point. He held a laissez-faire stance regarding the severity of enforcement of the anticlerical laws of the 1917 constitution. During his term, from 1920 until 1924, although rogue attacks on Catholic churches and organizations occurred at times, the persecution of the Church had come to a relative lull.

Archbishop Orozco took advantage of this lull and hosted the 1922 Catholic National Workers' Congress in Guadalajara. Interestingly, President Obregón provided a cavalry guard to stand outside the hall, and the guards saluted the archbishop every time he passed by during the congress. Twelve hundred Catholic worker delegates, representing eighty thousand Catholic union members throughout Mexico, attended, as did several bishops. At the same time, Obregón reopened Catholic schools and colleges and moved the Guadalajara seminarians to a retreat house that could accommodate two hundred people.

The Catholic National Workers' Union and the Mexican Catholic Youth Association, under the leadership of Anacleto González Flores, took their stand. Anacleto was a young Catholic lawyer who believed in nonviolence, had organized boycotts, and had founded the magazine *La Palabra* as a Catholic voice against the actions of the government.

However, when the cornerstone of Guanajuato's Christ the King statue on the Cerro del Cubilete mountain was laid by the Vatican's apostolic delegate to Mexico, Archbishop Ernesto Filippi, Obregón immediately retaliated by deporting him back to Rome. The days of laissez-faire were over. Historians mark this deportation of Archbishop Filippi as "the founding moment of the government's new emerging, scripted, strategic, anticlerical policy."[102]

In 1924, Plutarco Elías Calles won the presidential election, and a barbaric religious persecution began in Mexico. Calles had said that he would wipe out all religion from Mexico in a single generation, and he set out with a vengeance to do so.

Calles's vow to wipe out all religion in a single generation, however, remained unfulfilled. He had not foreseen the impact of the emerging Cristero Uprising.

During this growing political tension, life went on at the orphanage, the schools, and the hospital in Atotonilco. More women were entering Mother Luisita's community, and the need for the

---

[102] Curley, *Citizens and Believers*, 213.

sisters' intercessory prayer and charitable services increased as the danger intensified. About this time, with the Cristero Uprising looming on the horizon, Sister Carmen Josefa traveled with Mother Luisita from Atotonilco to Guadalajara. When they boarded the train, no seats were available until a man got up and gave Mother his seat. A second man did not want to give up his seat for Sister Carmen Josefa to sit next to Mother Luisita, so the two men began to quarrel angrily. When the train arrived in Ocotlán, both men left the train and shot each other.

When the religious persecution worsened in 1924, the school in Atotonilco had to be relocated to the house of Don Manuel Valle, about a block away from the hospital. The sisters began to wear lay clothes whenever they left their convent. The severity of the religious persecution increased even more after Calles assumed office on December 1, 1924. Three weeks later, José Guadalupe Zuno, the atheistic zealot who was now the governor of Jalisco, closed the major and minor seminaries of the Archdiocese of Guadalajara on the pretext that their sanitary installations were inadequate and did not come up to code. At the same time, suspicious persons began to visit the Hospital of the Sacred Heart in Atotonilco.

Much of the following information about what happened during the beginning days of the Cristiada is taken from *Rostro de Bondad*.

Letters still exist between Mother Luisita and the vicar-general of the archdiocese as well as to the vicar-general of religious in Guadalajara that reveal how the events unfolded. In a letter to Father Abundio Anaya, dated December 4, 1924, three days after Calles took office, Mother Luisita wrote, "I await your instructions regarding what we should do in the event that any alarming event may happen. Should we dress as lay people without our habits as a prudential precaution? Should we go out [only] when there is a real need? What should we do if they take the house away from us?" When Mother Luisita speaks of the house, she means the hospital and the attached convent, school, and orphanage. Sometimes she means only the convent.

Father Anaya replied, "With deep sorrow, I have learned that the municipal authority in Atotonilco has closed the Girls' School. I fear that all these schools will be closed by this hostile government."

At noon on Christmas Eve, the sisters were notified of impending danger. It was a terse order, like all those given in the face of imminent peril: "Everyone leave." The sisters slipped away to the homes of friends or to wherever God led them. Sister Josephine lay trembling under her bed when another sister found her and finally convinced her to get up and leave with her.

Mother Luisita wrote to Father Anaya on January 11, 1925, and informed him that on the previous day, just as the sisters were going to the school to begin classes, the mayor told them to put hospital patients in the school quickly. He did this in the hope that it would save the school, because the regime in Guadalajara wanted to put a government school in that place.

The mayor also told Mother Luisita that she needed to place immediately in the school a licensed government teacher who could sign the rental contract with the government to operate a school on that site. Furthermore, the mayor told her to have the sisters work quietly in the school as aides, because some townspeople were going to report to the government that the sisters were running a religious school.

The same was happening in Mexico City. Soon after the sisters had begun working as aides, on February 21, 1925, one hundred armed men entered La Soledad Church around eight in the evening. "Get out!" they ordered the three surprised priests. Surrounded by more armed men, an elderly clergyman arrived. He announced that he was the patriarch of Calles's newly created Mexican Catholic Apostolic Church, and La Soledad was now his headquarters. The seventy-three-year-old former priest was a Freemason who called himself "Patriarch Juan Heriz." Another former priest, Manuel Monge, was with him.

The next morning, when Father Monge was preparing for Mass, a group of parishioners rushed into the church and attacked him. He and Patriarch Heriz ran for their lives into the sacristy. The following day, a newly formed group who called themselves the "Knights of the Order of Guadalupe" and had been assembled by the authorities, surrounded the church. By this time, the parishioners' surprise had turned into righteous anger.

Not long after, a riot took place in the neighborhood surrounding La Soledad. The police soon arrived with high-pressure fire hoses to disperse the crowd of more than a thousand people. One was pronounced dead, and several were injured in the melee. La Soledad was never again used as a church. It became a library. Ultimately, "Patriarch" Heriz moved into another abandoned church in Mexico City, and Father Monge was reconciled with the Catholic Church. Calles's attempt to establish a state-run church had ended. Traces of the schismatic church remained for several years.

The event at La Soledad was seen as a harbinger of the Mexican government's strategy to confiscate all buildings of the Catholic Church and turn them over for civic use. Like La Soledad, they were used as public libraries or municipal buildings.

The La Soledad incident caused the Catholics in Guadalajara to begin to protect and defend their beloved priests. The National League for the Defense of Religious Liberty (LNDLR), a new Catholic civil rights organization, would play a crucial role in the upcoming Cristiada. The Mexican Catholic Youth Association soon joined them. When four members of the group were murdered, the pacifist Anacleto González Flores began to help the growing number of Catholic Mexicans who were preparing for an uprising against the government.

∞

When the time arrived for Mother Luisita and the original sisters to profess their final vows in 1925, no priest was available to them, given their unsafe situation, so Mother Luisita presented the retreat conferences herself. She told the sisters that they were truly the foundation of the community and conveyed the seriousness and beauty of their sacred vows to God.

On April 1, 1925, Father Macario Velázquez, in the name of the Catholic Church, received the final vows of chastity, poverty, and obedience of Mother Luisita and her sisters. Although canon law mandated five years of yearlong vows, the fifth year was waived after considering their many years of waiting. The ceremony took place between six and seven in the morning. In accordance with the ritual, Mother Luisita carried a simple white candle in her hand, but as she processed in, Father José del Valle took her candle and gave her another one, adorned with a beautiful white bow with golden tassels. They had waited twenty-one years to pronounce their "Forever!" to God through perpetual vows of obedience, chastity, and poverty.

Archbishop Orozco asked the pastor of San Miguel for a report regarding what the school and the hospital had suffered. On July 12, 1925, the pastor replied:

> I am pleased to report to Your Excellency regarding what the schools and the hospital in Atotonilco have suffered.

Several months ago, our mayor closed the girls' school that was in one of the departments of the hospital operated by the Carmelite Sisters of the Third Order of Guadalajara. He also closed a children's school which was situated in a private house that had been rented for this purpose. When a new government authority arrived in Atotonilco, he decided that it could continue as is for now and "join" [the government educational system] in due course. He also recommended that classes be given outside the hospital building to prevent the school from being seized. The schools were able to continue by renting houses that became their new classrooms.

Now, in recent days, a young man named Bancalari came to town and, with the authorization from the civil government, took the plans of both the parish school and the hospital. Because we did not want him to realize that they were operated by religious, we agreed that Doctor Martín del Campo would be put in charge as if it were a private hospital. The young government envoy asked the doctor for the documents and put them in his file. The property is still in the name of "Mr." Sánchez Aldana and the school in the name of Doctor Martín del Campo.[103]

On August 5, the sisters were expelled by the government authorities. About three weeks later, on August 25, the archbishop also asked Mother Luisita for a report of what had been happening. She replied:

> I gladly respond to Your Excellency's request to send a report regarding what has been happening in our recent

days of trial and persecution: In June, we were warned that a government official would visit us. We were cautioned to remove and hide religious articles of any kind, so we then moved them together with what we could of our clothing, furniture, and other items. Some sisters had to move into the house we had rented for a school until the danger had passed.

The result of the inspection was that we were given a month's time to verify that the house is private property, and as such will be free, but because it is in the name of Father Celso Sánchez Aldana, Mr. Pérez Sahagún [a lawyer] chose to wait silently to see what would happen. Then, on the twenty-ninth, a telegram was received demanding an answer to the request.

In July, we learned that it was General Romo who had denounced us, so it was thought necessary for us to leave Atotonilco and travel to San Francisco de Asís.... Several times, we have received a message from the mayor that the visitor is coming, so we dispersed so he would not find any Religious there. This is why eight or ten sisters are in the schoolhouse, coming only in the morning to hear Holy Mass.

All this has been done with the approval of Father Macario Velázquez. God save Your Excellency for many years.

Your daughter,
Maria Luisa Josefa del Santísimo Sacramento,
de la Peña, C.D.T.

Piecing together some of the memories of the founding sisters revealed more facts. Mother Luisita had been told to get the sisters out of Atotonilco so that when the next imminent inspection

came, the sisters would not even be there. The roads surrounding
Atotonilco were unsafe, so Mother Luisita decided to have the
entire community walk to San Francisco de Asís, about twenty-
five miles away, to get away from Atotonilco. Well before sunrise,
the sisters banded together and quietly began their climb up the
Los Altos hills. Around noon, when they were well into the hills
and out of harm's way, they saw a vehicle approaching them. The
pastor of San Francisco de Asís had sent the car to meet them and
transport Mother Luisita and a few older sisters on the last phase
of their journey. Father Toribio Bracho, S.J., began a retreat for
them that afternoon.

By fall, the Vatican was receiving urgent messages from both
clergy and laity to help the Mexican people. In September, the
LNDLR sent two men to Rome to tell the pope that unless something was done to change conditions, the people, "victims of violence and immorality, might abandon their Faith."[104]

It was still too dangerous to travel on any road. Although a
Cristero uprising had not yet been officially proclaimed, the approaching danger was obvious to all. In a letter, Mother Luisita
cautioned Sister Refugio "not to go out into the streets" and "to
pray in your own house" instead of in a church. On October 25,
1925, when it became unsafe to pray in the churches, Mother Luisita wrote to Sister Maria Socorro. There is a brief section in that
letter that has captured the essence of Mother Luisita's spirituality:
"Form a beautiful and rich tabernacle within your heart for Our
Lord and then do not let Him go. In that way, you will always
have Him with you. Enter within yourself, and meeting Him, tell

[104] David C. Bailey, ¡Viva Cristo Rey!: The Cristero Rebellion and the Church-State Conflict in Mexico (Austin: University of Texas Press, 1974), 59.

Him all your experiences." These three powerful sentences would sustain the sisters during the dark days of the Cristiada.

Pope Pius XI issued the encyclical *Quas Primas* on December 11, 1925, establishing the feast of Christ the King for the universal Church. The Vatican had chosen this slow-moving diplomacy as its way to help Mexican Catholics, but the situation in Mexico daily grew more urgent. The Vatican saw the persecution through a wider historical lens of almost two thousand years of experience. The pope's goal was to change the Mexican constitution itself. In his view, in the long run it would be a better solution than violent uprisings. The pope appointed Archbishop George Joseph Caruana as the Vatican's new apostolic delegate to Mexico on December 22.

The newspaper *El Universal* had published three anonymous reports by journalist Ignacio Monroy on January 27, February 4, and February 8, 1926, stating that Catholics were going to exercise their legal right to begin the process of reforming the new constitutional articles that made the life of the Church impossible. This enraged Calles and set in motion his groundwork for his infamous Calles Law. On January 7, 1926, the Mexican Congress had already given Calles the power to regulate any anticlerical laws.

On February 2, the pope wrote a letter of support and consolation addressed to the Mexican bishops. In it, he condemned the anti-Catholic attitude of the government and criticized Calles's treatment of the former apostolic delegate, Archbishop Serafín Cimino. He conceded that the Church in Mexico was being oppressed through unjust laws. Nonetheless, he instructed the bishops not to participate in politics. Neither could he permit the founding of any political party with a Catholic name. He did not want the Church's enemies to have any excuse to label Catholicism "political" because this would only strengthen the already widespread anticlericalism in Mexico. He advised the bishops "to inform Mexican Catholics as to what was good for Mexico and to encourage them to work actively to achieve that good."[105]

From the bishops' point of view, what the people of Mexico needed was for the Catholic Church to be able to continue her existence, with the hope that good results would somehow follow. When Archbishop Caruana arrived in Mexico in March, he evaluated the situation. He told the bishops to form an episcopal committee to be presided over by Archbishop José Mora y del Río and to include all bishops who happened to be in the vicinity at the time.

As it turned out, almost every bishop in the country made it to Mexico City to bring his voice to the life-altering decisions being discussed. The bishops reviewed the new Calles Law, which had been made available to them prior to the July 31 promulgation of the law.

The bishops met on July 9 to discuss their options. By July 14, they gave their support to the economic boycott proposed by Anacleto González Flores and other Catholic groups. It included a boycott of government transportation, movie houses, and public schools as well as any government-run business. Many Catholics joined this boycott, but it was unsuccessful. At the same time, to show that he meant to enforce the law, Calles seized more church property, expelled all foreign priests, and closed monasteries, convents, and religious schools.

Shortly after their meeting, Archbishop Orozco sent a letter on July 19 to all the religious in the Archdiocese of Guadalajara,

---

[105] Harriet Denise Joseph, "Church and State in Mexico from Calles to Cárdenes, 1924–1938" (Ph.D. diss., North Texas State University, 1976), https://digital.library.unt.edu/ark:/67531/metadc 500405/m1/1/.

ordering them to either go back to their families or find a pious family to shelter them.

The bishops knew full well that the new law was not compatible with fulfillment of their priestly ministry. Consequently, on July 22, the Episcopal Committee asked Pius XI if they could go ahead and suspend all Catholic religious services in Mexico before the new law went into effect. Permission was granted. Catholic priests would never agree to acquiring a government license in order to exercise their ministry. Never! They preferred to close all the Catholic churches in Mexico, and that is what they did. On July 31, all the Catholic churches in Mexico were closed.

When legal resources failed, and all legal means had been exhausted, Catholics resorted to weapons in self-defense against unfair tyranny. The armed movement sprang up spontaneously in many parts of Mexico. Those who fought for their rights were called Cristeros, a name taken from their battle cry, *¡Viva Cristo Rey!*, meaning "Long live Christ the King!"

Previously, the bishops had disapproved of any use of weapons, but in time they recognized the lawfulness of using them, although they refrained from participating in the Cristero Uprising. Some bishops quietly supported the Cristeros; others did not. Officially, the Mexican bishops never supported the rebellion.

The religious persecution intensified.

Mother Luisita and her community were targeted by the government.

Time was running out.

Chapter 12

Cristiada

¡Viva Cristo Rey!

The combat between good and evil continues as each generation confronts evil's current manifestation, whatever it may be. In Mother Luisita's generation in Mexico, the battle took place as thousands of men and women fought to their death for faith, family, and freedom in what has come to be known as the Cristiada. Saint Teresa of Ávila spoke about two visions she had experienced about a future battle.

Once, in prayer, with much recollection, sweetness, and repose, I saw myself, as it seemed to me, surrounded by angels and close to God. I began to intercede with His Majesty on behalf of the Church, and I was given to understand the great service which a certain Order would render in the latter days.

On another occasion, when I was at Matins in the choir, six or seven People who seemed to me to be of a certain Order appeared and stood before me with swords in their hands. The meaning, I think, is that they are to be defenders of the faith; for another time, when I was in prayer, I stood in spirit on a wide plain where many people were fighting with great zeal. Their faces were beautiful and, as it were, on fire. They defeated many; others they killed. It seemed to me a battle with heretics.[106]

Blessed Anne of St. Bartholomew, Saint Teresa's companion, clarified that Saint Teresa said, "a certain Order" because she did not want to mention that it was explicitly the Carmelite Order "lest others should be aggrieved."[107]

The Carmelite Order's shield, with its flaming sword of Elijah, symbolizes this spiritual battle in the great contest between light and darkness. The theme of light permeated Mother Luisita's life journey. The Carmelite Sisters of the Third Order of Guadalajara, under her leadership, were fully engaged in fighting the anticlerical laws of President Calles, a thirty-second-degree Mason who, according to the Masonic trestle board of February 1928,[108] was awarded a medal of merit from the head of Mexico's Scottish Rite of Freemasonry on May 28, 1926, because of his violent actions against Catholics.[109]

[106] Quoted in John Mathias Haffert, *Mary in Her Scapular Promise* (Sea Isle City, NJ: Scapular Press, 1942), 201-202.

[107] Haffert, *Mary in Her Scapular Promise*, 202n15.

[108] Denis Fahey, C.S.Sp., "Calles Is Supported by the U.S. and Russia," excerpt from chap. 5 of *Secret Societies and the Kingship of Christ* (1927), Tradition in Action, https://www.traditioninaction.org/History/G_017_Fahey_2.html. Fr. Fahey wrote *Secret Societies and the Kingship of Christ* in 1927, while the Calles government was striving to wipe out the Catholic Church and her influence from Mexico. He recorded the important role of Freemasonry in generating the revolution, citing original documents from Masonic journals.

[109] Olivier Lelibre, "The Cristeros: 20th-Century Mexico's Catholic Uprising," *Angelus* 25, no. 1 (January 2002), http://www.

"The Church has only one thing to do: disappear," Calles asserted. "We must uproot from Mexican soil all outdated religious ideas.... We must undertake the terrible struggle against the past, against all the things which we must cause to disappear forever from the surface of the earth.... The government is determined to execute its program without taking the slightest notice of the caretaker's wincing or the protests of the lazy monks. Three times in my life I have met Christ on my path and three times I have insulted Him."[110]

On July 31, 1926, Calles's anticlerical laws were promulgated. The thirty-three articles included the expulsion of foreign priests and closure of schools, colleges, and even diocesan seminaries. The law forced the closure of nursing homes, orphanages, and hospitals supported by religious corporations, with persecution of the press and propaganda against Catholics. It outlawed private worship and tried to relocate all priests in Mexico City who had not been exiled.

The mournful tolling from San Miguel Arcángel's bell tower resounded together with all the church bells throughout Jalisco the day the Calles Law was promulgated. Grief spread over the cities and towns like a mantle. The sisters' pastor in Atotonilco gathered them together in their little chapel to give them the sad news that they could no longer have the Blessed Sacrament there. He told them how the bishops had decided to close all Catholic churches in Mexico as the only option left to them. This was the

angelusonline.org/index.php?section=articles&subsection=show_article&article_id=2119.

[110] WesternMan, "The Freemasonic Hand behind Mexican History," *Middle Earth Magazine*, December 24, 2019, https://middleearth-mag.com/the-freemasonic-hand-behind-Mexican-history.

last day that the Holy Sacrifice of the Mass would be celebrated in the churches. After the sisters received Holy Communion, both the tabernacle in their small oratory and the one in the parish church were emptied.

The week before the law went into effect, the faithful lined the streets and plazas, awaiting their turn to go to Confession, to have their children baptized, or to have their marriages blessed by the Church. The morning Masses were filled beyond capacity, with attendees overflowing into the streets. Holy Communion during these Masses went on for hours. Only God knew if these faithful would be killed in the uprisings or how long it would be before the sacraments would be available to them again.

During the first week in August, the authorities began their aggressive program of expropriation of all Catholic churches. When soldiers tried to take over the Santuario de Nuestra Señora de Guadalupe (the Church of Our Lady of Guadalupe) in Guadalajara, four hundred armed Catholics shut themselves in the church. Committed to not allowing their church to be turned over to the government, they exchanged gunfire with federal troops and surrendered only when they ran out of ammunition. The battle resulted in eighteen dead and forty wounded. Catholics in other place also resisted the expropriation, which resulted in death threats, deaths, and many wounded. When authorities following Calles's orders told Archbishop Orozco to report to Mexico City with the other bishops to register in order to be certified to continue his ministry, he opted to go into hiding once again.

While the Vatican engaged in its diplomatic conversations with the Mexican government, something else was happening throughout the republic. Catholics, common workmen, farmers, lawyers, people of all stations in life, became enraged when they witnessed their local churches forcibly taken from them as government property. No one had the right to take their churches. To practice their religion was their God-given right as well as one of their civil rights as Mexican citizens, and they knew it. They fought with the energy that comes from deeply held convictions and, in the end, won many of these first encounters with the federal soldiers. In the rural areas especially, the people had the soldiers running for their lives. No government had the right to take away their priests. The people simply would not stand for it.

Soldiers in sandals and dressed in white linen, still filled with the communal spirit of their village, of their field, of their private undertakings, of their family, held steady under fire, did not hesitate to respond to supreme demands, and crossed that line beyond which one no longer loves oneself, beyond which one no longer thinks of preserving one's life. They stood up and marched calmly to the battle, hurled themselves machete in hand on the Federal machine-guns, and scaled heights at the summit of which simple peasants began to appear to us as great warriors.[111]

One night in early September, Mother Luisita arrived in Ocotlán with Sister Teresa, who was singing as she entered their convent. The sisters all knew that whenever Sister Teresa sang, it was an indication that she had a sorrow in her heart. When she stopped

---

[111] Jean A. Meyer, *The Cristero Rebellion: The Mexican People between Church and State, 1926–1929* (Cambridge, UK: Cambridge University Press, 1976), quoted in Gary Potter, "Valor and Betrayal—The Historical Background and Story of the Cristeros," Catholicism. org., January 30, 2006, https://catholicism.org/valor-betrayal-cristeros.html.

singing to announce that they had come to bring a surprise, the sisters waited anxiously to find out what the surprise would be. Mother told them about the recent order of Archbishop Orozco that all religious should return to their homes or remain with some pious family.

On November 18, 1926, Pope Pius XI issued another encyclical, *Iniquis Afflictisque* (On the Persecution of the Church in Mexico), to denounce the violent anticlerical persecution in Mexico. The pope had already been informed that the convents and rectories were among the first targets of the anticlerical laws. There were fifty-four Carmelites for Mother Luisita to move into the homes of trusted families. It took several weeks.

By December, the only sisters who remained at the hospital were the nurses. This saved the nursing sisters from peril because the wounded soldiers on both sides sought healing at their hospital. The federal soldiers (*federalistas*) took over the hospital from 1926 to 1929, when the peace accord was finally signed. The soldiers fired from the hospital windows during the skirmishes. During the day, the nursing sisters worked in the hospital. Every night, for safety, Mother Luisita and her companions stayed in the home of Don Isidro Cervantes, the mayor of Atotonilco and father of one of the sisters. This was the safest place for them because the police would not search the house of the mayor. He was a good person and a benefactor of the community.

As all of this was going on, Mother Luisita wrote to Sister Mary of the Trinity, "May the grace of the Holy Spirit be in your soul, my beloved daughter. Affectionate greetings! May your life in that little corner of the earth be as a bonfire of love, consuming itself in the love of God and zeal for souls."[112] Again, she uses the word

---

[112] Kennedy, *In Love's Safekeeping*, vol. 1, letter 17, 83.

soul. In Catholic theology, the soul is the still point, the center, the life principle of each human person. Within the soul are the powers of thinking, willing, and loving. Catholic teaching states that each human person has two essential parts: a body and a soul made in the image and likeness of God.

Saint Teresa of Ávila described the human soul in the following way:

> I thought of the soul as resembling a castle, formed of a single diamond or a very transparent crystal, and containing many rooms, just as in heaven there are many mansions. If we reflect, sisters, we shall see that the soul of the just is a paradise, in which, God tells us, He takes His delight....
>
> Nothing can be compared to the great beauty and capabilities of a soul; however keen our intellects may be, they are as unable to comprehend them as to comprehend God, for, as He has told us, He created us in His own image and likeness.[113]

It was during the religious persecution, with their churches closed, their removal from the public view extended, and their regular daily activities stripped from them that the inner spiritual life of the sisters flourished. This happened to the Carmelite mystic and author Saint John of the Cross in his nine months of solitary confinement when he produced his spiritual literary masterpieces. Carmelites are called by the very nature of their vocation to "intimacy with God through prayer."[114] To meditate

---

[113] Teresa of Jesus, O.C.D., *Interior Castle*, First Mansions, chap. 1, no. 2, Christian Classics Ethereal Library, https://www.ccel.org/ccel/teresa/castle2.v.i.html.

[114] Constitutions of the Carmelite Sisters of the Most Sacred Heart of Los Angeles, art. 31.

deeply on the indwelling presence of God within the human soul is life changing. To interiorize the concept of the immense dignity of the human person, made in the image and likeness of God, impacts every aspect of daily life.

Many scriptural references bear witness to this deep and abiding presence of God within the human soul.

> Do you not know that you are God's temple and that God's Spirit dwells in you? (1 Cor. 3:16)

> If a man loves me, he will keep my word, and my Father will love him, and we will come to him and make our home with him. (John 14:23)

> Abide in me, and I in you. As the branch cannot bear fruit by itself, unless it abides in the vine, neither can you, unless you abide in me. (John 15:4)

The sisters were no longer worried about threats. They were living the reality of extreme religious persecution day by day. Their personal relationship with Our Lord deepened as they suffered for Him and with Him. Sister Maria de las Victorias related the following incident to the author of A Zaga de Su Huella:

> One day, about three in the afternoon, the federal troops entered Atotonilco. Mother Manuela de la Concepción gave orders to all the novices to leave the house. My companion and I (both of us were novices) left immediately in great fear, trying in vain to find refuge from the bullets crossing over our heads. All the houses had their doors closed.
>
> Suddenly we met a lay co-worker from the hospital who took us to the place where Mother Luisita and other

professed sisters were hiding. The soldiers had advanced so quickly that the sisters were forced to make use of a hiding place in the corral of Don Nazario Flores's home, situated across from the hospital. Once inside the small opening, the entrance was covered with a bale of straw. Our Mother Luisita was sequestered there with fifteen professed sisters and two novices. Also hidden in that small area were statues of our Lady of Mount Carmel and our Holy Mother Saint Teresa of Avila. Vestments and sacred vessels used for the Mass were also there. The space was so small that we had to squeeze together in order to leave a space on the floor for someone to sit for a while and rest.

This is how we were situated when we heard the federal soldiers coming into the house. They brought their horses and were trying to find food for them. As we were hiding in the corral, an anguished fear showed on Mother Luisita's face and she said, "What are we going to do, my daughters? Place yourselves in the hands of God and make an act of contrition. If they find us, they will certainly kill us! Let us offer our lives. We belong to God. May His most Holy Will be done!" With her scapular, she blessed the entrance of the hole. I got close to her and whispered in her ear, "Mother, if they want to kill us, shall we profess our vows in our hearts even though we are only novices?"

"Yes, my daughter," she answered and continued to bless the entrance.

Meanwhile, the shooting between the federal soldiers and the Cristeros who had returned after retreating earlier, could be heard in the distance. The soldiers, threatening the owner of the house in order to get food for their horses, could also be heard. Nothing happened. The soldiers went away. No harm had been done. After a whole day of prayer, fasting and a good preparation for death, we left the house at dusk.[115]

Another sister remembered the following:

Another time, when Mother Luisita was in hiding with Mother Elena of the Cross, she said, "Ay, my daughter! This is more than my strength can bear." She had a deathly fear of soldiers. With an expression of dread on her face, she said, "What if the soldiers grab a sister ...?" Her voice broke and trailed off. She couldn't finish the sentence. Not long after, she went to Guadalajara and arranged for only eight sisters to remain at the hospital. Then the entire group of novices traveled to Guadalajara, where they were scattered in private homes. Mother told them that someone had warned her that her name was on the list of wealthy landowners' families and that they were looking for her to get the de la Peña fortune.

The hospital continued to maintain itself with donations from the Conference of Saint Vincent de Paul. The school was closed. The orphanage was operating on donations. Soldiers supplied medicine and food for the hospitalized soldiers, but they did not pay for any of the services rendered to them. The troops' doctor was Ignacio Cordoba. Two other physicians, Carlos Mercado and Esteban Martín del Campo, stayed with him to treat the other patients.

One day a wounded federal soldier being cared for in the hospital cried out, "Bring me a priest!"

---

[115] Personal remembrance of Sister Maria de Las Victorias Rodriguez, O.P.

Sister Magdalena, who was very witty and remained the steadfast protector of the hospital during the Cristiada, answered dryly, "Where am I going to find a priest? You have killed them all. Make an act of contrition." When a female federal soldier was taken to the hospital with tuberculosis, she also asked for a priest, and Sister Magdalena helped her make an act of contrition. She died in peace.

The soldiers would climb up to the dome of the chapel's tower to shoot from there, and the sisters had to crawl quietly, remaining very close to the wall, to go from one area to another to get anything they needed. The Blessed Sacrament Chapel was empty except for the *federalistas*, who were now quartered there. Father Velázquez arranged for a little girl to take the Blessed Sacrament to the sisters. Although they could not attend Mass, they received permission to keep the consecrated Hosts in the novitiate area of their convent and to receive Holy Communion with their own hands.

By taking their stand at the hospital, the sisters were able to endure and save it; otherwise, it would have fallen into the hands of the government. Sometimes the sisters would not have any nourishment until two in the afternoon, when Mother Manuela would pass little cups of chocolate through a window between the hospital and the patio of the enclosure.

Meanwhile, the sisters at San Francisco de Asís in Tepatitlán were enduring the same suffering. El Nacimiento, the Estate of the Nativity, in the Los Altos highlands was a property of the de la Peña family. One of the first biographies of Mother Luisita, *A Zaga de Su Huella*, contains three very telling sentences: "He [Don Epigmenio de la Peña] named that fringe of the property El Nacimiento (The Nativity). The armed uprising of the *Cristeros* would begin exactly there, on the perimeter of the de la Peña property. The wild highland of San Francisco where *El Nacimiento* was located would become the nucleus of the *Cristiada* in Jalisco."[116] In 1927, the Los Altos region became the focal point of the rebellion, with some of the bloodiest battles fought there.

The persecution of the Church worsened throughout Jalisco, but especially in Los Altos. The formal rebellion began on January 1, 1927, with the manifesto "A la Nación," by twenty-seven-year-old René Capistrán Garza, the leader of the Mexican Association of Catholic Youth. In it, he wrote that "the hour of battle has sounded.... The hour of victory belongs to God." Jalisco exploded with bands of rebels moving throughout Los Altos, mostly armed with only ancient muskets and clubs. The Cristeros cried, "*¡Viva Cristo Rey! ¡Viva la Virgen de Guadalupe!*" (Long live Christ the King! Long live the Virgin of Guadalupe!) Uprisings arose throughout Los Altos in Arandas, Tepatitlán, Ayo el Chico, and Atotonilco el Alto, with a group of approximately two thousand poorly armed men.

Mother Carmen of Jesus Chavez recounted to the author of *A Zaga de Su Huella* the following history about the day the sisters were forced to leave their beloved San Francisco de Asís.

Soon after January 1 manifesto, the pastor of San Francisco de Asís in Tepatitlán, Father José del Valle, ordered the sisters to leave the town. The Carmelite Sisters and the Sister Servants of the Blessed Sacrament, who were both residing there, were taken to the Rancho de San Juan, where they remained for some days in the homes of families of their students.

Soon it was no longer safe in that place and the sisters traveled to another ranch called La Violeta. Both communities walked there together under the light of the moon. The

---

[116] Caravacci, *Loving Kindness*, 13.

pastor there, Father Fernando Escoto, together with their choir children, walked with them. On arriving at La Violeta, they were placed in two rooms. The family took good care of all of them, and Father Escoto celebrated Mass and supplied them with food and milk. There were three Sister Servants of the Blessed Sacrament and seven Carmelites.

One day, when the Holy Mass had just begun, one of the choir boys arrived gasping, "They are here! They are here!" referring to the federal soldiers.

The priest very calmly asked, "Where are they, here or in San Francisco?"

"In San Francisco," said the boy.

The priest continued celebrating the Mass. All received Holy Communion and at the end of Mass, they quickly picked up and hid everything. Some realized they needed to take nourishment to give them strength. They found some bread and milk, the only meal of the day. Soon they were at the base of the hill and hid in some bushes behind a house. They remained behind the bushes all night. At two in the morning, they continued their journey toward a secluded forest where they felt that they would be safer and remained there two days, praying in silence. The pastor then told them to walk to the Rancho de San Rafael and to stay in the house of the parents of Sister Carmen of the Blessed Sacrament.

After a few hours of walking, they stopped on a small hill, where they ate some food sent to them by Sister Carmen's family. After resting for a while, the sisters continued until they arrived at the ranch at nine in the evening. No sooner had they reached the place, when Father del Valle informed the sisters that Mother Luisita wanted them to go all the way to Atotonilco, about ten miles from there. After blessing them, he obtained some donkeys for their journey. They returned using the road leading toward the de la Peñas' El Nacimiento Ranch.

After the sisters were on their way, they observed that the muleteers were afraid that people from the government would find out that they were guiding Catholic sisters. Thank God, nothing happened. They arrived safely at the house of Doña Secundina Rodriguez, the mother of Sister Concepción of Mary Immaculate Rodriguez, in Atotonilco. This good lady affectionately welcomed the sisters. As soon as they could, the sisters went to look for Mother Luisita. She lovingly embraced them, thanking God for having brought her daughters safely through so many dangers.

About this time, Mother knew that something needed to happen quickly to assure the family's safety and that of her sisters. She mulled over the words of Ramón Ugarte two years previously when the Carmelites arrived in San Francisco de Asís: "Today is the triumphal entrance; tomorrow, Good Friday will arrive." Good Friday had arrived, and Mother Luisita began her plan to escape from Mexico and find a place of refuge for her Carmelites across the border in the United States.

༄

In February 1927, President Calles ordered all priests to report right away to Mexico City. They all refused immediately in unified defiance. Calles then declared they were all criminals. Most went into hiding.

Three years of bloodshed would take place followed by a second wave of the Cristiada in the 1930s. By the early months of

1927, as the saying goes, the writing was already on the wall. The Catholics of Mexico knew what was coming and prepared for the worst. The Carmelite Sisters were in extreme danger. They lived in the area where the strongest battles of the Cristiada were taking place in Jalisco. Moreover, federal troops needed to pass through Atotonilco every time they wanted to reach any town in Los Altos.

The Cristeros in Los Altos learned the art of warfare. As it turned out, gifted natural military strategists emerged from within their ranks, and the Cristeros began to fight on their own terms. Guerilla warfare throughout the familiar Los Altos region gave them the advantage they needed. On February 23, 1927, the Cristeros defeated federal troops at San Francisco del Rincón, Guanajuato, followed by another victory at San Julián in Los Altos.

The whole region was named San Francisco de Asís, as was one of the towns in the region. It was the Cristiada's nucleus in Jalisco. Federal soldiers made a surprise attack on the town and rounded up the Cristeros and killed them. Sister Patrocinio of Our Lady of Mount Carmel, only ten years old at the time, remembers that her family searched for the bodies of dead relatives and found them hanging from trees. The family cut the nooses around their necks, took the bodies home, and prepared them for Catholic burial. Many Cristero leaders lived in that little town. Some were able to get away just as the federal soldiers entered. Leaving their homes and families behind, they fled to the United States.

On April 1, 1927, one of the main leaders of the Catholic resistance, Anacleto González Flores, was questioned, tortured, condemned, and executed. On April 19, a group of militant Catholics, seeking revenge for Anacleto's death, derailed and robbed a train traveling from Mexico City to Guadalajara. Father José Vega, against the orders of his bishop, had joined the Catholic forces and led the attack. When the army soldiers escorted the train, which held a shipment of money and gold destined for the Bank of Mexico, shot and killed Father Vega's brother, the priest became enraged. As he shouted, *"¡Viva Cristo Rey!"* the militant group poured oil on the train and lit it on fire. The entire crew and more than a hundred passengers lost their lives. The forty-two armed soldiers escorting the train died as well. News of this tragic event quickly traveled worldwide. Father Vega was killed two years later, in April 1929.

A *New York Times* article stated,

Mexico City: Harrowing scenes marked the arrival here at three in the morning of the relief train bearing survivors of the slaughter aboard a Mexico City to Guadalajara train near Limón in the state of Jalisco, on Tuesday night when revolutionaries or bandits wrecked the train and killed ... members of the military escort and, according to some estimates, more than one hundred of the passengers.[117]

Other sources added that the surviving passengers testified that the bandits, who had shouted *"¡Viva Cristo Rey!"* were led by three priests. Presented with this testimony, General José Alvarez, in charge of investigating the incident, concluded that the robbery had been "organized by the Catholic bishops." Calles agreed with this conclusion and ordered the arrests of Archbishop Mora y del Río, Archbishop Ruiz y Flóres, and four other bishops.

President Calvin Coolidge sent Dwight Morrow as the United States ambassador to Mexico. He held a secret meeting with the

---

[117] "Mexican Survivors Tell Train Horrors," *New York Times*, April 22, 1927, https://www.nytimes.com/1927/04/22/archives/mexican-survivors-tell-train-horrors-nervetorn-refugees-in-capital.html?searchResultPosition=1.

Mexican bishops on a train. At one point during the meeting, Morrow looked out the window and, to his horror, saw the dead bodies of Cristeros hanging from telephone poles. This incident propelled him to do whatever he could to stop the war.

During the last week in April, General José Ferreira issued the tragic order to transfer the entire civilian rural population into the larger cities. In this way, the farmers could no longer support the Cristeros with food from their abundant fields and orchards. All rural inhabitants were ordered to present themselves to the government in one of the five designated plazas no later than the first week in May. Guadalajara's plaza was among the five chosen. All the products from their ranches, animals, orchards, and fields and the buildings on their land now belonged to the government. In less than a week, this forced evacuation relocated fifty thousand people who lived within eight hundred thousand square miles. They had been told that if they did not leave, their property would be bombed. Some landowners bribed the soldiers carrying out the commands and remained on their haciendas, at least for a time.

Conditions throughout the region were dire. Thousands of displaced people left their ranches, but there was not enough room to shelter them, although the families throughout Guadalajara took in as many as they could. This is when the group of Discalced Carmelite nuns from the Monastery of Saint Teresa's in Guadalajara made their decision to leave Mexico as refugees seeking sanctuary in the United States. They left on May 18, about two weeks after the relocation order.

As for Mother Luisita, she had already received permission to leave Mexico from Monsignor Manuel Alvarado, vicar-general of the Archdiocese of Guadalajara, who was in charge while Archbishop Orozco was in hiding. With help from her family and trusted friends, she had acquired passports and the necessary immunizations for travel. Friends chose some appropriate outfits for the three Carmelite Sisters to wear so they would not arouse suspicion when they entered the train station and boarded their train. Mother Luisita's family purchased three first-class tickets for them.

The other two sisters who were chosen to accompany their foundress were forty-year-old Sister Teresa of Jesus Navarro, Mother Luisita's second cousin, and twenty-four-year-old Sister Margarita Maria of the Sacred Heart Hernandez, who had only recently professed her vows. Mother Luisita would celebrate her sixty-first birthday on the train. The rest of the sisters in the community were left behind.

The first available train was scheduled to depart on Tuesday, June 20, at noon from the Guadalajara train station. Mother Luisita's plan was to save as many sisters as possible from the growing threat of the federal soldiers by helping them cross the border. She planned for them all to return to Mexico when things calmed down. However, unknown to them at the time, God had another plan for her community to plant deep roots in the United States.

The three Carmelite Sisters boarded the new train without incident and were quick to notice that they were not the only refugees fleeing for their lives. Passengers were frightened. The daughter of President Calles was on the same train; her father was sending her to Our Lady of the Rosary Academy in San Diego after the recent death of her mother. She sat directly across the aisle from Mother Luisita. Lorenzo Valle, a relative of one of the sisters, was also on the train, heading to the United States to attend a seminary there. Mother Luisita's nephew José Arambula, the son of her sister Mariquita, accompanied them as their escort. This was the first time the new train was used.

After only four hours of travel, the train came to an abrupt stop. During a recent monsoon, a landslide had covered the tracks with mud and rocks. It was impossible to go on. A second train took them the rest of the way.

There was no ventilation and no lights on this second train as it passed through the sweltering Sonoran Desert. The site of Mother Luisita's smallpox immunization, a requirement for a passport, grew red and hot, and her infected arm throbbed constantly. When it came time to sleep, two inebriated passengers who had tickets for the upper berths wobbled in. The sisters in the lower berths got little sleep. Mother Margarita Maria told these stories to William Queen when he wrote his book on Mother Luisita, *The Doctor's Widow*.

Mother Luisita's family and friends told her to pray that all would go smoothly at the border because sometimes "there were problems." They understood that the three sisters with their first-class tickets would have more privacy on the train and get through the immigration process at the United States border more easily.

Before the early 1900s, Mexicans were able to move freely across the border without regulation. With the Mexican Revolution, American officials had an increased awareness of the open border, and Mexican immigrants were categorized as diseased and dirty. Mexicans were bathed every time they crossed the border. At the border, entrants were stripped naked, showered with kerosene, examined for lice and nits, and vaccinated against smallpox. This policy lasted into the 1920s. In 1917, an inspection and quarantine were issued based on a threat of typhus. The threat lasted several months, but the medical inspection continued into the 1930s, even after there was no longer a serious threat.

Medical inspection of Mexican immigrants was not opposed because health was a prerequisite for labor. The inspections were also differentiated by class, as a sizeable number of Mexicans—especially recognized commuters, those who were well dressed, and those who rode first-class on the train—were exempt from the disinfection drill.[118]

About noon on June 23, 1927, the train reached Nogales, the border town between Mexico and the United States. The Southern Pacific Railroad had two depots there: one on the Mexican side of the border and the other on the American side, in Nogales, Arizona. The first-class passengers were escorted off the train first. The other passengers disembarked next. Mother Luisita and the sisters watched them as they were directed another way to the disinfection baths.

As the sisters walked to the American side, Ignacio De La Torre, his wife, María, and one of their sons, who were good friends of Archbishop Orozco, met them at the United States depot. Their assistance greatly helped the sisters decide what to do next because Ignacio was familiar with the process. He took them to the immigration office, where the necessary documents were presented to the authorities.

As they had a few hours to wait before boarding the American train to Los Angeles, they accepted the De La Torres's offer of hospitality, to freshen up at their home and have a good lunch at a nearby restaurant. This was the beginning of a friendship between the De La Torre family and the Carmelite Sisters. The couple generously offered to meet and assist any Carmelite sister who would enter or leave the United States from that day forward.

[118] Howard Markel and Alexandra Minna Stern, "The Foreignness of Germs: The Persistent Association of Immigrants and Disease in American Society," *Milbank Quarterly* 80, no. 4 (January 2002): 757–788, doi:10.1111/1468-0009.00030.

The sisters boarded the final train, and as it picked up speed, Mother Luisita knelt in the aisle. The other two sisters joined her, and together they prayed aloud the Te Deum, the most ancient prayer of praise and thanksgiving of the Catholic Church. The small group continued praying until they realized that they were blocking the passageway. Calmly getting up, they returned to their seats, reopened their Little Office of the Blessed Virgin Mary, and continued their prayers.[119]

Mother Luisita asked Sister Margarita Maria to translate as best she could whatever was asked of them. Not knowing what else to do, she picked up the route itinerary and browsed through it: Nogales to Tucson—67 miles; Tucson to Yuma—240 miles; Yuma to Los Angeles—270 miles.

They reached Los Angeles on Friday, June 24, 1927.

It was the solemnity of the Sacred Heart of Jesus. On that day, in God's divine providence, the seeds of a second community founded by Mother Luisita were sown in the California soil to germinate and grow in that same providence.[120]

[119] The Little Office of the Blessed Virgin Mary is composed of psalms that are prayed several times a day, marking the hours of each day and sanctifying the day with prayer honoring the Blessed Virgin Mary.

[120] The companion book *In the Face of Darkness* details the beginnings of the Carmelite Sisters of the Most Sacred Heart in Los Angeles.

Part 4

The Later Religious Persecution Years
(1927-1937)

*Continued Religious Persecution and
the Death of Mother Luisita*

When I read Mother Luisita's words, they help me to pray. I am sure that they will help all of us to pray and to have that same confidence in God that she had. In her letters, she is always telling her sisters to trust in God. In fact, she says it so often that we can almost take it for granted, or think she is simply repeating nice little sayings. But I think it is not right to think that way because, as we all know, Mother Luisita's faith was hard-won. She was tested and tried. She knew the cross. And in the light of this pandemic, your Foundress's apostolate of healing and hope, her compassion for the sick and poor, is even more prophetic.

—Archbishop José Gomez of Los Angeles, 2021

Chapter 13

Refugees

Our beginnings have come at a tremendous
cost, as you will see in eternity.

—Letter of Mother Luisita to Mother Mary of the Eucharist, 1930

The religious persecution in Mexico that began in stealth, like an obscuring fog rolling in silently, suddenly overtook the country. One day things continued in a routine way, and then, before people realized what was happening, darkness held the country in its cold embrace.

When this happened, the people in and around Atotonilco wanted to be near Mother Luisita. Her presence brought them comfort. Her words redirected their thoughts to God. Mother Luisita's gaze seemed to reach their very souls. People said that when they were with Mother Luisita, she gave them the impression that she saw some distant shore on the horizon and was always moving toward it, and everything else was seen in relation to it.

Saint Thérèse expressed the same longing when she wrote, "Life is our boat, not our home." Mother Luisita used to quote, "Let us go forward, good seamen, for our Love is waiting on the seashore." She has come to be known by this ability to see the spiritual dimension of daily living. "For greater things you were born," she would often say.

Father Camillo Macisse, O.C.D., former superior general of the Discalced Carmelites, wrote, "The reading of her letters reveals with great clarity Mother Luisita's contemplative outlook, which led her to discover God in all that happened."[121]

Mother Luisita quite unobtrusively commanded respect in a way that is hard to describe. People felt comfortable around her. They felt at home with her. And somehow, they instinctively trusted her and looked to her for advice. Some said that they were convinced that Mother Luisita could read their souls.

Several women in Atotonilco had been watching Mother Luisita and her sisters from afar and now felt called by God to follow in their footsteps, to dedicate their lives to God in prayer and service like them. They had been deeply influenced by Mother Luisita and the way of life of her community and asked Mother Luisita if they could join her community. Many of these new postulants and novices were only teenagers when the Cristiada began. It was not uncommon for young girls to marry during their teens. Mother Luisita was fifteen when she married, as was her mother, Doña Luisa. Entering a convent at that young age was also accepted as the norm.

These young Carmelite postulants were deprived of any traditional instruction during their beginning days and months as sisters. Theirs was a baptism by fire into the Carmelite community. Constantly on the move, each night they opened thin bed mats that had been rolled into a tight bundle that morning with their few personal items tucked inside. Lying on their mats, they remained quiet in whatever home they were currently hiding, ready to leave at a moment's notice.

---

[121] Kennedy, *In Love's Safekeeping*, vol. 1, 1.

They could not enter any church. There were no Masses, except clandestine ones from time to time. At one time, they were eight months without the sacraments. It wasn't long before the young sisters who had been living with different families had to be quickly transferred to Guadalajara to protect them from becoming victims of the horrible outrages of war.

In the United States, Ramón Ugarte, Mother Luisita's brother-in-law who had previously fled to Los Angeles, met the sisters at Los Angeles's Central Station upon their arrival. He immediately took her to a hospital, where the infection on her arm was treated. Afterward, he escorted all three refugees to a rooming house in Los Angeles, where they would stay until more permanent lodging could be found.

The first item on Mother Luisita's to-do list the following day was a visit to Bishop John Joseph Cantwell of the Los Angeles–San Diego Diocese so they could present themselves as religious refugees and ask for his help and blessing. On Saturday, the day following their arrival, Bishop Cantwell welcomed them and introduced them to Father Leroy Callahan, the director of Catholic Charities and liaison with the Mexican refugees in the diocese.

Father Callahan found a temporary home for the three sisters in a nearby convent of the Daughters of the Most Holy and Immaculate Heart of the Blessed Virgin Mary, more commonly known as the Immaculate Heart Sisters. That community had left their native country of Spain at the request of Bishop Thaddeus Amat in 1871 and realized how much the Carmelites needed support and a safe place to rest. From June 26 until August 3, the three Carmelite refugees stayed at the Immaculate Heart convent on the campus of Immaculate Conception Parish in Los Angeles.

On July 3, only seven days after entering the United States, Mother Luisita sent her sisters in Mexico the first news from Los Angeles. She mentioned in a letter to Sister Carmen Chavez that they were already studying English. She shared how much her lack of English affected her and that she was trying hard to communicate but had much difficulty in understanding English.

She added that she just wanted to return to Mexico, that she could not live in Los Angeles because it was too cluttered with noise—automobiles and people and the hustle and bustle of crowded sidewalks—and it all overwhelmed her. It was difficult, she wrote, for her to even hear the chiming of the hours on the city clock.

Right away she observed the respect people showed them and how impressed she was with the organization of everything. The letter bore the return address of the Immaculate Heart Convent: 834 Green Street, Los Angeles.

One of the highlights of the Carmelite refugees' two-month stay with the Immaculate Heart Sisters was a surprise picnic with some of the Discalced Carmelite nuns from the Monastery of Saint Teresa in Guadalajara. They were also refugees and temporary guests of the Immaculate Heart Sisters, although residing in a different convent. Years later, Sister Teresa of Jesus still remembered that during that picnic she became aware that "even the little animals are treated with respect in this country."

On August 3, Father Callahan drove the sisters to Holy Innocents Parish in Long Beach, California, a parish that had recently been established by Bishop Cantwell on December 12, 1923, the feast of Our Lady of Guadalupe. Holy Innocents was a poor parish that had begun with only thirty families.

Father Francis Ott, Holy Innocents' first pastor, had already accepted many Mexican refugees into his parish, and most of them lived in nearby neighborhoods. Doña Nicolasa Flores, who had assisted many of the refugee bishops and priests, welcomed the sisters into her home at 1859 Locust Avenue. Knowing her generous hospitality, the neighbors had given her home the title "the Christian Soldiers' Home."

From the beginning of their stay in Long Beach, the sisters recognized Father Ott's special love for his refugees. He personally taught the sisters many practical things about the American culture and, with his keen eye for detail, found the right ministries for them. He also helped them fill out forms, explaining each document patiently with the help of Sister Margarita Maria as interpreter. When he asked Mother Luisita if they would take a parish census, she realized that this was something they could do despite the language barrier.

When the sisters discovered couples who had not been married in the Church or had not baptized their children, they prepared them for these sacraments and held catechism classes in their native Spanish. The families, the sisters, and the parish all benefited from the sisters' time spent in the Holy Innocents community.

It did not take long for Mother Luisita to become the friend and trusted confidante of the Mexican immigrants in the nearby neighborhoods. She would visit with them on Doña Flores's front porch or under one of the shady trees in her spacious backyard. From the Christian Soldiers' Home Mother Luisita advised and counseled these traumatized people who had given up so much for the sake of religious freedom. Her refugee neighbors came from all walks of life—lawyers, doctors, farmers, and many others. Being in Mother Luisita's presence brought them peace and healing.

More and more people found their way to her door.

Doña Nicolasa and her family, also from Jalisco, had wanted the sisters to feel at home, so she cooked tasty dishes from their native state. She also displayed a framed picture of Our Lady, a copy of the original painting in a chapel near Atotonilco, in her living room when she heard the sisters were coming. Her family had been most respectful of the sisters and had offered them a little section of their home that they could call their own. To this day, the sisters have kept in contact with this generous family.

One of the rooms in Doña Flores's home was set aside as a chapel. Here the sisters found quiet and a place to meditate. Throughout the day, the doors to the chapel would be closed if a sister happened to be at home, and the others in the house respected their privacy and spoke quietly.

When Father Ott learned that five more sisters would arrive from Mexico on September 12, he rented a "good-sized house" at 1891 Cedar Avenue, about a mile from Holy Innocents. It needed a lot of repairs, and the sisters had no money, so they worked on it themselves, painting and repairing as best they could. Mother Luisita held a candle for them at night so they could continue painting late into the evening after their work in the parish. The house was just around the corner from Our Lady of Guadalupe Mission Chapel. Father Ott was responsible for three sites: the parish church of Holy Innocents, Our Lady of Guadalupe Mission Chapel, and Mount Carmel Mission Chapel, all in Long Beach. The Carmelites usually attended Mass six days each week at Our Lady of Guadalupe Mission Chapel, within the parish boundaries. Once a week, the little group walked a longer distance to Our Lady of Mount Carmel for Mass.

The days were very long. The sisters were usually up at four thirty and began meditation at five, followed by the chanting of the Little Office of the Blessed Virgin Mary and Holy Mass. After a light breakfast, they left for their various assignments and often worked until twilight fell. They split into two groups for their work. One group went from home to home and took the parish census.

The other group taught catechism classes at Holy Innocents and Our Lady of Guadalupe. Both groups, but especially the census group, would come home exhausted and often having eaten very little during the day.

Mother Luisita fixed up the garage and held sewing circles there, teaching in Spanish and helping the women as they sewed. It was a healing release in a safe place for these women who had left everything for their Faith. The number of women who attended grew.

In a letter written to her brother Salvador at this time, Mother Luisita wrote:

> Well, here I am at the beach. This is a very beautiful city, truly picturesque and peaceful. We're nineteen blocks away from the sea and the weather is good and pleasant.... I want you to know that I've tried to take care of myself. I do get up a little later and cover myself very well. Whenever it's very cold, I don't go outside because of my aches and pains. What else can I do? I'm already very old and, imagine, although it's very foolish of me, I find myself not wanting to die away from my country, as if God were farther away. We have to do whatever God wants because He is wisdom itself and our Creator. Besides, He loves us without measure and arranges the events of our lives as He knows best. I have to make up my mind about this and be at peace. Isn't it true?
>
> We will see each other soon. In the meantime, I am sending you an embrace. Your sister who loves you and wishes for you to be a good man. L. Peña.[122]

Sister Margarita Maria wanted to open a little store and sell rosaries and other religious articles from their home, using part of

---

[122] Kennedy, *In Love's Safekeeping*, vol. 1, letter 28, 94.

the front room. Mother Luisita thought this was a bad idea at first, but knowing how badly they needed the money, she eventually said yes. In a short time, this little store became profitable, and soon Sister Margarita Maria was adding books and other devotionals to her stock. Later, she added used clothing that parishioners gave her.

They did not have a chapel in their new house. Although Mother Luisita had fixed up one room as an oratory, it did not have what Catholics know to be the Real Presence of Christ in the Blessed Sacrament. So, one day Mother Luisita asked Sister Teresa of Jesus to bring the small wooden tabernacle they had brought from Mexico and to put it on the table in their living room. Then she told them that she would keep the doors of the tabernacle open as an invitation to Our Lord to come and dwell in it. Her hope was that Father Ott would find a way to provide a chapel for them in their house.

Her desire was fulfilled when a donation from a deceased benefactor of Holy Innocents bequeathed one hundred dollars to use for whatever was necessary. Father Ott provided the sisters with the items for a little chapel, and on November 4, 1927, he celebrated the first Mass there. It was the first Friday of the month, so he celebrated the Mass of the Sacred Heart of Jesus.

While the three refugees were adapting to life in the United States, back in Mexico the religious persecution was escalating quickly. Many people were arrested. Others were hiding or were keeping a low profile. Priests continued to be sought out, and many were slaughtered, some while they were celebrating Mass. One of the most famous priests of the Cristiada, a recently ordained Jesuit, Father Miguel Augustin Pro, had returned to Mexico after his studies in Europe. After working clandestinely among Catholics in Mexico City for approximately a year, wearing various disguises and outwitting the authorities who were searching for him, he was martyred by a firing squad on November 23, 1927. The photos the government soldiers took before and after his death traveled around the world through various news services. The government took the photos to intimidate Catholics, but the opposite happened. The strategy backfired and fueled the Catholics' conviction to reclaim their right to worship.

The sisters in Long Beach learned a little more about events in Mexico through a U.S. newspaper clipping about a smallpox epidemic in Atotonilco that broke out shortly after Mother Luisita left for the United States. The relocation order had jam-packed people together. More and more of the wounded were brought to the Hospital of the Sacred Heart. With the shortage of food and the poor sanitary conditions came the smallpox outbreak.

Working conditions were desperately insufficient as the sisters treated the terrible disease, which brought many of the patients to madness. The federal troops also brought their wounded soldiers to the hospital, but there was no more room. They brought some field tents that were intended for about thirty patients, but the sisters ended up cramming up to 105 plague victims in them. In addition to treating smallpox patients, the sisters took care of wounded soldiers from 1926 to 1929. The federal troops had taken over the hospital and were quartered there. In fact, the *federalistas* had made the hospital their headquarters.

Doctor Esteban Martín del Campo, father of Sister Maria Dolores of Jesus in the Blessed Sacrament, and other doctors from Guadalajara arrived in Atotonilco to try to contain the spreading of the illness. sister Maria del Rosario gives vivid details:

> It was very sad to see the patients suffering so much. With only brooms, we swept the piles of scabs from the wounds

and the other body waste covering the floor. We boiled the bed linen and clothing in a big copper tub that we had borrowed from the mayor.

One day, one of the patients asked me if I was afraid. On the following day, I made myself overcome my fear of the disease, and I went near the patient and told her, "I will help you to sit up." At that moment, the doctors came in and saw me helping her sit up. They were surprised and said, "Just look at the courage of this young woman who is in danger of getting contaminated."

I was still there when the visiting reporter took a photograph, and my picture came out in the newspaper as I was giving milk to a patient. All of us made extraordinary efforts to eradicate the plague. We would fill our mouths with wine and then sprinkle the patients with it because they got well faster. I burned my mouth doing that with such a strong liquor.[123]

When Mother Luisita in the United States read the newspaper clipping, she said, "My daughters are heroines."

A few weeks later, Mother Luisita wrote in code to Sister Socorro, who had remained in Mexico.

Your father [God] hasn't allowed me to leave [the United States.] Nor does He say anything regarding your sisters coming over here. I cry out to Him every day to either send me to you or to bring the rest of the family here with me. I plead, but He keeps silence.

---

[123] Personal remembrance of Sister Maria Rosario of the Divine Heart Hernandez.

I do hope that one of these days He will be surprising me with the news that either I will be going over or that you will be coming. I want to be wherever we would have enough work to sustain us—not only can we work better if we are together, but my desire is to be with my daughters.[124]

Father Callahan was still searching for places of employment for his Mexican Carmelites when he learned that the Christian Brothers at Saint Mary's College in Moraga, California, were looking for domestic help for their newly built college. He thought that this would be a good fit for his Carmelite Sisters. Mother Luisita thought from the beginning that this might not be the best decision for them. They had come from Mexico fatigued, malnourished, and not knowing the culture or language. She thought that intense manual work might be too much for them.

In December 1927, Mother Luisita wrote to Father José Refugio Huerta, her dear friend and adviser from Atotonilco, who was also in the United States, asking his advice. When Father Huerta answered her letter, he counseled her to accept the offer. She also wrote to Father Pedro, who gave her the same advice.

On February 18, Mother Luisita wrote the following letter to the Christian Brothers in Moraga.

Dear Brother Joseph,

I look forward to meeting you in a few weeks so we can talk through the specific points of the contract. I think we would be able to commit to two years, and then we can decide at that time if we remain at Saint Mary's or return to Los Angeles.

---

[124] Kennedy, *In Love's Safekeeping*, vol. 1, letter 30, 96.

On behalf of all the sisters, thank you for the invitation
to join the domestic service staff of Saint Mary's College.
We pray that the construction is going well and on schedule.
Sincerely yours in Christ,
Sister Maria Luisa Josefa of the Most Blessed
Sacrament[125]

A few weeks later, the Christian Brothers traveled to Long
Beach to meet with Mother Luisita and Father Ott, who helped
Mother with the contractual decisions, which included the building
of a convent for them. He discussed every detail of the contract
with the brothers. Mother Luisita anguished over this decision.
Something within her seemed to hold her back from signing, but
she had no other alternative.

On April 2, she mailed the signed two-year contract back to
the brothers.

Father Ott knew the Carmelites would soon need a larger living
space. More sisters were expected, and so he began house hunting
for the Carmelite Sisters again. He found another house at 1830
Chestnut Avenue in Long Beach. Instead of renting this one, he
bought it outright and said that when escrow went through, they
could move in. It needed a lot of work before the next group of
sisters arrived, and they worked together again to repair and paint
the house. Eight more sisters arrived in March and settled in right
away. No one knew any English. Sixteen Carmelite refugees were
now in the United States.

Mother Luisita's practical advice, such as on how to find dis-
counts for train tickets or when it was safe to send packages through

---

[125] The original letter is in the archives of the Carmelite Sisters of
the Most Sacred Heart of Los Angeles. Sister Margarita Maria
translated documents for Mother Luisita.

trustworthy couriers, are short spiritual maxims that reveal her spirituality:

"Remember, for greater things you were born."

"¡Adelante! Onward!"

"God will provide."

"Look to God, your soul, and eternity. All the rest is a wisp of smoke."

"Live in hope!"

Mother Luisita had forbidden the sisters in Mexico to have their photos taken and had cautioned them to remain hidden, keeping a low profile so that they could continue their work among the people without being discovered by the government soldiers. The few existing photos of Mother Luisita and the sisters during these years were taken in the United States.

Preparations were soon underway for the move from Long Beach to Moraga, California. Sister Carmen and Sister Margarita Maria left in early May for Oakland, California, to find out more about Saint Mary's College. On May 18, Mother Luisita, accompanied by a few sisters, also traveled to Oakland. They stayed with Sister Carmen and Sister Margarita Maria for three months at Providence Hospital, across the street from the Christian Brothers' Saint Mary's College High School, which had recently closed.

While awaiting the completion of the Moraga convent, the sisters helped the brothers by sewing vestments and other items for the chapel as well as tending to other tasks that the brothers requested from time to time. The sisters especially loved their recreations in the evening with the brothers when they learned about American customs from these kind teachers.

The Catholic newspaper for the Archdiocese of San Francisco, the *Monitor*, published a series of three feature stories on the refugees. The article in the June 3, 1928, edition was written in the somewhat flowery style of the early 1900s. The reporter, Fred Williams, interviewed the Carmelite refugees at Old Saint Mary's College in Oakland, where the sisters were living during the construction of their Moraga convent.

The interview touched Williams, who had come to realize the underlying strength and virtue of Mother Luisita. So did the Christian Brothers. Sister Mary of the Angels of the Eucharistic Heart Salicido remembered many years later that Brother Edward would call Mother Luisita "*la santa madre Luisa*," which means "the holy Mother Luisa," whenever he spoke of her. Williams asked Mother Luisita if he could take a photograph of her with his daughter, Margaret Mary, and she agreed. (The library microfiche of the newspaper photo appears in the photo section of this book.)

In July, Mother Luisita and Sister Margarita Maria returned to Long Beach to receive the next group of sisters who would be coming up from Mexico at the end of August. They met the new sisters at Los Angeles's Central Station and accompanied them on their four-hundred-mile train ride to San Francisco and the seven-mile ferryboat trip to Oakland across the San Francisco Bay. Gratefully, they discovered, as had the other sisters before them, that the Bay Area was much cooler.

Meanwhile, back in Mexico, another epidemic had occurred in March 1928. When it began, the government called for the orphanage to be turned into a hospital department to be cared for by a government-appointed staff. Fortunately, no other staff was sent because the sister who served as superior told them that the sisters were willing to attend to anyone who was sick. When the government tried to confiscate the sisters' property, Mr. Carlos

Morales spoke to the government official at the sisters' request, and the community was able to retain their property. There were sixteen girls in the orphanage at the time. The orphanage and the school were being used by some of the many families who had been relocated to the cities by the government mandate. Up to sixty families had been housed there. As for material resources, the hospital still received the interest from Mother Luisita's donation to the archdiocese administered by Mother Luisita's brother Salvador. It was not enough, however, and those at the hospital suffered greatly from shortages of food and medicine. Sometimes they had no food at all because the number of patients kept growing. In addition, people who had assisted the sisters were forced to flee Atotonilco when their lives were threatened.

The sisters needed to be as creative as possible to find ways to survive. In Guadalajara, they used the money received from a property of Mother Luisita that was administered by her brother-in-law. Not much was collected from the school because many of the girls had been admitted free of charge. Because religious organizations could no longer own anything, the house in Guadalajara where the sisters were living, located at Jarauta 96, had to be rented to someone who was not religious. They did this through a mock sale to Mr. Antonio Vázquez Cisneros.

In California, in August 1928, just a few weeks before their move to Moraga, the sisters made their eight-day yearly retreat while still living in Oakland. A glimpse into Mother Luisita's soul comes through this sentence in her spiritual notes during that retreat: "I feel the necessity of prayer. It is my consolation and hope because without the help of God, I can do nothing. I am like a dry stick as regards doing anything that's good, and bad weeds grow in my soul with great velocity and strength whenever I neglect prayer."[126]

Now the group of sisters was complete. Eighteen sisters would remain to fulfill the two-year contract with the Christian Brothers, while Mother Luisita and Sister Margarita Maria would stay only for a while and then return to Long Beach. The two years in Moraga were difficult for the sisters. Because they were not in the best of health, they found adjustments difficult, emotionally and physically.

Letters from those two years, as well as remembrances of the sisters who worked there, tell of long hours of work, falling asleep at prayers, and having parts of the original contract removed because they just could not handle it all. When Archbishop Orozco visited them, he took Mother Luisita aside and told her, "Mother, as soon as possible, find a way to stop this domestic work and return to the apostolates for which your community was founded."[127] Many sisters remembered that during the time they were at the college "we worked like men."[128]

As fire refines gold, Mother Luisita's spiritual and physical sufferings brought about a greater surrender to the loving providence of God. A few months later, under the inspiration of the Holy Spirit on Christmas Eve, in the stillness of the night before Midnight Mass and with quiet determination, Mother Luisita knelt before the tabernacle. Reading from the paper she held in her hands, she made her Christmas offering to God:

---

[126] Kennedy, *In Love's Safekeeping*, vol. 2, 955.

[127] Personal remembrance of Sister Maria Refugio of the Sacred Heart Navarro.

[128] Personal remembrance of Sister Ines of Jesus Gonzalez Hernandez and many other sisters.

Lord, do me the charity of accepting me as Your own; I do not have any of the virtues required for You to accept me, but look at Your own merits and my desires.

Here I am, Lord. I offer myself to You without any reservations or conditions. I want to deny You nothing. Deign to accept me so that once and for all, I am in right relationship with You. I am here. I am Yours. Do with me as You will. Give me Your love and make me suffer whatever You like and in whatever manner You want. I do not want to be anything. I want to be the target of Your justice where Your chastising arm would rest.

If You are pleased with my life, here it is, Lord, any way You want it. Without breaking the fulfillment of my vows, I offer myself and all my life to You for sinners, in atonement for the sins that are committed every day and for priests. My Jesus, give me the necessary strength to suffer whatever You want to give me—or rather, cut off, burn, destroy, annihilate whatever You want.

Even though my desire is that my life will be consumed soon—and how I wish I could hasten its coming—yet I resign myself to Your Holy Will. My Lord, I promise to accept gladly any interior sorrow, sickness, contempt, calumny, false testimony, and my life, whatever way You are pleased to have me. And if my sufferings have any merit, I offer them for priests and in a very special way for my sisters.

December 24, 1928, Moraga, California[129]

Mother Luisita's plan had been to stay in California until the end of the uprising, but the Cristiada had no real victory on either

---

[129] Caravacci, *Loving Kindness*, 958.

side. Six months after her Christmas offering, diplomatic negotiations brought about a truce of sorts when, on June 21, 1929, the Mexican government and the Catholic Church signed a peace accord known as *los arreglos* – a tremendous gift on Mother Luisita's birthday and feast day.

Archbishop Orozco was the only Mexican bishop who had refused to sign the peace accord. He said that his conscience would not allow him to sign because true religious freedom had still not come to Mexico. As for Mother Luisita, she wrote immediately to the Christian Brothers to let them know that the sisters would complete their two-year contract and would not renew it. She clarified that the sisters would leave Saint Mary's College in June 1930.

The diplomatic process followed by the Vatican in achieving the signing of *los arreglos* culminated in these peaceful arrangements, which were seen by the pope as "the least evil to avoid the greater evil of the indefinite suspension of worship."[130]

Soon after the peace accord was signed, in August 1929, the Very Reverend Father William of Saint Albert, superior general of the Discalced Carmelites, arrived in the United States and included on his itinerary a visit to the sisters at Saint Mary's. Mother Luisita was already back in Long Beach, so Mother Mary of the Eucharist, local superior of the Moraga community, welcomed him and led him to the chapel. Father Pedro had told them how to prepare and what to expect during the visit. The superior general listened with interest to their personal stories of the beginnings of their community and the religious persecution during the Cristiada. Later, he also visited Mother Luisita in Long Beach and assured her of his blessing and support for her community.

[130] Orozco Mosqueda, *Rostro de Bondad*, 200.

That same month, Father Ott learned that he was being transferred from Holy Innocents in Long Beach to Saint Patrick's Church
in Los Angeles. The move took place quickly, and within a few days,
Father Ott's personal belongings were at Saint Patrick's, and a new
pastor was on his way to Holy Innocents. Father Ott had become
their dear and trusted friend and adviser. Before leaving he told
them, "Let's keep in touch, sisters. You know where to find me in
Los Angeles if you need me."

Before long, they needed him. The new pastor told Mother
Luisita right away that the parish could no longer afford the expense
of religious sisters to minister to the Mexican refugees in the parish.
When Mother Luisita telephoned Father Ott at his new rectory,
he was not surprised and immediately told her to bring the sisters
to Saint Patrick's because there were many Mexican parishioners
who needed the sisters' services.

Although Father Ott had no money to help the Carmelites
establish themselves at Saint Patrick's, he was able to find a convent left vacant by another religious community. He told Mother
Luisita that he could not afford to have it moved from its current
location to the empty lot near his parish. Mother Luisita asked
the diocese for a loan to have the convent moved to the new site
near Saint Patrick's. The bishop agreed and cosigned a bank loan
for $3,500. Father Ott gave this house to the Carmelite Sisters to
be their first property in the United States.[131]

---

[131] The Archdiocese of Los Angeles cosigned a bank loan with Mother
Luisita in 1929 so an abandoned convent could be moved onto
the empty lot in front of Saint Patrick's Church. Although it did
not take place until six years after Mother Luisita's death, the way
in which the $3,500 note was finally paid belongs to the story of
her first foundation in Los Angeles. The Salesians of Saint John
Bosco took over Saint Patrick's Parish in October 1943. The lot

In time, the Catholic Welfare Bureau began sending orphaned girls to the Carmelite Sisters and paid for their care. Other girls were also placed under the sisters' care by their families. Because of this, the sisters were finally able to make ends meet. Their apostolate with the young girls was successful and continued later as the Little Flower Missionary House on 2434 Gates Street in Los Angeles.

It seemed that as soon as things began to go smoothly, a new crisis would arise.

On October 29, 1929, just when things were looking up for the sisters, the United States stock market crashed, sending the country into a tailspin, and like many others, the sisters were caught in its wake.

---

had grown in value, carrying the building with it as an integral part of the realty. "Not a scrap of paper did the sisters have in evidence of their equity in the property, but their moral claim was recognized, and the Salesians paid them $3,800 for the house. After discharging the note, they still had three hundred dollars left, which helped them establish the Little Flower Missionary House on its present site of 2434 Gates Street" in Los Angeles. Queen, *The Doctor's Widow*, 95–96.

Chapter 14

Everything Is Grace

Pray and expect.

—Mother Luisita[132]

Atotonilco's streets were empty now. So, too, was its charming plaza. San Miguel Arcángel Church stood in silent witness to the remnants left after the pillaging. An eerie silence embraced the town as a pall embraces a coffin.

The cobblestones were stained with blood. The corpses were gone, but ghosts of memories remained.

And the sounds—of guns and rifles; of the death rattle of those who were slain; of the whispered "¡Viva Cristo Rey!" on the lips of the wounded who died alone, still clutching crucifixes or rosaries, old muskets or clubs, or simple farming tools used as weapons.

Some say that, standing near the Los Altos highlands when it is quiet, one can still hear the echoes of "¡Viva Cristo Rey!" reverberating through the silence.

This was the Mexico to which Mother Luisita returned together with Sister Margarita Maria on October 24, 1929. Evidence of the

---

132 Kennedy, *In Love's Safekeeping*, vol. 2, 958.

carnage was still apparent throughout Los Altos. The land, the ranches, the cattle and agricultural fields, and the financial holdings of many of Mother Luisita's friends and acquaintances—gone. Only remnants of the violent battles that covered the land remained.

Empty fields of destroyed crops greeted them. Friends and relatives told them how their land as well as that of other landowners had been confiscated by the government. The two Carmelites learned that friends were either missing or dead. In fact, throughout Jalisco, churches had been burned down. Others had been desecrated with filth from the horses that had been stabled there. Friends and relatives wore traditional mourning clothing. No words existed to express the depth of feeling in Mother Luisita's heart as her eyes caressed her beloved country.

Sadly, there was more.

In the Los Altos region of Jalisco where the Cristero uprising had begun, the war was not over. Former Cristeros were still being targeted by local militants called *agraristas* who had fought alongside the federal soldiers in exchange for land grants. They were now taking their own revenge in the small towns, killing former Cristeros despite the signing of the peace accord. In some places, the Cristeros were massacred even as they were laying down their guns at local churches.

Following the peace accord, the government began a more direct and personal persecution—the systematic, premeditated assassination of the Cristero leaders for the purpose of preventing the renewal of the movement. Although the number of Cristeros murdered after the peace accord was hard to come by, one study estimated the lives lost throughout Mexico during the postwar manhunt to be about five thousand victims.[133]

---

[133] Knights of Columbus, *For Greater Glory Study Guide*, www.kofc. org/en/resources/college-programs/10559-for-greater-glory-study-guide.pdf.

As she went from place to place, Mother Luisita learned more about the peace treaty between the Vatican and the Mexican government. Pope Pius XI had authorized Archbishop Leopoldo Ruiz y Flores to sign the peace accord, but he had imposed two conditions: (1) that amnesty would be granted to all those in arms who surrendered and (2) that houses, bishops' residences, and seminaries would be returned. Although the president immediately accepted both conditions, they were never fulfilled. Consequently, Mother Luisita returned to a country that was not at peace and where vengeance continued, especially in Los Altos, where both her community and the Cristiada were born.

Even though the peace accord was in effect, the persecution of Catholics was as strong as ever in Los Altos. The sisters still lived hidden away in various homes, secretly continuing their apostolate as best they could. Into the 1930s, they continued their "hide-and-seek" existence, frequently changing their locations, not wanting to stay too long in one place lest they put the families who sheltered them in danger. (In 1937, Mother Luisita would die in the "borrowed house" where she was still hiding.)

After a few days had passed, Mother Luisita received a letter from Sister Margarita Maria, who had remained in Guadalajara when they returned to Mexico. She was deeply distressed over what had happened during the past two years. Mother Luisita wrote, "May the grace of the Holy Spirit always be in our souls, Sister Margarita! Do not lose your presence of God but contemplate it with gentleness within your own self." From that time, the following phrase was repeated over and over in Mother Luisita's letters: "May the peace of God be in your soul!"

This positive mindset of Mother Luisita, who remained consistently optimistic through thick and thin, is reminiscent of the famed holocaust survivor, psychiatrist Viktor Frankl, whose

Man's Search for Meaning explored the way to emerge from traumatic horror as a victor, not a mere survivor. Mother Luisita, like Frankl, found a deep and profound meaning in what she and her community had experienced. They had accompanied their countrymen through the horrors inflicted on them—horrors that included assaults on their faith, their families, and their native country.

As the saying goes, "It is better to light a single candle than to curse the darkness." Mother Luisita and her sisters were those candles. Their lives were lit candles. Their Carmelite charism of prayer drew them and others closer to God's all-embracing light. If the churches were closed, if the killings continued despite the peace accord, the sisters themselves would be living monstrances carrying the light of Christ into the darkness.[134]

December 24, 1929, would mark the twenty-fifth anniversary of the beginning of Mother Luisita's new community and, amid the ruins and the rubble and her efforts to reorganize her ministries, Mother Luisita had an idea that she wanted to carry out. She wanted to have a celebration. It would need to be extremely simple and subdued, a quiet Mass followed by a grand fiesta, albeit a hidden one because of the persecution still going on throughout Los Altos.

She also visited the sisters living in various areas of Jalisco to learn how they were doing and especially to learn what their specific needs were. Many of them had subsisted for two years with almost nothing to eat and very few material goods.

---

[134] A monstrance is a vessel (usually of gold or silver) in which the consecrated Host—known by Catholics as the Blessed Sacrament or the Holy Eucharist—is enclosed and placed on the altar for adoration by all the faithful.

Several important community documents were finally attended to and finalized. Archbishop Orozco approved the sisters' constitution and ceremonial books right away, but when Mother Luisita saw his deletions, it affected her very much. She had wanted so much to retain the rituals and customs of the Discalced Carmelite nuns, but the archbishop did not. He had taken many of them out.

Mother Luisita was so affected personally by the archbishop's changes to their way of life that she became ill. For his part, Archbishop Orozco realized that Mother Luisita's contemplative heart yearned for and thrived in that prayerful atmosphere she remembered so well in the cloister, but he strongly believed that in time it would prove to be too much for her sisters to retain all their traditions while working a full day as apostolic Carmelites. At times, he was very strict with Mother Luisita, but she always obeyed her archbishop, even though her obedience usually came at a cost. He used to say that Mother Luisita was a saint but not in his mold.

Sister Margarita of Christ remembered one of the times when Archbishop Orozco reproved Mother Luisita:

I witnessed His Excellency manifest his displeasure with Mother because of her way of being so recollected. He humiliated her and told her that he wanted her to be like a superior of a different community. I do not remember her name. He wanted Mother Luisita to be as active as she was. He requested that little by little she should be taking away many little rules from our constitutions because it seemed as if we were cloistered nuns, and we were not.

How I admired her, seeing how she accepted these humiliations and as I heard her say in her sweet voice to him, "Your Excellency, I am going to try to do everything your Excellency is advising." And when we came back, she informed the community of the archbishop's decisions. She was always submissive and obedient.[135]

That deep relationship with God that Mother Luisita treasured as her first priority and that of her Carmelite Sisters remained, but without retaining all of the cloistered customs.

Ever since Mother Luisita had closed the novitiate out of prudent discretion during the Cristiada, no new women had entered the community. Now the archbishop finally gave permission to reopen the novitiate, but its location was changed from Atotonilco to Guadalajara, which was safer.

Mother Luisita had been back in Mexico only a few months and had been trying her best to reorganize the hospital, schools, and convents when, to her surprise, Archbishop Orozco, still living in exile in the United States, wrote to her. He told her that he wanted to discuss the future of the congregation in the United States with her and for her to return to the United States immediately.

Mother Luisita responded promptly, and on January 20, 1930, she left Mexico again, bringing Sister Margarita Maria with her as her companion. When Archbishop Orozco met with her, he discussed the future of the community in the United States. He told Mother Luisita that he wanted her to establish a novitiate in the United States close to the border to save the vocations of the sisters. He knew that the persecution was far from over.

Mother Luisita fully agreed with him. She, too, had hoped that the community would remain in the United States and be canonically (according to Church law) established there. He also asked Mother Luisita to return to Mexico and, because of the

---

[135] Personal remembrance of Sister Margarita of Christ Hernandez.

circumstances, to appoint rather than elect a new governing body for the community.[136]

Before she returned to Mexico, Mother Luisita went to see her old friend and adviser Father Callahan. When the two met, he shared with her his growing concern for her community in the wake of a new Mexican Repatriation Act, which had already begun to send Mexican refugees back to Mexico. There was, in his estimation, a great probability that if the sisters did not sink deeper roots into American soil by owning property and establishing a stable apostolate, they would be repatriated back to Mexico like the others.

Father Callahan was an astute scholar who wrote and spoke seven languages. He kept up on current affairs and feared that the Mexican refugees he had sponsored would be sent back to Mexico. He did not want this to happen to his Carmelite Sisters.

Father Callahan had observed the needs of the Spanish-speaking patients in the Los Angeles County tuberculosis sanatorium. Many of the Mexican immigrants had contracted tuberculosis, yet few doctors and nurses spoke Spanish. Father Callahan urged Mother Luisita to consider as her first institution in the United States a tuberculosis sanatorium for young Spanish-speaking girls. He told her that it was essential that she begin to act right away to prevent the forced repatriation of her sisters.

Before Mother Luisita returned to Mexico, she quietly told Sister Mary of the Eucharist that if the decision was made to open a sanatorium, she would become the future superior of that foundation. Sister Mary of the Eucharist asked Mother Luisita to allow Sister Margarita Maria to remain with her in California to be the administrator of the new sanatorium because of her knowledge in English and her experience in business.

---

[136] Kennedy, *In Love's Safekeeping*, vol. 1, letter 93, 175.

Mother Luisita then took Sister Margarita Maria aside and asked her candidly if she would prefer to return to Mexico or remain to help with the foundation of a sanatorium in the United States. Mother Margarita Maria's remembrances tell us that her reply was "Mother, I do love it here in California and I love Mexico, too." With that said, she left the decision to the Holy Spirit and Mother Luisita.

Mother Luisita returned to Mexico on Easter Monday, April 21, 1930, leaving Sister Margarita Maria in California. Mother Luisita beseeched God to enlighten her so she would accomplish His will in making this decision. In one of her letters, she writes that she did not know if the sisters could establish, operate, and develop a sanatorium so soon. They were not prepared for this specialized care. They still did not know the language. They had very little money. Yet what was the alternative?

So many decisions needed to be made at this time: finalizing the negotiations with the Christian Brothers regarding the departure of the Carmelite Sisters from Saint Mary's; determining where to send the eighteen Sisters who were leaving Moraga at the end of June 1930; finally, choosing which sisters would remain in the United States.

It was May before Mother Luisita made her decision. She wrote to Mother Mary of the Eucharist and Sister Margarita Maria to tell them that they should move ahead and begin specific plans with Father Callahan for a tuberculosis sanatorium. She directed them to go to Bishop Cantwell's office to let him know of her decision to begin a sanatorium in the United States.

After that, it all happened so fast.

A few days after receiving the letter, Mother Mary of the Eucharist, Sister Margarita Maria, and Father Callahan met with Bishop Cantwell. The bishop listened attentively. At first, he was very reluctant to give his approval and spoke candidly of the financial risk involved, the sisters' lack of experience, and the youth of Father Callahan and the sisters who were present. Father Callahan, Mother Mary, and Sister Margarita Maria were all under thirty years of age. At last, the bishop said, "All right. You have my approval, but you must start on a small scale."[137]

Father Callahan found a three-acre property in Duarte, California, about thirty-five miles from Los Angeles. When he drove the sisters to see the Duarte property, they immediately fell in love with the plot, which reminded them so much of their home in Jalisco. It was in a lovely valley and, just like Atotonilco, was surrounded by beautiful mountains with temperate weather most of the year. Standing on their new property for the first time left them nostalgic. Right away, they saw that it needed a lot of work. But they were willing to roll up their sleeves and begin again.

It would be up to Mother Luisita to give them permission to purchase it. From Mexico, Mother Luisita prayed anew, this time about the purchase of the property. The purchase price was $17,500. She knew all too well that the recent stock market crash of October 29, 1929, had drastically impacted finances throughout the United States, including the ministries of the Catholic Church.

So, plans now needed to be shaped according to the dire financial circumstances in the United States. As in most places, money was tight in the Diocese of Los Angeles–San Diego. As a result, Mother Luisita needed to find a way to buy the property. The bishop was not able to help with its purchase. She was on her own. After considering her few options, she decided to secure a bank loan.

---

[137] Helenita Colbert, *To Love Me in Truth: Mother María Luisa Josefa of the Most Blessed Sacrament* (Alhambra, CA: Carmelite Sisters' Printing, 1987), 63.

Mother Luisita gave the sisters' permission to borrow $17,500 from the bank to purchase the property and another $5,000 for the most essential equipment, with a first and a second mortgage on the property. The bishop was able to help the sisters by giving permission for the diocese to guarantee the loans because the sisters, without any funds of their own, were assuming a large debt. This was another huge leap of faith on the part of both the bishop and Mother Luisita.

With Mother Luisita's approval, Sister Margarita Maria proactively mailed handwritten appeal letters asking for donations toward the establishment of their new sanatorium. Only ten people replied, and she acquired a mere $200, but a list of friends and benefactors began with this original request.

During July 1930, several Carmelite Sisters left Saint Patrick's to take possession of the three-acre tract twenty-two miles east of Los Angeles. They began to live in the dilapidated farmhouse on the property. Mother Mary of the Eucharist was the local superior. Sister Maria de la Soledad was the local vicar, a role like that of a vice president. Sister Margarita Maria was assigned as the administrator of the sanatorium. They had only a few days to get the property ready for the arrival of their first patients.

The sisters worked at trimming and weeding; some helped clean up the property. They improvised tools and furnishings. Mother Mary of the Eucharist spent every morning sweeping the property and battling the huge pockets of undergrowth throughout the three acres that were home to snakes and other reptiles.

On July 29, the sisters placed an ad in the *Los Angeles Examiner* requesting furniture—anything usable—for the sanatorium. Many odds and ends came in, and every item was used. Stacked wooden packing crates became patients' nightstands. Sixteen unmatched chairs graced the dining tables for the patients. The only new items were dishes the sisters bought at the five-and-dime.

Father Callahan, with help from his family, converted the garage into a recreation hall for ambulatory patients, and the two existing run-down shacks, renamed "cottages," became wards for the patients.[138] He asked the Christian Brothers to donate an old school bus from Cantwell High School in Los Angeles to the sisters. One day, the sisters were startled to see him driving the old bus onto the property. They took out the seats and put them in the recreation hall for the girls. The bus seats worked perfectly!

The sisters rented a sewing machine for two days—for that was all they could afford—and used it around the clock. They took eight-hour sewing shifts and sewed patient gowns, curtains, rugs, towels, washcloths, bed linen, and whatever else could be made from cloth.

On July 31, 1930, Father Callahan came to celebrate the first Mass for the sisters. There was only a makeshift altar and no vestments for him. They had expected Father Callahan to bring his own vestments, but he forgot even his cassock, the long black robe worn by Catholic priests. The sisters unsewed the sleeves from a new habit. Fr. Callahan put it on. Next, a ribbon became his cincture. As there was no stand for the missal, one of the sisters filled a pillowcase with stuffing from a packing box.

On August 2, 1930, the feast of Our Lady of the Angels at that time, five young girls from Olive View Sanatorium arrived at Santa

---

[138] Colbert, *To Love Me in Truth*, 67.

Teresita. The beginning days at Santa Teresita were during the heart of the country's depression years. Everything was scarce. They worked extremely hard and learned how to make use of whatever they had on hand.

In those beginning months, there was no hot water on the property. In a clearing near the cottages, the sisters chopped firewood from old, dying trees and built fires to boil water. Both dishes and clothing were left in large pots of boiling water with the recommended solution to sterilize them for the required amount of time.

By using their common sense and asking questions of knowledgeable friends, the sisters learned what they needed to do to open and operate the new sanatorium.

It was hard work.

These first young patients grew to love the sisters, who, in turn, loved the girls. Under the direction of Sister Mary Rose, the girls published a newsletter called the *Rose* and a bound collection is in the archives of the Carmelite Sisters of the Most Sacred Heart of Los Angeles. It contains the thoughts and feelings, hopes and dreams of these young girls stricken with tuberculosis. Dotted with anecdotes from their daily lives, the *Rose* provided interesting and often inspirational reading as well as a creative outlet for them.

Many times, the sisters found themselves with very little to eat. They had no other staff members to help them, so they took turns on night duty after working all day.

It was a very difficult beginning.

Saint Thérèse of the Child Jesus, Carmelite Doctor of the Church who died of tuberculosis at only twenty-four years of age, wrote, "Everything is grace." The Carmelite Sisters knew that.

They lived by it.

They lived by it during the difficult beginning years of setting down roots in the United States: when they had no money
to buy shoes and were grateful when they could finally afford
to purchase fifty-cent tennis shoes; or when a peddler dropped
by their house in Long Beach and "just happened" to have the
exact framed painting of Saint Ignatius of Loyola that they were
searching for and that they purchased for only ten cents; when,
at Saint Patrick's, Mother Luisita needed medicine and they "just
happened" to find some money in the gutter that no one claimed;
or when Father Callahan appeared on the horizon driving the
old school bus in Duarte—to name only a few of the many graces
with which they were blessed.

"Everything is grace."

As with their sisters in Mexico, when life was hardest, the refugees' faith became strongest. Saint John of the Cross, the Carmelite
mystic and Doctor of the Church, wrote, "Where there is no love,
give love and you will draw forth love." This is what was happening at Santa Teresita. Love became the characteristic trademark of
the charism of Mother Luisita's new community—to bring God's
healing love, the love of His Sacred Heart, to body and soul.

This is how her community began.

This is how the community has continued.

Although the early days at Santa Teresita were very difficult, as
the days passed, each cottage became home to the six or eight girls
living there. Visitors noticed the tangible family spirit. The girls
began to share stories about their lives before they came to Santa
Teresita and how their lives were now so much happier with the
guidance of the sisters.

Quietly, the Holy Spirit worked within the hearts of the young
patients, healing, uplifting, and restoring. All that the sisters were
and did was not unnoticed by the patients at Santa Teresita, as

shown by some of the surviving diaries and other writings of the young women receiving treatment.

One story is about Jenny Gifford, a seventeen-year-old college student. A terminal case, Jenny arrived at Santa Teresita a self-pronounced agnostic. She was aware that she would not recover and manifested an active, hard courage born from desperation. Her roommate in the cottage, Belia, was a gentle girl of deep faith, with warm love and understanding flowing from her faith. Each morning, Belia received Holy Communion and silently prayed for Jenny. Sister Genevieve, a Dominican nun dying of tuberculosis in the room next to theirs, was also praying for Jenny.

In December, Jenny asked to meet with the priest. "I don't want to die like this, Father. I'd better try some religion."

Belia, who was in the next bed, smiled and reached her hand across the aisle to Jenny, whispering gently, "You don't try religion, Jenny. You humbly ask your Father God for it."

And that is what Jenny did. In ten lessons from Father Carlos, who visited Santa Teresita from time to time to minister to the girls, she had a clear picture of the Faith. On Holy Thursday she was wheeled into the chapel to make her First Holy Communion. It was the first time she had ever been in a Catholic chapel.

"What brought you into the Faith, Jenny?" one of the other girls asked her.

Jenny replied, "Two things: the example and kindness of my roommate, Belia, and the heroism of Sister Genevieve. You see, the walls between our two rooms are so thin that during the night when I couldn't sleep, I could hear Sister Genevieve, who wasn't sleeping either, praying softly, saying repeatedly, 'Jesus, mercy!' and 'Jesus, I love You!' She suffered so much, yet never complained. And she spoke so beautifully of her approaching death. Only a Catholic can die like that. That is why I wanted to be one." She was a daily communicant from her First Holy Communion until the day of her death, less than a month later.[139]

Sister Margarita Maria called the girls *primorosas* to acknowledge their beauty and dignity. The Spanish word's literal meaning is "exquisite." To be a *primorosa* was to be a young woman who was poised and filled with grace, self-worth, dignity, and self-respect. This endearment was just what the girls needed, and they loved it.

About this time, the sisters in the United States noticed that Mother Luisita began using her code more frequently in her letters to them and her words were getting briefer and more guarded.

Mexico was submerged in the second wave of the religious persecution.

---

[139] Sister Timothy Marie Kennedy, O.C.D., *In the Face of Darkness: The Heroic Life and Holy Death of Mother Luisita* (Manchester, NH: Sophia Institute Press, 2019), 213–214.

Chapter 15

Second Cristiada

*The interior soul knows how to work and live and remain
recollected at the same time. Between Jesus and the soul there flows
a current that no one sees and a dialogue that no one hears.*

—Mother Luisita[140]

The ordination ceremony of a Catholic priest is at least two hours
long and often longer. People who attend an ordination do not
seem to mind that it is so lengthy. On the contrary, they are happy
to stand for two hours or more if there are no seats available. Even
with extra chairs lining the aisles, the church's vestibule is likely
to be full with the overflow of attendees.

At some deep level, people know that an ordination is a sacred
moment. They intuitively realize that something utterly profound
happens at a Catholic ordination. Each gesture, each symbolic action, holds a world of meaning within it. The Sacrament of Holy
Orders has been passed from bishop to candidate for two thousand
years. The priesthood of Jesus Christ is passed on yet again each
time the bishop wordlessly lays hands on a candidate for ordination.

---

[140] Kennedy, *In Love's Safekeeping*, vol. 2, 928.

Is it any wonder, then, that evil forces target the Catholic priesthood?

The physical battles of the Cristiada were now over, but another battle targeting the priesthood began in full force when Governor Adalberto Tejeda passed a law in 1931 based on an overlooked clause of Article 130 of the Mexican constitution. The article declared that each state in Mexico had the right, through its legislature, to determine the number of priests allowed in the state "based on the needs of the people." Tejeda turned this clause into a lethal weapon. There were 1,100,000 people in his state of Veracruz, and Tejeda proceeded to enact through his submissive legislature a law that allowed only one priest for every 100,000 people. That came out to only eleven priests for the entire state of Veracruz.

The same thing happened in the federal district that included Mexico City. Their new law stated that there would be only 219 priests for the 1,500,000 Catholics, and they had to be approved by the governor, not by the archbishop. The movement spread like wildfire. On December 23, 1931, Archbishop Díaz addressed an open letter to the president of Mexico regarding the situation. Lawyers drew up petitions, which the people circulated, but all of these efforts were in vain.

Praying for priests is an essential part of the Carmelite Order's charism. Supporting priests, especially by prayer, was of primary importance to Mother Luisita's community and remains so today.

In his 1936 book *Mexican Martyrdom*, Father Wilfrid Parsons, S.J., describes the dire plight of priests after Tejeda's 1934 ruthless enforcement of Article 130 of the constitution:

Two men, an American and a Mexican, were standing at a window overlooking the Zócalo, Mexico City's great plaza that is bounded by the Cathedral on one side and the National Palace, one of Spain's gifts to Mexico, on another.

The Mexican pointed to two struggling figures that were passing. They were clad in rags; their shoes were torn and full of holes; their hats looked as if they had been picked up from a trash pile. They were walking toward the Cathedral in Mexico City.

"You see those men?" he asked. "They look pretty poor. They are two priests from Veracruz. They come here every day to visit the Cathedral, and later go to the offices of the archbishop for a handout. There are nearly two thousand priests like them in the city, and most of them are poor, or nearly as poor as those two. Hardly one of them has a peso to his name. They live on the scant resources of the Catholics of the city."[141]

In 1926, there had been 4,500 priests in Mexico. By 1934, there would be only 334 priests. Looking ahead, in 1935, seventeen states would have no priests left at all.

Archbishop Orozco continued his support of the Carmelite Sisters. In October 1932, he gave Mother Luisita permission to establish a province of the community in the United States with a novitiate: the Province of Saint Raphael. Mother Mary of the Eucharist was named provincial superior, and Sister Margarita Maria was named the provincial vicar. Mother Luisita was well aware that these vital steps forward were an affirmation by the Church that her new

---

[141] Wilfrid Parsons, S.J., *Mexican Martyrdom, 1926–1935: Firsthand Experiences of the Religious Persecution in Mexico* (Rockford, IL: TAN Books, 1987), 165.

community and its mission were accepted by the Church. This was a huge blessing and a profound consolation to her. Mother Luisita never stopped. Although there were intervals when prudence dictated that she hide herself away, her planning continued. She established her next foundation, a school in Mexico City near the Basilica of Our Lady of Guadalupe, in October 1932. Father Abundio Anaya, vicar for religious, told the sisters that if they were interrogated by the police, each one should identify herself as a consecrated woman, a religious sister. He told them not to be afraid and to have great confidence that the Holy Spirit would answer for them. He asked them to remember that the martyrs never prepared their answers.

On October 22, 1932, five sisters were taken to jail as prisoners. Their stay was shortened because one of the Carmelite Sisters had a relative of high status who had intervened for them. One of the books on Mother Luisita, *The Doctor's Widow*, adds the following detail: "As the sisters left, the warden expressed his regret and complimented them on the fact that during their incarceration the jail had known some semblance of order for the first time since the Revolution began."

Another facet of the Second Cristiada was the atheistic, socialistic agenda forced on Mexican schools during the presidency of Lázaro Cárdenas. When Cárdenas became president in 1934, he initiated a new system of liberal, godless education. Beginning in the early 1930s, the Mexican government had stepped up the momentum of incrementally teaching more and more socialism in its public schools. Mandatory sex education was enforced in all schools. Sexual acts were done in the presence of the school-children, some as young as kindergarten age.

According to stories that have been handed down, some parents went to their children's classrooms and shot the teachers dead after learning what the new sex education had put their children through. In one small town, the entire populace rose up against a school. The townspeople showed up at the school, armed with sticks and stones, while the teacher was speaking with the mayor, discussing the new curriculum. When the two heard the mob outside, they scurried up to the roof of the school. The townspeople took turns guarding the school, leaving the two stranded on the roof for two days and two nights without shelter or water.

In Guadalajara, in a single day, eighty-six schools closed, affecting tens of thousands of students. The teachers who remained in the schools, public or private, were forced to take an oath that they would teach this new curriculum. Each state formed its own oath. Part of the oath in one state included the following words and is representative of all the states: "I declare that I am an atheist, an irreconcilable enemy of the Catholic Church and Roman religion, and that I will endeavor to destroy it, detaching conscience from the bonds of any religious worship and that I am ready to fight against the clergy anywhere and wherever it will be necessary."

One would think that things couldn't get worse, but they did. Mother Luisita heard the stories as they were passed from person to person and then from town to town. Mother Luisita anguished at the sight of so many priests who became homeless and unemployed overnight. It was more than shameful; what had been done to them was sacrilegious. People gave them food and clothing when they could, but that was not enough. These priests without churches, deprived of exercising their priesthood, were pathetic to see as they roamed aimlessly through the streets. Some were able to leave the country, but not all.

The Carmelite Sisters were still hiding in private homes. Groups of students were formed, and the sisters found obscure places to teach without having to implement the government's mandated socialist program.

Mother Luisita's deep spirituality is revealed in the many letters written during the Second Cristiada: her total trust in God's divine providence, her priority of spending as much time as possible in the presence of the Most Blessed Sacrament, especially during Holy Communion, and her heart-to-Heart conversations with God dwelling within her.

> I am a beggar before the Blessed Sacrament, always praying for you.

> God will provide for our needs. Let us trust that we will receive all from Him Who loves us so much and is always watching over us.

> May the Sacred Heart of Jesus be our refuge.

> Pray as close to the tabernacle as you can.

> Be a true religious with solid virtues. Women have a vivid imagination and a compassionate heart, but their so-called virtue might be likened to the blaze of a palm mat on fire, which leaves behind nothing but ashes. We must be practical, austere, and hardworking even to the utmost of our strength so that we may be resolved and become what we are supposed to be and not merely phantom religious. ¡Adelante! Onward! God will provide.[142]

In January 1934, Mother Luisita wrote a letter to Mother Teresita of the Child Jesus Chavez. Times were so bad that the letter was very brief, and there was no code used and no signature. Mother

---

[142] Kennedy, *In Love's Safekeeping*, vol. 1, letter 207, 336.

Teresita was going through a rough period of illness, and Mother Luisita encouraged her spiritually and physically. After telling her to rest extra and to eat enough, she offered the following counsel:

> Do not feel alone because you're not. Our Lord in the Blessed Sacrament wants to be your Confidant, your Friend, your Consoler. He wants to fill your soul with His love. Perhaps that's why He is making you feel the emptiness of creatures. How good our God is and by how many different paths He leads souls! Don't doubt it. You have been very dear to Him and it's only natural that He will be jealous with those souls He loves so much. He wants you all for Himself.[143]

The year 1935 was a very difficult one for the Church in Mexico. Mother Luisita used aliases in her letters. Often there were no return addresses, and most letters were carried by hand instead of being delivered by mail. Some letters were censored despite Mother Luisita's code. The government search for Catholic sisters intensified. It was becoming more and more difficult for the sisters to find people who were willing to risk hiding them in their homes.

On April 25, 1935, Mother Luisita wrote to Sister Margarita Maria, who was still in Duarte, California. The letter is heavily coded and refers to the purchase of a property of Mother Luisita, an orchard named La Labor. She wanted a purchase transaction to take place between an American citizen and the owner (herself) in order to protect it from seizure by the federal government, but she did not intend any money to be transacted. The sentence "I have a lot of sewing to do" refers to the dire poverty of the

---

[143] Kennedy, *In Love's Safekeeping*, vol. 2, letter 318, 532.

community in Mexico at that time. This letter is a good example of the creative writing that Mother Luisita had to use to get her point across in language that would not be fully understood by the government censors.

April 8, 1935

My dear Margie:

I greet you with all affection, my dear friend. When will I have the joy of seeing you? Please excuse this short notice on this very poor piece of paper, but circumstances require it. I have a lot of sewing to do. I am writing to tell you about a friend of mine who finds herself in difficult financial and economic circumstances and wishes to sell an orchard. She wants to know if you will be able to buy it with the money you have saved in that country. It is a real bargain, so ... dear friend you are already an American citizen and already have your citizenship papers. Answer me immediately and tell me if this is true, because she may not want to sell the orchard to people from another country. You know how much provincialism there is in Mexico.

In case you buy that orchard, perhaps you will have to give the power of attorney to someone here so they can take care of the deeds. Well, think it over carefully and if you wish to purchase that very beautiful piece of property tell me soon. Goodbye, dear friend. Greetings to your mother and sister!

Maria Carrillo[144]

---

[144] Kennedy, *In Love's Safekeeping*, vol. 2, letter 441, 685. Maria Carrillo was one of Mother Luisita's aliases.

∞

Toward the end of April 1935, Mother Luisita traveled to the United States, where she became very ill from a serious infection. After she had been in California for a few weeks, her condition began to worsen. Doctor Walter Holleran, a surgeon, examined her, and surgery was performed the following day. He told Mother Margarita Maria, who was the local superior at Santa Teresita at the time, that Mother Luisita was suffering from a grave condition of advanced septicemia, with no longer than two years to live. He went on to say that her case was the worst infection that he had seen in his career as a physician.[145]

Mother Luisita was placed in isolation in a room in the hospital basement. This was the standard protocol at Queen of Angels Hospital in Los Angeles during the 1930s. She remained in California until she had recovered sufficiently to travel back to Mexico, but she never fully recuperated. This was her final trip to the United States.

Mother Luisita had traveled back and forth between Mexico and the United States to visit her scattered sisters. In Mexico, she had to travel often on foot. There was no money for transportation. Her energy was dwindling now, and her already fragile health was worsening. She would tell the sisters every time she left, "I am leaving, but the Tabernacle remains. I am not taking the key to the Tabernacle."[146]

Her letters at this point are undated and heavily coded. Here are a few excerpts:

> The secret police are around here, and the soldiers are chasing the children.... They [the soldiers] already know the

---

[145] Caravacci, *Loving Kindness*, 174.

[146] Personal remembrance of Mother Socorro of the Holy Spirit Cholico Rodriguez.

address of the house where Jesus Teresa [Mother Jesus Teresa of the Virgin of Carmel Gutierrez Ortega] and her family were, and they had to get out and separate. This situation is just terrible. Blessed be God! I haven't gone to see you because I don't want to put the lady or you in any danger.

Maria must have told you already that we're on an outing [looking for a place to live] and that we left the house on Hidalgo, and the one in Mezquitan is closed but we haven't turned it in yet.

In August 1935, the family unit came under attack by President Cárdenas. His new law stated that the government would confiscate any building, including a family's home, if any type of religious activity whatsoever was carried out within that home, even if the supposed actions were inferred or implied. After about a year, in 1936, he quite unexpectedly adopted a more conciliatory policy regarding religion. This was a huge step on the part of the Mexican government in burying the hatchet that had been wielded for ten years against the Mexican Catholic population. The *New York Times* ran an article on it, quoting Cárdenas:

> The government will not commit the error of previous administrations by considering the religious question as a problem preeminent to other issues involved in the educational program. Antireligious campaigns would only result in further resistance and definitely postpone economic revival.[147]

---

[147] J. Lloyd Mecham, *Church and State in Latin America: A History of Politico-Ecclesiastical Relations* (Chapel Hill: University of North Carolina Press, 1934), 409, citing a *New York Times* article of March 31, 1936.

This major policy change brought hope to the hearts of the Carmelite Sisters in Mexico. Taking advantage of Cárdenas's temporary lessening of some restrictions, Mother Luisita forged ahead, opening three more schools in 1936: in Jamay, Jalisco; Mexticacán, Jalisco; and Santo Tomás de los Plátanos in the state of Mexico. Sadly, this lessening of restrictions took place slowly, and the sisters remained in hiding. Socialist teachings were still mandated in private schools, and churches and convents that had been confiscated were not yet returned. It would not be until four years later, with the election of Manuel Ávila Camacho in 1940, that the sisters could finally stop hiding.

In 1936, when the sisters had to find a new place to live, they could not find any family willing to give shelter to an extremely ill sister, Mother Luisita. Over the years, many courageous families had risked their lives by hiding the sisters in their homes. The sisters had lived in a home on Independence Street, which they named "the House of Straits" because of the narrowness of its corridors. Later that same year, they had moved to another residence on the same street. They called it "the House of Bedbugs" because of the huge insect population. It had once served as a chicken coop.

Now, a house had finally became available to them on Garibaldi Street in Guadalajara, not far from Holy Name of Jesus Church, also on Garibaldi. The new house was small with poor accommodations. Mother Elena of the Cross Heredia remarked, "Mother, this awful house looks like a sepulcher." Mother Luisita answered, "It doesn't matter; it doesn't matter. From this sepulcher to heaven."[148]

Her words proved to be prophetic.

---

[148] Personal remembrance of Mother Socorro of the Holy Spirit Cholico Rodriguez.

Chapter 16

Fragrance of Roses

Let us go forward, good seamen,
for our Love is waiting on the seashore.[149]

—Mother Luisita

Birth and *death*: two of life's most evocative words.

Images of these words vary as much as the individuals speaking them. Consider the unmatched beauty of a mother with her newborn infant or the travail etched on the face of someone mourning a beloved spouse or child or another loved one. The words hold both uncertainty and confidence, both joy and sorrow. Birth, a joyous event, comes with labor. Death, with its underlying sorrow, brings peace.

Is death an end or a beginning?

It depends.

In fact, the answer is more likely to be not an either-or but a both-and, in order to capture the fullness of the feelings experienced.

How one answers the question "Is death a beginning or an end?" reveals that person's core values and philosophy of life. Death

---

[149] Kennedy, *In Love's Safekeeping*, vol. 2, letter 329, 558.

is a deeply personal topic. One must enter into it softly and respectfully, as if crossing a threshold and walking onto sacred ground, the place where time and eternity meet. Reflecting on death brings to the light both questions and answers and reveals faith or lack of faith and hope or lack of hope.

Saint Joseph Cafasso said, "We are born to love; we live to love, and we will die to love still more." Saint Thérèse of the Child Jesus, whom Saint Pius X called "the greatest saint of modern time," wrote, "I do not fear a separation that will unite me to God forever." She also wrote "I will spend my heaven doing good upon earth." Saint Teresa of Ávila proclaimed, "I want to see God." And Saint Elizabeth of the Trinity's dying words were "I am going to light, to love, to life!"

These thoughts from some of the saints open a door to the final days and death of Mother Luisita through eyewitnesses who described her last illness, death, and funeral from their personal memories.

Sister Patrocinio of Our Lady of Mount Carmel remained with Mother Luisita during her final months as a nursing aide and attended to her needs during her final weeks. During an interview in 2016, she recalled those final days with Mother Luisita:

> It was a very small house in Guadalajara. Our Mother Luisita was in a small, private room. A brown couch sat against one wall, and Mother Luisita's bed was near the opposite wall. The room was so very small that it seemed more like a little parlor. There were two old chairs. No rug. The floor was red brick. A window with curtains was near her bed. The curtains were a muted, tan color, and Mother Luisita always kept them closed because the light bothered her eyes, so the room was always in the semidarkness.

The only division in the room was a screen that separated her from the couch used by the sister who stayed overnight and took care of her. You see, Mother Luisita was in a house without a bedroom. There were only three rooms. A little parlor, a little kitchen, a small indoor patio behind the kitchen and the dining room. That was it. Mother Luisita had become very sick, and the sisters realized that they needed to move to a safer place. Because of the religious persecution, it was harder for the sisters to find people who would take them in. Conchita Hernandez, Mother Margarita Maria's mother, owned two houses in Guadalajara. One of the houses was next door to the house where Mother Luisita finally found refuge. Conchita moved into her second house so that the sisters could live all together on Avenida Garibaldi so that they could be near Mother Luisita.

There were daisies in the garden, and the water faucet was there. The water came from the city. We filled a bucket with water from the faucet and then warmed it in the kitchen to bathe Mother Luisita. Her legs retained water. Ever since 1935, she had swollen legs because of fluid retention. She also suffered from a chronic infection of the nose, a consequence of her diabetes. There were no antibiotics. A syringe was used to wash out the nose and put in medication. Mother Luisita always had a headache because of this infection. I was the one who did this procedure as often as Mother Luisita needed it.

I was eighteen years old when Mother Luisita died. During the last year and a half of Mother Luisita's life (ever since my profession), I was with Mother Luisita at her request. In the Garibaldi house, I would sit on the couch behind the screen and wait for Mother Luisita to ring a little bell, and then I helped with any personal needs and assisted Mother Luisita by rolling up and placing pillows to make her more comfortable. I would also help Mother turn over from side to side.

Visiting sisters would come by and pray with Mother Luisita, but by then Mother was too sick to give advice. A lot of priests would come by and visit her—at least one priest each day. Bishops, doctors, sisters, and Monsignor Anaya, vicar for religious, also came to visit her. Archbishop José Garibi y Rivera, the successor to Archbishop Orozco came to visit, and she again put the Congregation into his hands. He told her that a priest from the parish would bless her with the Eucharist at the moment of her death.

The Blessed Sacrament was hidden in one of the corners of the dining room. When Mother Luisita was dying, Father Modesto Sánchez blessed her with the little reliquary that he had taken from the hiding place in the dining room.[150] It looked like a tiny monstrance, and it held one single small consecrated host. When she quietly stopped breathing, Father blessed her with the Eucharist. The Council members were present at her death.

Other eyewitnesses to her final days and her funeral recorded their memories. Mother Carmen of Jesus, who stayed by Mother Luisita's bedside during her final weeks, recalled the following:

---

[150] A reliquary is a container for a holy relic. A relic is an object or article of religious significance; it usually consists of the physical remains of a saint or the personal effects of the saint or venerated person preserved for purposes of veneration as a tangible memorial.

Mother Luisita knew perfectly well that her last hour had arrived, and she asked me, "How many of our little houses do we have?"

"Nine," I answered.

"Oh, then, now I shall die," she said. She remembered that a priest had told her the following prophetic words, "Mother Luisita, you will not die until you have established seven houses."

By now there were already nine.[151]

She knew that the time had come, and so it happened.

Sister Catalina of the Cross shared her remembrance:

When I was on retreat before my perpetual profession, Mother was resting in the small patio. The sister who was making the crown of white flowers for my profession-of-vows ceremony approached her and said to her, "Mother, Sister Catalina is on retreat. On whom shall I take the measurements for her crown?"

"My daughter," Mother Luisita said while inclining her head, "measure it on me. I am going to need it."

That is what happened. A few days more, and that crown adorned the head of our good Mother at her funeral.

Sister Refugio recalled the morning of Mother Luisita's death:

---

[151] At the time of her death, Mother Luisita had established several foundations in Mexico: Atotonilco (school, orphanage, and hospital), San Francisco de Asís (closed during the religious persecution), Guadalajara, Ocotlán (closed during the religious persecution and reopened in 1933), Jamay, Mexticacán, Santo Tomás de los Plátanos and two in the United States: Saint Patrick's in Los Angeles and Santa Teresita in Duarte, California.

By now, Mother was gravely ill. Because I was frail due to my poor health, and they thought that her sickness made a great impression on me, they sent me to sleep at the house next door, belonging to Conchita Hernandez, Mother Margarita Maria's mother.

The night before Mother died, I was not able to sleep. Finally, in the morning I fell asleep and dreamt that Mother was dead, and her body lay in the place where I actually saw her later. She was wearing her habit. Near to her was a little girl dressed in white as if she were waiting for something, and the sisters were calling out, "The soul of our Mother Luisita!" At that I awoke and heard the cathedral bells that were ringing at dawn.

In about five minutes, Mother Teresa knocked at the door and I asked her, "How is Mother?" She didn't want to tell me the truth, and that is why she answered, "She is in her agony." "I dreamt that she was dead," I told her. Mother Teresa reacted, and then she told me, "She just died."

The day before, around four o'clock in the afternoon, Archbishop José Garibi y Rivera had come to see her. He had looked at her and said "Mother Luisita," and then he prayed with her, "Lord, may Your will be done on earth as it is in heaven." It seemed as if she tried to kneel. That same day in the morning, Father Refugio Huerta had come by and said these beautiful words to her: "Mother Luisita, Our Lord has you on His Cross, but from there you are going to soar to heaven." Our Mother seemed to have been in a state of drowsiness, but she moved her little head as if affirming that she heard. Her illness impeded her from getting up. That lasted about a month, from January 9 until February 11, when she died.

Mother Mary of the Eucharist was with Mother Luisita during those final days. She recounts:

> On February 5, 1937, our Mother fell ill. She had uremia and was very close to death's door. I returned from Atotonilco to be with her. On the sixth, she made an effort to go down to the Profession Ceremony of Sister Catalina. On the tenth, in the morning, I began to pray because she told me, "I am asking Our Lord the grace of having you help me in my immediate preparation for my death." I did pray for her until she died. She was in agony, in a state of coma, for thirty-two hours. She constantly moved from side to side. The agitation would stop momentarily, and she would become confused, and then another attack would begin again.

Father Modesto Sánchez was also with Mother Luisita when she died. At an advanced age, he recalled what happened.

> I had been in the church on February 10, Ash Wednesday, still helping to administer the ashes to the faithful when the pastor came and said to me, "Go and assist a sister who is critically ill."
>
> It was about 10:00 p.m. when I left the church. As I entered her room, I saw that she was already unconscious, her breathing labored, and her eyes closed. I stayed there, seated on the sofa, a short distance from her bed.
>
> Around midnight, Archbishop Garibi and Monsignor Navarro, vicar-general, arrived. They stayed a little while, and when they were about to leave, Archbishop Garibi told me, "Father, I leave you here." So, I remained with her. Between three and four in the morning, her breathing began

to decrease, and I went to pray with her and commended her soul to God until she sighed her last breath, peacefully. I gave her the last absolution at the moment of her death, and I blessed her with the Most Blessed Sacrament in the monstrance, because it was what the sisters asked me to do.

She looked as if she had fallen asleep. Immediately, the sisters improvised an altar, and there, in the room, I celebrated Holy Mass for her. It was February 11, 1937. Without a doubt, she was taken by the Immaculate Virgin of Lourdes on her day.

This is all that I had the good fortune to do in order to assist her as she left this world, to commend her soul to God, and with a blessing and Holy Mass her sisters celebrated her entrance into Heaven.

Sister Paulina of Jesus shared this remembrance:

When I arrived, I stood near Mother Luisita to see how she looked. She seemed as if she were smiling, very serene, but pale. Some cotton had been placed in her nasal passages, because for some time a sore had been there. It had not healed due to her diabetes, and the odor it released was unpleasant. About five in the morning the cotton fell out. I got up to replace the cotton. It was then I realized that the bad odor had been replaced by a fragrance as of fresh roses coming out from her body. There were no flowers around her. Sister Maria Celina Velázquez and I bent over in order to kiss a crucifix she had on her, and as we did this, we confirmed that the aroma of roses came directly from her, and it was so very pleasant! We looked around and realized that all the sisters present noticed this very pleasant fragrance of fresh roses. A young girl, not a sister, who also noticed the fragrance, said, "I am going to go and see where they put the flowers," without knowing that the scent was from Mother Luisita's body.

Mother Socorro, Sister Maria Celina, Sister Eugenia, and Sister Carmen Teresa were witnesses to this incident.

Mother Mary of the Eucharist recalled:

Later that evening, when Sister Maria of the Assumption and I arrived from Atotonilco, they were already having the wake. I still remember what Father Aurelio Vidrio said on that day: "What a remarkable sight! All the sisters are experiencing deep sorrow, but there is no loud wailing." There was an immense line on the way to the cemetery, all her daughters, priests, friends.

On that day, very early, before Mother was placed in the coffin, we were called by order of seniority, and we kissed her forehead. The novices did also. Between eight and nine in the morning, Archbishop José Garibi y Rivera arrived. He prayed over the body and said, "Mother Luisita has left us. And now, I shall see about you sisters whom she entrusted to me." A few days later, he would return to celebrate a funeral Mass for her in the Chapel of Jesus in Atotonilco.

People came by quietly during the day to pay their last respects. They laid their rosaries and medals upon Mother Luisita's body and gazed upon her for the final time. That night when the sisters kept vigil at her bedside, several of them continued to notice the fragrance of roses surrounding Mother Luisita's body. Two Masses were celebrated in that little room the day of her death and two more the next morning before the funeral Mass.

Mother Mary of the Eucharist also recalled that "after the coffin was closed, everyone set out for the Mezquitán Cemetery where Don Sabás Castañeda and his wife, Cuquita, who was Mother Luisita's sister, had a plot. I still remember when we were in the cemetery. Other people were also there to bury their dead, and they left them so as to take their rosaries and touch them to Mother Luisita's coffin and then they kissed them."

Sister Carmen Celina remembered that "the whole community bade her farewell. In twos we approached her and kissed her forehead. We also did this while we were with her in the room where she died. Because I entered on February 11, 1930, what Mother said to me on my entrance day remained engraved in my memory. She told me, 'What a beautiful day you have entered Carmel, the feast of Our Lady of Lourdes. Oh, how I wish this could be the day that I would enter heaven!'"

Mother Luisita also used to say, "Death is to fall into the arms of God." On February 11, 1937, the feast of Our Lady of Lourdes, her desire was fulfilled. At five in the morning, Mother Luisita fell gently into the arms of God.

The bells of San Miguel Arcángel were announcing the morning Angelus.

It was the beginning of a new day.

Afterword

My mission is finished. To me belonged a hidden life.
The Congregation will have a brilliant future.
That does not pertain to me now, but to another person.

—Mother Luisita[152]

Mother Luisita died as quietly as she had lived. She "fell into the arms of God," while lying in a borrowed bed, hiding in a borrowed house. The following day, she was buried in a borrowed grave with the borrowed crown of Sister Catalina still on her head.

Mother Luisita's life and death have not been forgotten. Then and now, people continue to be captivated by her. There is a quality of Mother Luisita that draws them to her. She had a maternal strength with a spiritual dimension that still holds a mysterious appeal.

People long for the same serenity she possessed. A simple way, really—the way of a right relationship with God; the way of faith, hope, and love with complete, utter trust in God's loving providence. During her life, those who had observed her and had spent time with her experienced not only peace but a deep satisfaction.

[152] Queen, *The Doctor's Widow*, 116.

She nourished them on a level they did not even realize—the spiritual level. Some call this quality her spiritual motherhood.

Mother Luisita spoke to God simply, deeply, and constantly, heart to Heart, friend to Friend. Her prayers were not simply directed to Him. No, her prayer was always a conversation with Him.

The amazing thing about Mother Luisita was the fact that she continued this amid revolutions and religious persecutions. People wondered, "How does she maintain such peace and serenity during such troubled times?" Today many are asking the same question.

Archbishop José Gomez of Los Angeles answered this question when he spoke to the Carmelite Sisters of the Most Sacred Heart of Los Angeles in February 2021, on the eighty-fourth anniversary of Mother Luisita's death.

> Sisters, in the life and spirituality of Mother Luisita, you have a beautiful privilege and opportunity in this moment, in this world that is emerging from the pandemic. By your witness of trust in God—by doing your work with serenity and joy, seeking God's holy will in everything and by sharing the life and teachings of Mother Luisita—you can bring people to trust in God again.

In 1938, only one year after Mother Luisita's death, the Carmelite Sisters in California were no longer classified as refugees. That same year, the California Department of Health commended Santa Teresita as "one of the loveliest sanatoria in the United States."[153]

---

[153] Letter from State of California Department of Public Health, October 26, 1938. The name Santa Teresita Rest Home had been changed to Santa Teresita Sanatorium in 1937.

Blessed Pedro Heriz, O.C.D., Mother Luisita's adviser and confidant, was martyred in November 1936 during the Spanish Civil War and beatified on October 13, 2013, by Pope Francis.

Blessed Ezequiel and Blessed Salvador Huerta were martyred on April 3, 1927, after being tortured. They were beatified in 2005 by Pope Benedict XVI. They never divulged the whereabouts of their priest brothers who were Mother Luisita's friends, both mentioned in this book, Fathers José Refugio and Eduardo Huerta, whom the government had wanted to find and kill.

On April 25, 1949, Mother Luisita's community was given the *Decretum Laudis* (Decree of Praise) by the Catholic Church. The *Decretum Laudis* is the official approval that the Holy See grants to institutes of consecrated life and societies of apostolic life in recognition of ecclesiastical institutions of pontifical right—that is, not under the juridiction of the bishop but directly responsible to the Holy See.

On June 18, 1981, in the chapter hall of the cathedral church in Guadalajara, the ceremony of the opening process of the beatification of Mother Luisita took place.

On February 2, 1983, the California province was raised to the status of an autonomous institute of pontifical right with the name the Carmelite Sisters of the Most Sacred Heart of Los Angeles. This decree sealed the Vatican's approval and gave the province the right to depend immediately and exclusively on the Vatican in the matters of internal governance and discipline.

On September 21, 1992, President Carlos Salinas de Gortari of Mexico reestablished full diplomatic relations with the Vatican after a break of more than 130 years, completing a reconciliation based on the government's restoration of legal rights to religious groups earlier in 1992. The government ratified its informal policy of not enforcing most legal controls on religious groups by, among other things, granting religious groups legal status, conceding them limited property rights, and lifting restrictions on the number of priests in the country.

The Mexican people lived under the 1917 constitution for eighty-three years. It was not until the election of Vicente Fox as president of Mexico in 2000 that the constitution's chokehold on the religious practices of the Mexican people finally ended. President Fox stated: "After 1917, Mexico was led by anti-Catholic Freemasons who tried to evoke the anticlerical spirit of popular, indigenous President Benito Juarez of the 1880s. But the military dictators of the 1920s were a lot more savage than Juarez."[154]

On July 1, 2000, Mother Luisita was declared Venerable by Pope Saint John Paul II.

In February 2007, the cause for the beatification and canonization for Servant of God Archbishop Francisco Orozco y Jiménez was opened.

Anacleto González Flores, leader of the Catholic Association of Mexican Youth (ACJM), founder of the magazine *La Palabra*, and founder and president of the Popular Union (UP), was beatified on November 20, 2005 by Pope Benedict XVI.

A new basilica in honor of the Mexican martyrs from Jalisco, el Santuario de los Mártires de Cristo Rey, honors the twenty-five Mexican martyrs who died for their Faith during the Cristiada. Construction began in 2007. The massive shrine is funded solely by the people and businesses in Guadalajara and is being built as donations are received. Its construction has been slow but is steadily progressing.

---

[154] Vincente Fox and Rob Allyn, *Revolution of Hope: The Life, Faith, and Dreams of a Mexican President* (New York: Viking, 2007), 17.

Afterword

Today, Mother Luisita's two communities, the Carmelite Sisters of the Most Sacred Heart of Los Angeles and the Carmelitas del Sagrado Corazón de Mexico, continue to bring God's love to people throughout the Americas and beyond.

Mother Luisita's communities have kept a collection of favors, graces, and healings attributed to her intercession. The members of the de la Peña family continue the tradition of getting together once a year on the feast of Saint Joseph, a tradition begun by Mother Luisita's father, Don Epigmenio de la Peña, and carried on by his children and their descendants. Mother Luisita's remains are located in a side chapel at the motherhouse of the Carmelite Sisters of the Sacred Heart of Mexico in Atotonilco el Alto, Jalisco. People visit this beautiful chapel to pray through her intercession.

Appendices

Appendix A

Mother Luisita's Cause of Beatification and Canonization

The official petition to introduce the Cause of Mother Maria Luisa Josefa of the Most Blessed Sacrament (Mother Luisita) was sent to the chancery of the Archdiocese of Guadalajara on November 11, 1968. Father Finian Monahan, O.C.D., superior general of the Discalced Carmelites, authorized Father Simeón Tomás Fernandez, O.C.D., to be the postulator in charge of the Cause.

At the completion of the preliminary works assigned by the postulator of the Cause and fulfilled under his guidance, the corresponding procedures were initiated in Rome in the Congregation for the Causes of Saints.

During the Synod on the Family in 1980, Cardinal Pietro Palazzini, prefect of the Congregation for the Causes of Saints, in two synodal interventions, mentioned the Servant of God, underlining the introduction of her Cause:

> There are other causes to be introduced, and they concern the Servant of God María Luisa de la Peña Rojas, also Mexican of the Diocese of Guadalajara, Foundress of the Congregation of the Carmelite Sisters of the Sacred Heart (1866-1937). In the world María Luisa de la Peña Rojas

received the Sacrament of Matrimony at 15 years of age. She had no children and together with her husband dedicated herself to the works of charity. After becoming a widow, she joined the Order of Carmel and founded a new Religious Congregation.

On December 12, 1980, the same cardinal prefect signed the decree of the Congregation for the Cause of Saints and gave the *nihil obstat* for the opening of the investigation in the Diocese of Guadalajara, Mexico. On January 26, 1981, His Holiness John Paul II confirmed the response to the Congregation for the Causes of Saints. The postulator of the Cause traveled to Guadalajara, taking the rescript with the faculties of Cardinal José Salazar López of Guadalajara to initiate the process in his archdiocese.

On June 14, 1981, the Edict of Introduction of the Cause was published. It was read at all the Masses in all the parishes of the Archdiocese of Guadalajara and kept in a conspicuous place for the faithful to see for one week. Everything was ready to begin.

On the feast of Corpus Christi, June 18, 1981, in the chapter hall of the cathedral church in Guadalajara, the ceremony of the opening process of the beatification of Mother Luisita took place. The ceremony was private and very simple. Those present were the priests of the tribunal who had been named by the cardinal and his representative, Auxiliary Bishop D. Adolfo Hernández Hurtado. Many of the Carmelite Sisters witnessed this historic moment.

On July 1, 2000, Mother Luisita's heroic virtues were confirmed by the Church, and she was declared Venerable.

On December 14, 2020, the tribunal for the archdiocesan phase of the investigation of a potential miracle through the intercession of Mother Luisita was established in Guadalajara.

On June 28, 2021, the archdiocesan phase by the Archdiocese of Guadalajara of the investigation of the potential miracle was closed. Documents were forwarded to the Vatican dicastery for the Roman Phase of the potential miracle to begin.

Prayer for the Beatification of
Mother María Luisa Josefa of the
Most Blessed Sacrament
(Mother Luisita)

O Jesus in the Holy Eucharist, King and Center of all Hearts, look with merciful love upon the petitions we present to You through the intercession of Your servant, Mother María Luisa Josefa of the Most Blessed Sacrament. (Here mention your petition.)

We humbly beseech You to glorify her who was always such a fervent lover of Your Sacred Heart by granting us these favors if they are for Your greater honor and glory. Amen.

Please report any graces or favors received to the superior general of the Carmelite Sisters.

Superior General
Carmelite Sisters of the Most Sacred Heart of Los Angeles
920 East Alhambra Road, Alhambra, CA 91801
(626) 576-4910
contacts@carmelitesistersocd.com

Appendix B

Affiliation to the Carmelite Order
(English Translation of the Documents)

**Letter to Archbishop Francisco Orozco y Jiménez
asking to be annexed to the Carmelite Order as
Carmelite Sisters of the Third Order of Guadalajara:**

Illustrious and very Reverend Excellency, Doctor and
Teacher, Francisco Orozco:

Guadalajara.

I, Luisa de la Peña, and all the young women who make
up this community, with reverence and respect, and for the
greater honor and glory of God, set forth the following before you, dear Father, that we ardently desire that this house
which for so many years has granted innumerable services
to the people of this town of Atotonilco el Alto, and which
at the present time dedicates itself to the care of the sick
and to providing a home for orphans and education for the
young, be formally joined to some religious institute since
the most fervent wish of each of us is that God grant us to
be professed religious.

The Order to which we are most attracted is the Third
Order of Carmel because it has as its protectress the Most

Holy Virgin Mary, and at the same time this Third Order dedicates itself to the care of the sick, the orphans, and to teaching, as does our community. We humbly beg your Illustrious and Reverend Excellency to deign to see that these your poor daughters be joined to the Third Order of Carmel and that God will grant us the grace to do the good that Your Reverence determines.

May Our Lord guard and keep the life of your Reverence for many years.

Atotonilco el Alto, August 22, 1920

Signed: Maria Luisa Josefa del Santísimo Sacramento

Mother Luisita's request was accompanied by the following recommendation from the pastor of San Miguel Arcángel, Father Macario Velázquez, who had known the community from its beginning.

Recommendation from Father Macario Velásquez, pastor of San Miguel Arcángel in Atotonilco el Alto, Jalisco, Mexico:

I humbly and respectfully allow myself to add my recommendation to the previous request, assuring Your Excellency that all the members of this Community are endowed with great virtues and that with selflessness, through many trials, they have always been dedicated to the services of the sick of the hospital and now lately to the care of orphans and the teaching of children.

I therefore believe, Your Excellency, that formalizing this community will be of great benefit to the people of Atotonilco. It will also be a great help to the pastor and a very purposeful place for many girls who ardently wish to surrender to God's service under the Rule of Life and who are entirely subject to any prerequisites and stipulations of Your Excellency.

May God sustain the life of Your Excellency for many years.

Atotonilco el Alto, August 1920.

I, presbyterer, Macario Velázquez [Rubric]

At the bottom the following note was written:

This petition for the aggregation to the Order of Carmel to the Father General of the Carmelites was dated September 6, 1920.

Archbishop Franciso Orozco y Jiménez's letter to the Carmelite Superior General in Rome asking for affiliation to the Carmelite Order:

In the Archdiocese of Guadalajara, there is a Community in Atotonilco el Alto that ardently desires to be added to the Third Order of the cloistered Carmelites [Tercera Orden Enclaustrada de Nuestra Señora del Carmen]. These religious are dedicated to the sick, orphan care, and teaching. It should be noted that the Community is exemplary because of the selflessness and virtue of all the sisters.

In view of this, I sincerely plead with Your Reverence to grant the aggregation of this community as a Third Order of Discalced Carmelites. Any further information that you request will be provided to Your Reverence, and this Community will be subject to any necessary conditions. I anticipate with confidence Your Reverence's consideration of my request. May our Lord God sustain Your Reverence for many years.

Guadalajara, September 7, 1920.

+ Francisco Orozco y Jiménez,
Archbishop of Guadalajara

Official Document from the Superior General of the Discalced Carmelites affiliating the Sisters of Atotonilco to the Carmelite Order with the name Carmelite Sisters of the Third Order of Guadalajara: Discalced Carmelites of the Blessed Virgin Mary of Mount Carmel

Superior General of the Discalced Carmelite Brothers Order of the Blessed Virgin Mary of Mount Carmel. Prior of same Holy Mount, to the Reverend Mother Superior of the Nuns of the Institute of the Third Cloistered Order of Our Lady of Carmel in Atotonilco el Alto. Archdiocese of Guadalajara in Mexico.

Everlasting Health in the Lord:

We strongly desire to promote all that serves the honor of God, the salvation of souls and the flourishing of our Order. For the same reason, since the Most Reverend Archbishop of Guadalajara has asked us in his letter of September 7, 1920, to add to our Order your Institute, founded in Atotonilco el Alto with the approval and under the dependence of the same Ordinary:

We, knowing that in this Institute the rule is observed, and the habit of the Third Order of Carmel is worn, and having frequently heard with great joy in our hearts of your zeal, mutual charity, and holy emulation with which God is served there, graciously accept your request.

By these letters, we receive and add to our Order of Carmel each and every one of the present and future Sisters of that Institute, those that are in the houses already erected and those that are to be founded in the future.

We also declare that both present and future religious, each and every one, enjoy all the spiritual indulgences and graces that the Roman Pontiffs have granted or will grant to our First and Second Orders, according to the wording of the Decrees of the Holy See.

We pray that the Divine Goodness will always direct you in everything to God's greatest glory and to the good of souls and to infuse in you the true spirit of our Holy Mother Teresa of Jesus.

In faith of which, given in Rome from our General House on October 18, 1920,

Fray Lucas de María Santísima O.C.D.

> Friar Eugene of San Juan de la Cruz.
> Secretary [Rubric]. *Nihil obstat*: Manuel
> Alvarado, Vicar General. [Rubric] A.
> Correa (Secretary).

Appendix C

A Sampling of the Spiritual Maxims of Mother Luisita

A maxim is a short, pithy statement expressing a general truth or rule of conduct. Especially during the religious persecution, most of Mother Luisita's letters were written using the simple code she created. In fact, many people know and love Mother Luisita through her maxims. Here is a sampling of them, taken from *In Love's Safekeeping*.

How beautiful it is to be in the hands of God, searching His Divine gaze in readiness to do whatever He asks. (vol. 1, letter 207)

Form a beautiful and rich tabernacle for Our Lord within your heart and then do not let Him go. In that way, you will always have Him with you. Enter within yourself and, meeting Him, tell Him all your experiences. (vol. 2, letter 12)

The interior soul knows how to work and live and remain recollected at the same time. (vol. 2, 928)

Between Jesus and the soul there flows a current that no one sees and a dialogue no one hears. (vol. 2, 928)

Courage, and find refuge in prayer. (vol. 2, letter 604)

What answer are we supposed to give to our senses when they try to drag us down toward those miserable pleasures that the earth is offering? The answer is this — I was born for greater things. (vol. 2, 936)

Trust in God our Lord. Ask Him to help you every morning before you start your work and have the aspiration "Most Sacred Heart of Jesus, I place my trust in You" constantly in your heart. (vol. 2, letter 279)

Meditate upon the love God our Lord has for you. Be sure to meditate very close to the tabernacle, peacefully and without being apprehensive about this or that because anxiety is bad. It springs from pride. (vol. 1, letter 181)

Love our Blessed Mother very much. Make her your confidante. Talk to her about whatever is worrying you. (vol. 1, letter 59)

Fix your gaze on heaven, not on earthly things, which all pass away like a breath, leaving behind nothing but remorse and sadness like smoke, which disappears with only reality remaining. (vol. 2, letter 626)

May your life be filled with blessings. May they, like the valuable rain, help the seeds of those virtues most pleasing to God our Lord to germinate within your souls, embellishing them. (vol. 2, letter 513)

We should be like immovable rocks so that when the waves do come, they will wash over us, taking away with them all of the dirt that was on us. (vol. 1, letter 114)

The proud soul is like a peacock that spreads its colored tail and struts along. It sees itself from the front view as very beautiful, but if it looks back, it becomes sad because it is ugly. (vol. 1, letter 157)

Just as a drop of water gets absorbed into the ocean and becomes part of it, or as wax taken from different honeycombs is totally melted and then fused into one. That is the way that union with God takes place. (vol. 2, 938)

There can be storms in our souls more terrible than those at sea, but we were told not to fear because God our Lord is with us. In His own time, He will calm the storm, and we will be safe and have peace. (vol. 2, 952)

Don't worry and don't allow yourself to drown in a drop of water. You're all right. You are all right. (vol. 1, letter 206)

Let's rid ourselves of those tinsel-like virtues that shine but at the least touch fall apart. Be as strong as oak trees, not like straw, which is always knocked down by the wind. (vol. 1, letter 176)

How about your soul? Is it taking little steps toward heaven, or is it flying up there? Are you like the eagle or like some little animal preferring the mud of this world? (vol. 1, letter 150)

There is no doubt that at times we ourselves can be our own worst enemies. Maybe it's because our self-love makes us see little mosquitoes as if they were elephants, or perhaps it might be that we lack submission to the will of God. (vol. 1, letter 33)

Do not fear, in spite of the scarecrows that the devil is placing on your path. (vol. 1, letter 3)

We have to be very calm to be able to think.... We shouldn't come to any important decision right away. Learn to let some time pass. Take time to pray. Let the sun go down, and then make the decision the following day or even later. (vol. 1, letter 279)

Don't feel alone—because you're not. Our Lord in the Blessed Sacrament wants to be your Confidant, your Friend, your Consoler. (vol. 1, letter 318)

Always talk things over with our Lord before you take action. (vol. 1, letter 290)

The prayer of one soul alone, united to ... Jesus in the tabernacle, can save the world. (vol. 2, 928)

Appendix D

Mother Luisita according to Those Who Knew Her

A few personal memories of people who knew Mother Luisita:

"Mother Luisita does not 'walk' toward heaven; she soars."
— *Father Daniel Arias, associate pastor at*
San Miguel Arcángel Church in Atotonilco el Alto

"Every time I saw her, I thought of the Blessed Virgin Mary."
— *Agapita Cores Jiménez*

"I always saw her smiling."
— *Maria Luisa Jiménez*

"She reflected God in her whole being."
— *Ignacia Aceves de Miranda*

"What was Mother Luisita to her Carmelite Sisters? She was an angel who spent her whole soul, her whole fortune, and also her body in the congregation she founded, which has given so much glory to God, to the Church, and to society. She was a model religious, an unblemished superior, and a reservoir of tenderness and charity for the whole world. Her main virtues were modesty, abnegation, piety, and constancy, but what was most outstanding about her is that she left in her magnificent work her whole exquisite personality and all the sweetness of her incomparable charity."

—*Father Macario Velázquez Abarca, the pastor in
Atotonilo el Alto who received Mother Luisita's final vows
in 1925 and knew her and the members of the new
community well*

"She was a friend to all the townspeople. They called her 'the heart and soul of Atotonilco.' She was kind to everybody, and each felt especially loved by her. Consequently, Mother was a person whom everyone loved. The sisters used to wrap Mother Luisita in a small white blanket (called a *zarapito*) when she was ill, and she was carried in a small cart [in the early days]. I was then a schoolgirl. Mother's special devotions were a great love for the Most Blessed Sacrament, the Sacred Heart, the Blessed Virgin, Saint Teresa of Jesus, and Saint John of the Cross."

—*Mother Maria de la Divina Eucaristía, who was with
Mother Luisita in the United States and was the first
local superior of Santa Teresita*

"Mother Luisita had a very distinguished personality, just seeing her, one felt respect and at the same time confidence and affection toward her. Many of us felt loved by her, as if that love were only for each one of us personally."

—*Mother Socorro of the Holy Spirit Cholico Rodriguez*

"Mother's joy always seemed to me as a gentle reflection of her pure and upright heart. Her joy was sweet, simple, gentle, modest, never ostentatious or boisterous. Her face reflected sweetness, since this was one of her characteristics. She never raised her

voice. We could say we saw her laugh, but we did not hear her laugh."
    —*Mother Carmen of Jesus, one of the first sisters*
      to come to the United States during the persecution

"Mother Luisita is a saint, but she is in a mold which is not mine."
    —*Archbishop Orozco y Jiménez*

"In 1928, I traveled to the United States to join the sisters working at Saint Mary's College. The work there was very hard, and we broke many dishes. They [the Christian Brothers] even had to ask Mother to tell us not to break so many, but she said, 'Poor sisters, they get so tired. Let them take it out of our salary.' She was very considerate, and she suffered for her daughters in Mexico, and those in the United States."
    —*Sister Maria del Rosario, whose photograph was taken*
      during the smallpox epidemic and shown in the newspapers

"Every day after breakfast she would go to the chapel to make her hour of adoration before the Blessed Sacrament, and she used to say, 'From this little while in which I am with His Divine Majesty, I draw the strength necessary to endure the sufferings of the present day.' She would enjoy hearing music during these hours and had an innate affinity to this. When she was on her way to the chapel, she frequently called me to tell me not to forget my piano practice. I knew well what she wanted, and after a few minutes of technical practice, I would carry out her wish, playing classical music, which was her preference.

"This love for music she communicated to several of her daughters, and she implemented practices so that all those who were naturally talented or disposed would take lessons. She looked for the best teachers for these sisters. During the recreations, she would ask that there be singing and playing, but she did not allow dance music. At times when she was tired or weary, she would say to me, 'My daughter, sing something that will lift the soul to God.'"

—*Mother Elena de la Cruz, one of the sisters sent by*
Father Pedro Heriz to teach in the early days of the community

"During the revolution, I [was assigned] to Atotonilco. We would go to see Mother Luisita and the sisters. Our Mother was in hiding, sometimes alone or with Mother Elena de la Cruz. 'Oh, my daughter,' she would say, 'this is beyond my strength.' Fear of the persecution was very intense, very great, very great. Again, she would repeat: 'My daughter, I expose you to danger. What if the troops will take one of our little sisters?'

"From Saint Mary's I came to Los Angeles, but only just for the time it took for me to prepare to return to Mexico. When I was there, just about ready to return to Mexico, I had engraved in my mind the poverty of that little house located in front of Saint Patrick's Church, which by then already belonged to the community. I almost went crazy there, because we were in front of an emergency center, and there was noise all night long; I could not sleep. At Saint Patrick's, we did the same kind of mission work as we did in Long Beach. Soon after I left, it became a boarding school. Mother recommended we pray much in order to be able to suffer whatever would come upon us."

—*Sister Maria Refugio of the Sacred Heart, who arrived*
with the second group of Sisters to the United States in 1927

"In Long Beach, there was a church in honor of Our Lady of Guadalupe, especially for the Mexican people. When more sisters arrived, they dedicated themselves to serve in this mission church. They used to call us the exiled Mexican sisters. Within six months of this apostolate in the mission church, the Protestant church building had become a laundromat because it had been abandoned by the people. Soon after, the proposal came to Mother to take us to work at Saint Mary's. We did, but then Mother used to cry at seeing us work so hard."

— *Sister Teresa of Jesus, Mother Luisita's second cousin,*
who was one of the original three sisters to come to the
United States as a refugee

"During the Cristeros' revolution, I had the good fortune to be with her in hiding, with four other sisters. We were 'walled in' in Don Jesús Camacho's house; and for one hour, each one of us had to stand with arms extended in prayer, so that the Cristeros would win. When it was my turn, I lowered my arms very soon. Then Mother Elena told me to lift them up again, and Mother Luisita said to me, 'My daughter, I will take your place. Sit down,' and I sat down. At that time, I did not understand that this was great charity and kindness on her part, but now I see that it was a heroic charity.

"What can I say of her angelic purity? One could see in her eyes the purity of her soul. And now I can say, as did Saint John the Evangelist, 'She, who speaks, has seen it and gives testimony to the truth.' Mother Luisita's motto was 'Unite the apostolate to prayer.' She taught by example. She suffered in silence. She loved Christ and her brethren."

— *Sister Margarita of Christ, one of the refugee*
sisters in the United States

"In Mexico, we were very poor, and we did not have any light. One night, I told [Mother Luisita] that I had not slept because I was very much afraid. She prepared some small candles and a match and lighter, and she spent the whole night holding a small wire with the match lighter, which gave out light. This she did for my sake. It seems to me that this could not have been done by anyone but a saint. On another occasion, when I arrived from school, she was writing at a little table. I sat down next to her on a small floor mat, and as I leaned on her knees, I fell asleep. When I woke up, I realized that all the sisters were in the chapel, so I told her. She told me that she had remained still so as not to wake me up. This seemed to me to be a very maternal act."

— *Sister Ines of Jesus, one of the refugee sisters in the United States*

"Once [Mother Luisita] asked the sister cook, 'For whom do you prepare the meals? Is it not true that you do so for the spouses of Christ?' In this way, she admonished Sister because out of carelessness or whatever the cause, the food was not well cooked, and it was partially burnt. The sister was troubled and asked pardon. Mother saw to it that she would reflect and correct what she needed to do. When the sister confessed that she had been tired of being in the kitchen and that she had gone to Our Lord, Our Mother sent Sister to her cell, and she herself continued cooking the rest of that day so Sister could rest. That is the way she would correct us, in such a way that we would grow in humility and never do it again.

"One time I saw her looking very tired and the Community bell was ringing. I told her, 'Rest. Lie down, Mother. I will pray for you.' She answered, 'Away with you, Satan, I can still do it.'"

— *Sister Maria Ana de la Sagrada Familia*

"One day we went to spend the day with her. When we shared with her that we had not slept that night, immediately, she sent us to bed and saw to it that no one made any noise."

— *Sister Josefa de Cristo Anguiano*

"When she saw me, she said, 'Don't you have a little coat or shawl?' It was a cold afternoon with a bit of rain coming. I answered that I did not have any. She then took off her woolen shawl that she was covered with, but since it was a very large one, she folded it in half and then put it on me saying, 'Yes, it fits you well. Bring me those scissors and cut it.' I resisted; I did not want to cut her shawl, and besides, it was very pretty. But she repeated, 'Cut it quickly.' There was nothing I could do but to cut it. I did so, and she herself covered me with the half of the shawl, and she put away the other half and later she gave it to another sister."

—*Sister Maria Estela De Los Angeles Custodios Carrillo*

Appendix E

Vignettes from Catholic Life
By Fred W. Williams

Editor's note: This is one in a series of word pictures on religious life and places by one of the best-known feature writers in the West.

A ray of sunshine, filtering through a crack in the curtain penetrates the cool shadows of the improvised chapel of the Carmelites at old St. Mary's College in Oakland and forms a halo above the figure of the Christ on the Crucifix above the altar.

On its way to the Cross, it lingers caressingly on a solitary figure in the brown habit of Carmel that kneels many hours in prayer.

This is Maria Luisa, the Mother General of the exiled nuns of the Little Flower from Mexico.

The Sisters at the door to the chapel tell you the Mother General is not well, that she has not been well for a long time, ever since in fact, the Holy Mother Church went under the iron heel of bitter persecution in Mexico.

Letters reach her every day. They are in Spanish, and they come from the faithful in the homeland. They tell of many things that sadden her heart, of the murder and torture of friends, of the striking down of good priests, so many of them, of the robbing of the Church and the scattering of her flocks.

Downstairs a little group of nuns place flowers at the feet of a statue of St. John Baptiste de la Salle, he who founded the Christian Brothers in the seventeenth century, who carried the light of education into the cellars and tenements of the poor.

They are so grateful to the Christian Brothers, these good nuns, for the Christian Brothers have been so good to them. When all the world, it seemed, had turned against them, when they were upon the streets and without homes, the Christian Brothers did a splendid, gracious thing. They offered a haven from the conflict; they are building them a convent with a cloistered garden at Moraga, site of the new St. Mary's.

And so, each day they place fresh flowers at the feet of the statue of St. John Baptiste de la Salle, whose sons came to their aid in the answer to their prayers.

They pray for their Church now in Mexico, these little nuns, and for their Catholic countrymen and for their beloved Mother General, whose heart is so heavy and who, hour upon hour, like a statue carved in stone, kneels before the Blessed Sacrament.

Maria Luisa comes slowly down the stairs. She has finished with her prayers. Her nuns put forth willing hands to help her. Though not old, she has become feeble.

A gracious lady. A Spanish aristocrat. A woman who must have been a great beauty in her youth. Her eyes are big and brown and alight with strange fires. Now and then a troubled shadow quenches them. When she smiles, which is seldom, her whole face brightens and the vista of years [is] swept away.

Her eyes look on and past you. You sense she sees something you do not. Those eyes, so wondrous in their penetration, have looked upon tragedy and yet much happiness. Reverently you touch the hand she extends.

The Mother General does not speak English, but through a nun who acts as interpreter, she tells you something of her sorrows and of her unhappy land in which the Church lies so sorely wounded.

Her heart bleeds for the priests in Mexico, the priests who remained behind, who are cut down in their acts of mercy by the ruthless gunmen of "The Butcher," and who die with prayers of forgiveness for their murderers.

A bell tinkles softly against the coming night and summons the exiles of the Little Flower to Benediction. They gather their habits closely about them and silently, by twos, leave for the chapel.

Later in the evening, when all is silent about the deserted college building, golden voices rise from the Chapel singing the Laudate Dominum.[155]

---

[155] Fred V. Williams, "Carmelites Grateful for St. Mary's Offer," *San Francisco Monitor*, May 12 and June 3, 1928.

Timeline of Venerable Maria Luisa Josefa of the Most Blessed Sacrament (Luisa de la Peña Navarro)

July 15, 1859   Don Epigmenio de la Peña, a widower, and Maria Luisa Navarro are married in the town of Capilla de Guadalupe. They make Saint Joseph the patron of their new home.

Two children, Maria Magdalena Clotilde de Jesus and Maria Clotilde de Jesus, later die in childhood.

June 21, 1866   Luisa de la Peña, the third child and first to survive, is born in Atotonilco el Alto, Jalisco, Mexico. It is her mother's birthday.

Despite fears that she will not survive, the child clings to her fragile hold on life.

June 27, 1866   Luisa is baptized in the parish church of San Miguel in Atotonilco el Alto, Jalisco, Mexico.

She is given the name Luisa to honor Saint Aloysius Gonzaga, on whose feast day she was born, and also to honor her mother, who shares the same name and birthday. Her godparents are Don Manuel Rojas and Doña Rafaela de la Peña.

June 1874	Luisa receives Confirmation during the pastoral visit of Archbishop Pedro Loza y Pardavé, archbishop of Guadalajara. The exact date is unknown.
February 9, 1882	Pascual Rojas and Luisa marry.
January 6, 1892	Pascual and Luisa open the little Hospital of the Sacred Heart in Atotonilco el Alto, Jalisco, to serve the poor.
April 3, 1896	Pascual Rojas dies on Good Friday. In his last hours, he tells Maria Luisa that she can now follow her desire to become a religious. In the same year, she applies at the Visitation convent but is refused due to health reasons. Luisa is left a widow at the age of twenty-nine.
March 3, 1904	Luisa enters Saint Teresa Carmel in Guadalajara. She remains there three months and is imbued with the Carmelite spirit.
June 26, 1904	After prayer and in consultation with the archbishop, Luisa leaves the cloister to return to Sacred Heart Hospital, which has fallen into neglect and disrepair during her absence.
October 4, 1904	Together with other companions, Luisa prays for discernment to know God's will. Father Arcadio Medrano seeks the approval of the archbishop for them to begin living a regular community life.
December 24, 1904	Luisa and six companions begin life in community with a simple ceremony at which Father Arcadio Medrano presides.

December 24, 1905	For the first time, Mother Luisita and companions make a promise to the Sacred Heart of Jesus to keep poverty, chastity, and obedience for one year and to provide for the sick and for children.
March 1909	Archbishop José de Jesus Ortiz gives Mother Luisita and companions their first rule of life.
February 1910	At the request of the archbishop, Mother Luisita and companions begin the unification process with the Sisters of Perpetual Adoration.
1910	Beginning of the Mexican Revolution. From this time on, there are changes of power and civil war in Mexico.
June 19, 1912	Archbishop José de Jesus Ortiz dies. The annexation process comes to a halt.
May 22, 1913	The new archbishop, Francisco Orozco y Jiménez, asks the community to merge with the Sister Servants of the Blessed Sacrament. Twenty Sisters leave to join the Sister Servants. Mother Luisita leaves with the last group on July 22.
September 24, 1913	Luisa makes her novitiate in a private home due to dispersal of religious because of fear of arrest. She receives the name Sister Juana Francisca de Chantal of the Blessed Sacrament, after Saint Jane France de Chantal, who was also a widow and a religious foundress.
1914–1918	World War I. Persecution of the Church in Mexico begins again.

March 1915	Sister Juana Francisca de Chantal of the Blessed Sacrament makes her first profession of vows as a Sister Servant of the Blessed Sacrament.
May 22, 1917	Archbishop Orozco y Jiménez authorizes Sister Juana Francisca de Chantal, and any of her companions who so desire, to separate from the Servants of the Blessed Sacrament and return to Atotonilco to administer the Hospital of the Sacred Heart, which has again fallen into neglect and disrepair without Luisa's leadership.
	Three of the original twenty companions return with Luisa. They are dispensed from their vows. Two other sisters who had previously left the Sister Servants of the Blessed Sacrament again join her when she returns to Atotonilco. More women begin to join her in Atotonilco.
1917	Mexico's new constitution is enacted. Attack on the Church is renewed.
November 19, 1919	Mother Luisita, as she is now called, and companions open an orphanage for girls in Atotonilco. She also opens the "Little School of the Spelling Book" and gives reading and writing classes. A Sunday school for young girls for their Christian formation is also established.
	The sisters wear a black dress with pleats and a black translucent veil. They also wear a black cape with a collar and a crucifix with a chain.

September 7, 1920	Archbishop Francisco Orozco y Jiménez makes a pastoral visit to Atotonilco. While there, he tells Mother Luisita that the Holy Father does not want a proliferation of new religious communities and that they must annex themselves to an existing religious congregation.
	Mother Luisita and her companions with the blessing of Archbishop Orozco y Jiménez petition Rome for affiliation to the Carmelite Order.
December 1920	Archbishop Orozco informs Mother Luisita that the official Document of Affiliation to the Carmelite Order has been received. It is dated October 18, 1920.
February 2, 1921	Mother Luisita and her twelve companions begin living the Carmelite Rule. A Mass of Thanksgiving is offered by Reverend Macario Velázquez. Mother Luisita is fifty-four years of age.
April 1, 1921	Mother Luisita and six sisters receive the Carmelite habit in the morning and make their vows in the afternoon of the same day.
	Mother's religious name is now Maria Luisa Josefa of the Blessed Sacrament.
	Archbishop Orozco y Jiménez appoints Mother Luisita the first superior general of the congregation.
May 25, 1922	Archbishop Orozco y Jiménez grants permission to open the novitiate and to receive the first postulants.

December 1922	Mother Luisita accompanies the sisters to the first new foundation in Guadalajara, which is established amid great poverty.
May 1923	Mother Isabel Rioseco, R.F.R., a Franciscan Religious of Our Lady of Refuge, arrives to form the first novices by order of the archbishop. She remains exactly one year.
September 24, 1924	Mother Luisita accompanies sisters to the second foundation of the House of Saint Francis of Assisi in Tepatitlán.
	Persecution of the Church in Mexico continues.
April 1, 1925	Mother Luisita and first group of sisters make their final vows. The archbishop dispenses with the fifth year of temporary vows.
May 1926	Mother Luisita accompanies sisters to the new foundation of Ocotlán, Jalisco.
July 19, 1926	Archbishop Francisco Orozco y Jiménez signs a document stating that all religious should immediately return to their homes or remain hidden in the house of some pious family.
July 31, 1926	All Catholic churches in Mexico are closed by the Catholic bishops. President Plutarco Elías Calles issues his anticlerical laws. Persecution of the Church escalates, and numerous priests, religious, and laypeople give their lives to defend the Faith.
January 1, 1927	The Cristero Uprising begins in Mexico.

June 20, 1927   Mother Luisita, feeling the need of safeguarding the vocations of her religious daughters, leaves her beloved Mexico in disguise and comes to the United States. Her companions are Sister Teresa of Jesus Navarro and Sister Margarita Maria of the Sacred Heart Hernandez. They travel by train. Sister Margarita Maria is the only one who knows English, and this knowledge is very limited.

    The following day marks Mother Luisita's sixty-first birthday. Sister Margarita Maria is twenty-four years old and has been professed for slightly less than two years. Sister Teresa is forty years old.

June 23, 1927   Mother Luisita and companions cross the border into the United States and arrive in Nogales, Arizona.

    Mother Luisita asks her companions to kneel with her in the Pullman car and recite the Te Deum in thanksgiving that they are now in a free country.

June 24, 1927   Mother Luisita and her companions arrive in the Archdiocese of Los Angeles on the feast of the Sacred Heart of Jesus. Arrangements are made with the Immaculate Heart Sisters on Green Street in Los Angeles to provide hospitality.

August 3, 1927   Mother Luisita and her companions move to Long Beach, California, and are welcomed into Holy Innocents Parish by Father Francis C. Ott, the pastor.

Mrs. Nicolasa Flores opens her home to the sisters, who are from her native state of Jalisco. The sisters accept the gracious hospitality at this home at 1851 Locust Street in Long Beach.

September 12, 1927

Five sisters arrive from Mexico. Mother Luisita and companions are provided with a large house on Cedar Avenue in Long Beach. A third house is later acquired on Chestnut Avenue in Long Beach.

In March, May, and August, additional sisters arrive in the archdiocese until there are more than thirty sisters.

1928

The sisters do catechetical work among their fellow refugees. They also take the parish census, teach Spanish, and establish sewing circles for women. They operate a secondhand store in order to support themselves.

Twenty sisters begin two years of domestic service at Saint Mary's College in Moraga, California.

Mother Luisita remains at Saint Mary's in Moraga for eight months and shares the austerity of the life with her sisters.

June 29, 1929

The churches in Mexico are reopened.

August 28, 1929

The sisters who remained at Holy Innocents Parish in Long Beach move to Saint Patrick's Parish in Los Angeles, where Father Francis Ott has been transferred as pastor.

August 29, 1929	Mother Luisita is present for the move from Long Beach to Saint Patrick's Parish.
	The sisters secure a $3,500 bank loan to move an abandoned convent to an empty lot in Saint Patrick's Parish. Archbishop John J. Cantwell cosigns the bank note as security for its payment.
1929	Mother Luisita establishes an Association of Christian Mothers and a group of young women known later as the Youth of Catholic Mexican Women.
	The sisters also begin to accept young girls as boarding students, and the foundations of the future Little Flower Missionary House are laid.
October 24, 1929	Mother Luisita returns to Mexico.
	The novitiate in Mexico is reopened in Guadalajara.
December 24, 1929	The community quietly celebrates the silver jubilee of its founding.
January 1930	Mother Luisita is summoned to return to the United States by Archbishop Orozco y Jiménez, who is living in exile in Los Angeles.
May 1930	Mother Luisita returns to Mexico, where she lives in dire poverty, moving from house to house.
August 2, 1930	Santa Teresita Sanatorium is opened in Duarte, California, for the care of girls with tuberculosis.

August 10, 1930	Mother Luisita is confirmed as superior general of the congregation.
	The constitutions and ceremonial of the congregation are approved by the Archdiocese of Guadalajara.
June–August 1932	Mother Luisita again visits her religious sisters in the United States.
October 22, 1932	Five sisters are arrested by the government in Mexico, causing Mother Luisita severe anguish.
October 24, 1932	An American province of Saint Raphael and novitiate are established in Los Angeles. Mother Luisita expresses in her letters her hope that the sisters will be able to establish permanent residence in the United States so as no longer to be considered refugees.
	In Mexico the persecution of the Church continues. Mother and the sisters continually change residences, live in constant danger, and suffer from hunger, cold, and insecurity.
February 1933	Mother Luisita establishes the foundation in Mexico City near the Basilica of Our Lady of Guadalupe. She suffers a serious illness that leaves her with the kidney disease that will ultimately cause her death.
December 22, 1934	At this time, Mother Luisita writes her last will and testament to the community.

April–August 1935	Mother Luisita makes her last visit to the sisters in the United States.
February 18, 1936	Archbishop Francisco Orozco y Jiménez dies. He is succeeded by Archbishop José Garibi y Rivera.
March 19, 1936	Mother Luisita establishes the foundation in Jamay for the education of children.
June 11, 1936	Mother Luisita establishes the foundation in Mexticacán for the education of children.
July 1936	At a General Chapter, Mother Luisita is again elected superior general. She pleads to be left without a position, but she is again reelected and confirmed in office by the new archbishop, José Garibi y Rivera, who at that time suppresses the California province of Saint Raphael.
August 24, 1936	Mother Luisita establishes the foundation in Santo Tomás de los Plátanos. Although Mother is not able to go herself to the foundation, she continues to guide and direct the new foundation through her letters and counsel.
November 1936	An official letter from the Chancery Office in November 1936 informs the sisters of the danger of being discovered by the government. The sisters are ordered to leave the convent immediately and disperse into houses of trustworthy friends or their own families.
	Mother Luisita moves to the house on Garibaldi Street, which is her last earthly home.

February 11, 1937	Mother Maria Luisa Josefa of the Most Blessed Sacrament enters into eternal life shortly before 5:00 a.m.
	Before she loses consciousness, she blesses the congregation. She receives a blessing with the Blessed Sacrament moments before her death.
	Throughout the day, the sisters arrive to bid farewell to their beloved Mother. People from the town come to the convent to honor the body of Mother Luisita. They touch rosaries, medals, and other objects to her body. They pray for help through her intercession.
February 12, 1937	His Excellency José Garibi y Rivera blesses the grave and says the ritual prayers. The body of Mother Luisita is laid to rest in the Cemetery of Mezquitan in Guadalajara.
December 24, 1941	The remains of Mother Luisita are removed clandestinely due to the sociopolitical circumstances of the country. They are taken to Atotonilco el Alto and placed in Calvary Chapel, at the motherhouse of the congregation. The sisters wish to ensure that they will always have their beloved foundress among them.
April 25, 1949	The Holy See grants the "Decree of Praise" to the Congregation.
June 22, 1966	The remains of Mother Luisita are again exhumed and transferred to a new tomb under the main altar of Calvary Chapel in Atotonilco.

July–August 1968	During the Special Chapter of the congregation, after consultation with all of the members of the congregation, the name of the congregation is changed from "Carmelite Sisters of the Third Order of Guadalajara" to "Carmelite Sisters of the Sacred Heart."
February 2, 1976	Mother Elisa Graciela, superior general, appoints Father Simeón Tomás Fernandez, O.C.D., general postulator of the Discalced Carmelite Order, as postulator for the Cause of Mother Maria Luisa of the Most Blessed Sacrament.
December 12, 1980	The cardinal prefect for the Congregation for the Causes of Saints, Cardinal Palazzini, signs the decree of the Congregation for the Causes of Saints, which gave the *nihil obstat* for the beginning of the process in the Archdiocese of Guadalajara.
January 26, 1981	His Holiness John Paul II grants confirmation of the response of the Congregation for the Causes of Saints.
June 18, 1981	On the solemnity of Corpus Christi, in the chapter hall of the Cathedral of Guadalajara, the ceremony of the official opening of the Cognitive (Informative) Process for the beatification of Mother Luisita takes place.

February 2, 1983	With ecclesial approval, the Province of the Sacred Heart in California separates from the Carmelite Sisters of the Sacred Heart in Mexico and, at the personal decision of Pope John Paul II, becomes an autonomous pontifical congregation, the Carmelite Sisters of the Most Sacred Heart of Los Angeles.
July 3, 1984	The last session of the Cognitive Process of the beatification of Mother Luisita is held to close this stage, which has lasted three years.
July 1, 2000	Mother Luisita is declared Venerable by Pope Saint John Paul II.
December 14, 2020	The tribunal of the Archdiocesan Phase of Inquiry into a potential miracle through the intercession of Mother Luisita opens in Guadalajara.
June 28, 2021	The Guadalajara Archdiocesan tribunal concludes, and the documents are forwarded to the Vatican for the Roman Phase of Inquiry into the potential miracle through the intercession of Mother Luisita.

Carmelite Sisters
of the Most Sacred Heart of Los Angeles

*To stand in the Presence of the Living God, and with Mary,
to make known to the world the love of the Sacred Heart of Jesus.*

From our own life of prayer that flows into our service of the whole person,
we accompany others through all stages of life through education, retreats
and healthcare sharing the personal love of the Sacred Heart of Jesus
with those entrusted to our care.

For more information, visit us at **carmelitesistersocd.com**

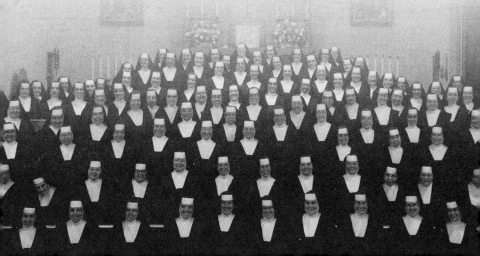

Where We Serve

RETREATS

Sacred Heart Retreat House
Drawing closer to the heart of Jesus
920 E. Alhambra Rd., Alhambra, CA 91801
Toll Free: (866) 598-4389 | (626) 289-1353
www.sacredheartretreathouse.com

HEALTHCARE

Sponsored by the Carmelite Sisters

Santa Teresita
A Neighborhood of Care

Assisted Living – Skilled Nursing Rehabilitation
819 Buena Vista Street
Duarte, CA 91010
(626) 408-7802
www.santa-teresita.org
contact@santateresitainc.com

Marycrest Manor
At the Service of the Family for LIFE

Skilled Nursing & Rehabilitation Community
10664 St. James Drive
Culver City, CA 90230
(310) 838-2778
www.marycrestculvercity.com

EDUCATION

ARCHDIOCESAN SCHOOLS
Staffed by the Carmelite Sisters

St. Philomena School
21832 S. Main Street
Carson, CA 90745
stphilomenaschool.org
(310) 835-4827

Holy Innocents School
2500 Pacific Avenue
Long Beach, CA 90806
lbcatholicschool.com
(562) 424-1018

Sacred Heart School
43775 Deep Canyon Road
Palm Desert, CA 92260
sacredheartpalmdesert.com/school
(760) 346-3513

St. Theresa School
2701 Indian Mound Trail
Coral Gables, FL 33134
stscg.org | (305) 446-1738

Sts. Peter and Paul School
3920 Pierce Street
Wheat Ridge, CO 80033
sppscatholic.com | (303) 424-0402

Archbishop Coleman F. Carroll High School
10300 SW 167 Avenue
Miami, FL 33196
colemancarroll.org | (305) 388-6700

Bibliography

Arquieta, Sister Piedad of Jesus, O.C.D. Interview with author. Alhambra, California, November 24, 1997.

Bailey, David C., ¡Viva Cristo Rey!: The Cristero Rebellion and the Church-State Conflict in Mexico. Austin: University of Texas Press, 1974.

Bartoli, Lucia. Interview with author. Duarte, California, September 25, 2016.

Boudinhon, A. "Canon Law." Catholic Encyclopedia. New York: Robert Appleton, 1910. http://www.newadvent.org/cathen/09056a.htm.

Brenner, Anita. The Wind That Swept Mexico. Austin: University of Texas Press, 1971.

Buchenau, Jürgen, and William H. Beezley, eds. State Governors in the Mexican Revolution, 1910–1952: Portraits in Conflict, Courage and Corruption. Lanham, MD: Rowman and Littlefield, 2009.

Caravacci, Ariadne Katherine. Loving Kindness. Alhambra, CA: Carmelite Sisters' Printing, 1983.

Carmel of Buffalo. Love Can Do All: 75th Edition Commemorative Booklet of the Carmel of Buffalo. New York, 1995.

Carmelite Sisters of the Most Sacred Heart of Los Angeles. *Community Hymnbook of the Carmelite Sisters of the Most Sacred Heart of Los Angeles*. Alhambra, CA: Carmelite Sisters' Printing, 2013.

Coderre, Sister Mary Jeanne, O.C.D. "Mother Luisita: The Marriage Years." *Carmelite Sisters Newsletter* 1, no. 3 (June 21, 2003). Revised in 2018.

——. "Mother Luisita: The Final Journey—The Death of Mother Luisita." *Carmelite Sisters Newsletter* 1, no. 13 (2003). Revised in 2018.

Colbert, Helenita. *The Flower of Guadalajara*. Alhambra, CA: Carmelite Sisters' Printing, 1956.

——. *To Love Me in Truth: Mother María Luisa Josefa of the Most Blessed Sacrament*. Alhambra, CA: Carmelite Sisters' Printing, 1987.

Congregation for Institutes of Consecrated Life and for Societies of Apostolic Life. *Verbi Sponsa: Instruction on the Contemplative Life and on the Enclosure of Nuns* (May 13, 1999).

Constitutions of the Carmelite Sisters of the Most Sacred Heart of Los Angeles. Alhambra, CA: Archives of the Carmelite Sisters of the Most Sacred Heart of Los Angeles, 1987.

Curley, Robert. *Citizens and Believers: Religion and Politics in Revolutionary Jalisco*. Albuquerque: University of New Mexico Press, 2018.

De la Cruz, Jaime, O.C.D. *A Zaga de Su Huella*. Mexico: Los Talleres Graficos de La Editorial Helio-México, S.A., 1961.

De la Peña, Carlos Hector. *Biografía de Mi Muy Amada Tía, Luisa Josefa del Santísimo Sacramento*. Guadalajara, 1945.

——. *A Biography of My Beloved Aunt*. Translated by Sister Mary Gonzaga Martinez, O.C.D. Alhambra, CA: Carmelite Sisters' Printing, 2005.

Early History of the Carmelite Sisters of the Most Sacred Heart of Los Angeles: 1927–1937. Compiled by Sister Mary Jeanne Coderre, O.C.D. Alhambra, CA: Archives of Carmelite Sisters of the Most Sacred Heart of Los Angeles, 2002.

Echevarria, Antonio Unzueta. *Beato Pedro De San Elías: Biografía y Espistolario.* Vitoria-Gasteiz: Ediciones El Carmen, 2005.

Fahey, Denis, C.S.Sp. "Calles Is Supported by the U.S. and Russia." Excerpt from chap. 5 of *Secret Societies and the Kingship of Christ.* 1927. Tradition in Action. https://www.traditioninaction.org/History/G_017_Fahey_2.html.

Federal Constitution of the United Mexican States (1824). University of Texas at Austin. Tarlton Law Library's Jamail Center for Legal Research. Last updated January 29, 2020. https://tarlton.law.utexas.edu/c.php?g=813224.

Fox, Vicente, and Rob Allyn. *Revolution of Hope: The Life, Faith, and Dreams of a President.* New York: Viking, 2007.

Heath, Earl. *75 Years of Progress: An Historical Sketch of the Southern Pacific.* Transcribed and edited by Bruce C. Cooper. San Francisco: Southern Pacific Bureau, 1946.

Hernández, Sister María Victoria, O.P. *Ministry Under Fire: The First Foundations of Mexico Researched and Compiled.* Mission San Jose, CA: Dominican Sisters' Printing, 2002.

Horvack, Marian, Ph.D. "Catholic Funeral Etiquette, Part 3: The Mourning Period." Tradition in Action, August 6, 2008. https://www.traditioninaction.org/Cultural/A048cp Civility_Funeral_3.htm.

Inasmuch as Ye Have Done It unto One of the Least of These. Duarte, CA: Santa Teresita Guild, 1948.

Joseph, Harriet Denise. "Church and State in Mexico from Calles to Cárdenes, 1924–1938." Ph.D. diss., North Texas State

University, 1976. https://digital.library.unt.edu/ark:/67531/metadc500405/m1/1/.

Kelley, Most Reverend Francis Clement. *Blood-Drenched Altars: A Catholic Commentary on the History of Mexico.* Rockford, IL: TAN Books, 1987.

Kennedy, Sister Timothy Marie, O.C.D., ed. *In Love's Safekeeping: The Letters and Spiritual Writings of Mother María Luisa Josefa of the Most Blessed Sacrament.* 2 vols. Alhambra, CA: Carmelite Sisters' Printing, 1999.

————. *In the Face of Darkness: The Heroic Life and Holy Death of Mother Luisita.* Manchester, NH: Sophia Institute Press, 2019.

Kenny, Michael, S.J. *No God Next Door.* New York: William J. Hirten, 1935.

Knights of Columbus. *For Greater Glory Study Guide.* www.kofc.org/en/resources/college-programs/10559-for-greater-glory-study-guide.pdf.

Laurentius, J. "Diocesan Chancery." *Catholic Encyclopedia.* New York: Robert Appleton, 1908. http://www.newadvent.org/cathen/04798c.htm.

Lelibre, Olivier. "The Cristeros: 20th-Century Mexico's Catholic Uprising." *Angelus* 25, no. 1 (January 2002). http://www.angelusonline.org/index.php?section=articles&subsection=show_article&article_id=2119.

Markel, Howard, and Alexandra Minna Stern. "The Foreignness of Germs: The Persistent Association of Immigrants and Disease in American Society." *Milbank Quarterly* 80, no. 4 (January 2002): 757–788. doi:10.1111/1468-0009.00030.

Mary of Jesus, O.C.D. *The Dove with the Scarlet Collar.* Australia: Treasure of Carmel Publications, 2013.

Mecham, J. Lloyd. *Church and State in Latin America: A History of Politico-Ecclesiastical Relations.* Chapel Hill: University of North Carolina Press, 1934.

Memorial Book of the 400th Anniversary of Founding of Atotonilco. Atotonilco, Jalisco, 1951.

"Mexican Survivors Tell Train Horrors." *New York Times*, April 22, 1927. https://www.nytimes.com/1927/04/22/archives/mexican-survivors-tell-train-horrors-nervetorn-refugees-in-capital.html?searchResultPosition=1.

Meyer, Jean A. *The Cristiada: El Conflicto Entre el Estado y La Iglesia.* Delegación Coyoacán, Mexico: FCE-Clío, 2012.

———. *The Cristiada: The Mexican People's War for Religious Liberty.* New York: Square One Publishers, 2013.

———. *The Cristero Rebellion: The Mexican People between Church and State, 1926–1929.* Cambridge, UK: Cambridge University Press, 1976.

Morales, Donna S., and John P. Schmall. *The History of Jalisco.* Houston: Houston Institute for Culture, 2004.

Neumayr, George. "The 'Private Idea' of Parental Rights." *Crisis Magazine*, April 11, 2013. https://www.crisismagazine.com/2013/the-private-idea-of-parental-rights.

New World Encyclopedia. S.v. "Anti-clericalism." http://www.newworldencyclopedia.org/entry/Anti-clericalism.

"100 Years after the Pandemic That Killed 300,000 Mexicans." *Puerta Vallarta Daily News*, September 1, 2018. https://www.vallartadaily.com/100-years-after-the-pandemic-that-killed-300000-Mexicans/.

Original Letters of Father José Refugio Huerta to Mother Luisita. Compiled by Sister Mary Jeanne Coderre, O.C.D. Alhambra, CA: Archives of the Carmelite Sisters of the Most Sacred Heart of Los Angeles, 2002.

Original Letters of Father Pedro Heriz, O.C.D., to Mother Luisita. Compiled by Sister Mary Jeanne Coderre, O.C.D. Alhambra, CA: Archives of the Carmelite Sisters of the Most Sacred Heart of Los Angeles, 2001.

Original Letters to Mother Luisita from Brother Gregory Mallon, F.S.C., and Brother Ralph McKeever, F.S.C. Compiled by Sister Mary Jeanne Coderre. Alhambra, CA: Archives of the Carmelite Sisters of the Most Sacred Heart of Los Angeles.

Orozco y Jiménez, Right Reverend Francisco. "Why I Became an Exile." *Little Flower Magazine,* 1930.

Orozco Mosqueda, Fray José de Jesus, O.C.D. *Rostro de Bondad: Biografía de la madre María Luisa de la Peña Navarro.* Guadalajara: Amate Editorial, 2021.

"PablotheMexican." "Patroness of Our Seminary: Mother Mary Elias of the Blessed Sacrament, OCD (1879–1943)." Our Lady of Mount Carmel Church, Seminary, and Convent, October 24, 2013. http://ourladyofmountcarmelusa.com/patroness-of-our-seminary-mother-mary-elias-of-the-blessed-sacrament-ocd-1879-1943.

Parsons, Wilfrid, S.J. *Mexican Martyrdom, 1926–1935: Firsthand Experiences of the Religious Persecution in Mexico.* Rockford, IL: TAN Books, 1987.

Personal Remembrances of Mother María Luisa Josefa of the Most Blessed Sacrament. Compiled by Sister Joseph Louise Padilla, O.C.D. Alhambra, CA: Archives of the Carmelite Sisters of the Most Sacred Heart of Los Angeles, 2016.

Queen, William M. *The Doctor's Widow.* Fresno: Academy Library Guild, 1956.

Ruiz, Ramón Eduardo. *Triumphs and Tragedy: A History of the Mexican People.* New York: W. W. Norton, 1993.

Sánchez, George. *Becoming Mexican American: Ethnicity, Culture, and Identity in Chicano Los Angeles, 1900–1945.* Oxford: Oxford University Press, 1993.

Saunders, Father William. "The Use of Sacramental Oils." *Arlington Catholic Herald.* Reprinted at Catholic Education Resource Center. https://www.catholiceducation.org/en/culture/catholic-contributions/the-use-of-sacramental-oils.html.

Sullivan, Reverend Philip, O.C.D. Interview with author. Alhambra, California, October 20, 2015.

Teresa of Jesus, O.C.D. *Interior Castle.* Catholic Treasury. http://www.catholictreasury.info/books/interior_castle/ic5.php.

Tennyson, Alfred Lord. "Morte d'Arthur." In *Idylls of the King.* London: Edward Moxon, 1859.

Ugarte, Henry. Interview with author. Alhambra, California, 1999.

¡Viva Cristo Rey! A Compilation of Articles on the Persecution of the Catholic Church in Mexico. Compiled by Sister Mary Jeanne Coderre, O.C.D. Alhambra, CA: Carmelite Sisters' Printing, 2007.

Williams, Fred V. "Carmelites Grateful for St. Mary's Offer." *San Francisco Monitor,* May 12 and June 3, 1928.

About the Author

Sister Timothy Marie Kennedy, O.C.D., is a member of the Carmelite Sisters of the Most Sacred Heart of Los Angeles. She was born and raised in Long Beach, California, the third of five children. She attended Mount St. Mary's College in Los Angeles and has a B.A. in English and an M.S. in educational administration. She has served in the retreat and education ministries of the Carmelite Sisters as retreat directress and vocation directress as well as teacher and principal in various schools. She currently resides at Casa Convent in Duarte, California.

Sister Timothy Marie edited the two-volume *In Love's Safekeeping: The Letters of Mother Luisita*. She is the author of *In the Face of Darkness: The Heroic Life and Holy Death of Mother Luisita* (Sophia Institute Press, 2019). She comes from a family of Irish writers and storytellers.

Sophia Institute

Sophia Institute is a nonprofit institution that seeks to nurture the spiritual, moral, and cultural life of souls and to spread the gospel of Christ in conformity with the authentic teachings of the Roman Catholic Church.

Sophia Institute Press fulfills this mission by offering translations, reprints, and new publications that afford readers a rich source of the enduring wisdom of mankind.

Sophia Institute also operates the popular online resource CatholicExchange.com. *Catholic Exchange* provides world news from a Catholic perspective as well as daily devotionals and articles that will help readers to grow in holiness and live a life consistent with the teachings of the Church.

In 2013, Sophia Institute launched Sophia Institute for Teachers to renew and rebuild Catholic culture through service to Catholic education. With the goal of nurturing the spiritual, moral, and cultural life of souls, and an abiding respect for the role and work of teachers, we strive to provide materials and programs that are at once enlightening to the mind and ennobling to the heart; faithful and complete, as well as useful and practical.

Sophia Institute gratefully recognizes the Solidarity Association for preserving and encouraging the growth of our apostolate over the course of many years. Without their generous and timely support, this book would not be in your hands.

www.SophiaInstitute.com
www.CatholicExchange.com
www.SophiaInstituteforTeachers.org

Sophia Institute Press is a registered trademark of Sophia Institute.
Sophia Institute is a tax-exempt institution as defined by the
Internal Revenue Code, Section 501(c)(3). Tax ID 22-2548708.